Rendezvous with
Arthur C. Clarke

A *Gylphi Limited* Book

First published in Great Britain in 2022
by Gylphi Limited

Copyright © Gylphi Limited, 2022

All rights reserved.

No part of this publication may be reproduced, stored in a retrieval system, or transmitted, in any form or by any means, without the prior permission in writing of the publisher, nor be otherwise circulated in any form or binding or cover other than that in which it is published and without a similar condition including this condition being imposed on the subsequent purchaser.

A CIP catalogue record for this book is available from the British Library.

ISBN 978-1-78024-108-1 (pbk)
ISBN 978-1-78024-109-8 (hbk)
ISBN 978-1-78024-110-4 (Kindle)
ISBN 978-1-78024-111-1 (EPUB)

Cover image used with permission of the Everett Collection. British science-fiction author Arthur C. Clarke in 1965. Design and typesetting by Gylphi Limited. Printed by Amazon.

Design and typesetting by Gylphi Limited. Printed by Amazon.

Gylphi Limited
Canterbury, UK

Rendezvous with Arthur C. Clarke

CENTENARY ESSAYS

edited by
Andrew M. Butler and Paul March-Russell

SF Storyworlds

Edited by Paul March-Russell, this new and exciting book series aims to explore the evolution of Science Fiction (SF) and its impact upon contemporary culture. The series will argue that SF has generated a series of storyworlds: first, in terms of SF's own internal landscape – the extent to which SF has grown self-referentially – and second, in terms of SF's external effect – the extent to which SF storyworlds have influenced the vocabulary of political, social and cultural discourse. The series is interested in rethinking the possibilities of the genre, in particular, by engaging with different media (literature, film, television, radio, the Internet and the visual arts), critical and aesthetic theory, and reading in translation, including SF from Africa, Asia and Latin America. Although the series focus is on SF, it is open to writers who have alternated between genres (M. John Harrison, Ursula Le Guin) or who have cross-fertilized SF with Gothic and fantasy (China Miéville, Christopher Priest). We are interested in the current and future directions of SF.

Series Editor
Paul March-Russell (Cardiff Metropolitan University)

Editorial Board
Andrew M. Butler (Canterbury Christ Church University)
Gerry Canavan (Marquette University)
Caroline Edwards (Birkbeck, University of London)
Farah Mendlesohn
Adam Roberts (Royal Holloway College)
Jennifer Woodward (Edge Hill University)
Lisa Yaszek (Georgia Institute of Technology)

Series Titles

Science Fiction Across Media: Adaption/Novelization (2013)
Edited by Thomas Van Parys and I.Q. Hunter

The Empires of J. G. Ballard: An Imagined Geography (2015)
David Ian Paddy

Art and Idea in the Novels of China Miéville (2016)
Carl Freedman

Science Fiction Adapted to Film (2016)
Nicholas Ruddick

The Science Fiction of Iain M. Banks (2018)
Edited by Nick Hubble, Esther MacCallum-Stewart
and Joseph Norman

The Science and Fiction of Edgar Rice Burroughs (2018)
Conor Reid

Science Fiction and Catholicism: The Rise and Fall of the Robot Papacy (2019)
Jim Clarke

The Unstable Realities of Christopher Priest (2020)
Paul Kincaid

Rendezvous with Arthur C. Clarke: Centenary Essays (2022)
Edited by Andrew M. Butler and Paul March-Russell

CONTENTS

Acknowledgements ix

Select Bibliography: Works by Arthur C. Clarke

Introduction: Clarke's Mysterious Worlds 1
Andrew M. Butler and Paul March-Russell

1 'It's just my job five days a week': 'Rocketmen'
   of the 1950s 15
   Andy Sawyer

2 Clarkaeology: Arthur C. Clarke's Time Capsules 35
   Patrick Parrinder

3 Leaving the Cradle: Apocalypse, Transcendence and
   Childhood's End 53
   Thore Bjørnvig

4 A Space Bodhi Tree: The 'Crypto-Buddhism' of
   Arthur C. Clarke 75
   Jim Clarke

5 No Future? Queering Deep Time in *The City and
   the Stars* 95
   Paul March-Russell

6 Arthur C. Clarke and the Limitations of the Ocean
   as a Frontier 115
   Helen M. Rozwadowski

7	The Extensions and Obsolescence of Man in *2001* and *2010* *Andrew M. Butler*	139
8	'All these worlds are yours except Europa': Transhumanism and the Ethics of Terraforming *Alexey Dodsworth-Magnavita*	157
9	Dark Forest or Grand Central: Self and Other in Liu Cixin and Arthur C. Clarke *Lyu Guangzhao*	175
10	'Big Dumb Objects', Conceptual Breakthroughs and the Technologiade in Arthur C. Clarke and Iain M. Banks *Joseph S. Norman*	193
11	Clarke Dare Speak Not its Name: Defining Sexuality in *Imperial Earth* *Mike Stack*	213
12	Thirty Years is Ample Time: The Clarke Award and Literary Science Fiction *Nick Hubble*	235

Afterword *Stephen Baxter*	253
Notes on Contributors	261
Index	265

Acknowledgements

The current book began life as a centenary conference at Canterbury Christ Church University in December 2017. We remain grateful to our hosts, the former Department of Media, Art and Design, now SCANDI, and especially to Jill Mason; for financial support from the Serendip Foundation; to Martin Latham of Waterstones for hosting an evening event with Stephen Baxter; and to our participants, including practical support from the London Science Fiction Research Community, and our keynote speaker Charlotte Sleigh.

Since then, it has been a stop-go process due to the precariousness of higher education in the UK and an uncannily science fictional apocalypse, and we are grateful that all of our contributors have stayed the course. We thank them for their patience and goodwill. The one chapter that did not have its origin at the conference is by Helen M. Rozwadowski. We are grateful to Helen and Oxford University Press for granting us permission to reprint her article from *Environmental History* 17(3) (2012). We are also grateful to Anthony Levings of Gylphi Press, and to the editorial board of SF Storyworlds for their scrutiny of our proposal.

Andrew would like to thank all those who have thrust sf books at him over the decades and Colin Odell and Mitch Le Blanc, the prefab two, for thoughts for *2010: The Year We Made Contact* many years ago. And all those much-missed second-hand bookshops, with reading copies cheap enough for pocket money. Paul would like to thank his brother, John, for insisting they saw *2001: A Space Odyssey* at a local cinema in 1978; the inexplicability of which compelled him into reading the novel. Things, as they say, were never the same again.

Select Bibliography
Works By Arthur C. Clarke

Compiled by Andrew M. Butler

Individual articles, reviews, prefaces, introductions, afterwords, story notes, letters and interviews are not included. Books listed are first US and UK editions, with significant revisions. Short stories listed are first appearance, reprints from newspapers and new titles.

Short Fiction

'Travel by Wire!' *Amateur Science Stories*, December 1937.

'How We Went to Mars.' *Amateur Science Stories*, March 1938.

'Retreat from Earth.' *Amateur Science Stories*, March 1938.

'Into the Past.' *The Satellite*, December 1939.

'At the Mountains of Murkiness, or Lovecraft into Leacock.' *The Satellite*, March 1940; in *At the Mountain of Murkiness and Other Parodies*, compiled by George Locke. London: Ferret Fantasy, 1973.

'The Awakening.' *Zenith*, February 1942; revised, *Future Science Fiction Stories*, January 1952.

'Whacky.' [As by Ego] *Fantast*, July 1942.

'Loophole.' *Astounding Science Fiction*, April 1946.

'Rescue Party.' *Astounding Science Fiction*, May 1946.

'Nightfall.' *King's College Review*, December 1946; as 'The Curse', *Cosmos SF&F*, September 1953.

'Technical Error.' *Fantasy*, December 1946; as 'The Reversed Man', *Thrilling Wonder Stories*, June 1950.

'Castaway.' [As by Charles Willis] *Fantasy, The Magazine of Science Fiction*, April 1947.

'The Fires Within.' [As by E. G. O'Brien] *Fantasy* 3, August 1947.

'Inheritance.' [As by Charles Willis] *New Worlds*, October 1947.

'The Forgotten Enemy.' *King's College Review*, December 1948.

'Critical Mass.' *Lilliput*, March 1949; revised, *Space Science Fiction Magazine*, August 1957; in *Tales from the White Hart*. New York: Ballantine, 1957.

'History Lesson.' *Startling Stories*, May 1949; also as 'Expedition to Earth', in *Expedition to Earth*. New York: Ballantine, 1953; London: Sidgwick and Jackson, 1954.

'The Wall of Darkness.' *Super Science Stories*, July 1949.

'Transience.' *Startling Stories*, July 1949.

'The Lion of Comarre.' *Thrilling Wonder Stories*, August 1949.

'Hide and Seek.' *Astounding*, September 1949.

'Thirty Seconds – Thirty Days.' *Thrilling Wonder Stories*, December 1949; as 'Breaking Strain', in John Carnell (ed.) *No Place like Earth*. London: T. V. Boardman, 1952.

'Silence, Please!' [As by Charles Willis] *Science-Fantasy* 2, 1950; *Tales from the White Hart*. New York: Ballantine, 1957.

'Time's Arrow.' *Science-Fantasy* 1, 1950.

'Nemesis.' *Super Science Stories*, March 1950; as 'Exile of the Eons', *Expedition to Earth*. New York: Ballantine, 1953.

'Guardian Angel.' *Famous Fantastic Mysteries*, April 1950; *New Worlds*, Winter 1950; expanded into *Childhood's End*.

'A Walk in the Dark.' *Thrilling Wonder Stories*, August 1950.

'Sentinel of Eternity.' *10 Story Fantasy*, Spring 1951; as 'The Sentinel', *Expedition to Earth*. New York: Ballantine, 1953; as 'Peak of Promise', *Summertime*, June 1968, July 1968.

'The Men in the Flying Saucer.' *Lilliput*, February 1951; as 'Trouble with the Natives', *Marvel Science Stories*, May 1951; as 'Captain Wyxtpthll's Flying Saucer', in Peter Haining (ed.) *The Wizards of Odd: Comic Tales of Fantasy*. London: Souvenir Press, 1996.

'Holiday on the Moon.' Serialized in *Heiress*, January–February 1951; *The Collected Stories of Arthur C. Clarke*. London: Gollancz/Orion, 2000; New York: Tor, 2000.

'Seeker of the Sphinx.' *Two Complete Science-Adventure Books*, Spring 1951; as 'The Road to the Sea', Everett F. Bleiler and T. E. Dikty (eds) *Year's Best Science Fiction Novels*. New York: Frederick Fell, 1952.

'Earthlight.' *Thrilling Wonder Stories,* August 1951.
'Second Dawn.' *Science Fiction Quarterly,* August 1951.
'Superiority.' *The Magazine of Fantasy and Science Fiction,* August 1951.
'"If I Forget Thee, Oh Earth ..."' *Future,* September 1951.
'All the Time in the World.' *Startling Stories,* July 1952.
'The Nine Billion Names of God', in Frederik Pohl (ed.) *Star Science Fiction Stories.* New York: Ballantine, 1953.
'So You're Going to Mars?' *Holiday,* March 1953; *The Challenge of the Spaceship: Previews of Tomorrow's World.* New York: Harper, 1959; London: Frederick Muller, 1960.
'The Possessed.' *Dynamic Science Fiction,* March 1953.
'The Parasite', in Sol Cohen (ed.) *Avon SF&F Reader.* New York: Stratford Novels, Inc., April 1953.
'Jupiter Five.' *If,* May 1953; as 'Jupiter V' in Mike Ashley (ed.) *The Best of British SF 1.* London: Futura, 1977.
'Encounter in the Dawn.' *Amazing,* June/July 1953; as 'Expedition to Earth', in *Expedition to Earth.* New York: Ballantine, 1953; London: Sidgwick and Jackson, 1954; 'Encounter at Dawn', in *Across the Sea of Stars.* New York: Harcourt Brace and World, 1959.
'The Other Tiger.' *Fantastic Universe,* June/July 1953.
'Publicity Campaign.' *The Evening News,* 9 June 1953; *Satellite Science Fiction,* October 1956.
'Armaments Race.' *Adventure,* April 1954; in *Tales from the White Hart.* New York: Ballantine, 1957.
'No Morning After', in August Derleth (ed.) *Time to Come.* New York: Farrar, 1954.
'The Invention.' *Argosy,* November 1954; as 'Patent Pending', in *Tales from the White Hart.* New York: Ballantine, 1957.
'Deep Range', in Frederik Pohl (ed.) *Star Science Fiction Stories No. 3.* New York: Ballantine, 1954 and *Argosy,* February 1956; expanded into novel *The Deep Range,* New York: Harcourt, Brace and World, 1957.
'This Earth of Majesty.' *The Magazine of Fantasy & Science Fiction,* July 1955; as 'Royal Prerogative', *New Worlds Science Fiction,* January 1957; as 'Refugee', in *The Other Side of the Sky.* New York: Harcourt, Brace and World, 1958; London: Gollancz, 1961.
'The Star.' *Infinity Science Fiction,* November 1955.
'What Goes Up ...' *The Magazine of Fantasy and Science Fiction,* January 1956; in *Tales from the White Hart.* New York: Ballantine, 1957.

'Security Check.' *The Evening News*, 13 January 1956; *The Magazine of Fantasy and Science Fiction*, June 1957.
'The Starting Line.' / 'Double-Crossed in Outer Space.' *The Evening Standard*, 23 May 1956; *The Magazine of Fantasy and Science Fiction*, December 1956; as part of *Venture to the Moon* from 1957; in *The Other Side of the Sky*. New York: Harcourt, Brace and World, 1958; London: Gollancz, 1961.
'Robin Hood, F. R. S.' / 'Saved! By a Bow and Arrow.' *The Evening Standard*, 24 May 1956; *The Magazine of Fantasy and Science Fiction*, December 1956; as part of *Venture to the Moon* from 1957; in *The Other Side of the Sky*. New York: Harcourt, Brace and World, 1958; London: Gollancz, 1961.
'Green Fingers.' / 'Death Strikes Surov.' *The Evening Standard*, 25 May 25 1956; *The Magazine of Fantasy and Science Fiction*, January 1957; as part of *Venture to the Moon* from 1957; in *The Other Side of the Sky*. New York: Harcourt, Brace and World, 1958; London: Gollancz, 1961.
'Diamonds! ... and then divorce.' *The Evening Standard*, 26 May 1956; as 'All That Glitters', *The Magazine of Fantasy and Science Fiction*, January 1956; as part of *Venture to the Moon* from 1957; in *The Other Side of the Sky*. New York: Harcourt, Brace and World, 1958; London: Gollancz, 1961.
'Watch This Space.' / 'Who Wrote That Message to the Stars? ...in Letters a Thousand Miles Long?' *The Evening Standard*, 28 May 1956; *The Magazine of Fantasy and Science Fiction*, February 1957; as part of *Venture to the Moon* from 1957; in *The Other Side of the Sky*. New York: Harcourt, Brace and World, 1958; London: Gollancz, 1961.
'Alone on the Moon.' *The Evening Standard*, 29 May 1956; as 'A Question of Residence', *The Magazine of Fantasy and Science Fiction*, February 1957.
'Reckless.' *Adventure*, October 1956; as 'Big Game Hunt', in *Tales from the White Hart*. New York: Ballantine, 1957.
'The Pacifist.' *Fantastic Universe*, October 1956; in *Tales from the White Hart*. New York: Ballantine, 1957.
'The Reluctant Orchid.' *Satellite Science Fiction*, December 1956; in *Tales from the White Hart*. New York: Ballantine, 1957; 'An Orchid for Auntie – Part One', *Speed & Power*, 14 March 1975, 'An Orchid for Auntie – Part Two', *Speed & Power*, 21 March 1975.
'The Next Tenants.' *Satellite Science Fiction*, February 1957; in *Tales from the White Hart*. New York: Ballantine, 1957.
'Cold War.' *Satellite Science Fiction*, April 1957.
'The Case of the Snoring Heir.' *Infinity Science Fiction*, April 1957; as 'Sleeping Beauty', in *Tales from the White Hart*. New York: Ballantine, 1957.

'Venture to the Moon.' [As 'À nous la Lune!'] *Fiction*, December 1957; incorporates 'The Starting Line', 'Robin Hood, F. R.S.', 'Green Fingers', 'All That Glitters', 'Watch This Space', 'A Question of Residence'; in *The Other Side of the Sky*. New York: Harcourt, Brace and World, 1958; London: Gollancz, 1961.
'The Ultimate Melody.' *If*, February 1957; in *Tales from the White Hart*. New York: Ballantine, 1957.
'The Defenestration of Ermintrude Inch', in *Tales from the White Hart*. New York: Ballantine, 1957.
'Moving Spirit', in *Tales from the White Hart*. New York: Ballantine, 1957.
'The Man Who Ploughed the Sea.' *Satellite Science Fiction*, June 1957; in *Tales from the White Hart*. New York: Ballantine, 1957.
'Feathered Friend.' Part of 'The Other Side of the Sky', *Infinity Science Fiction*, September 1957; in *The Other Side of the Sky*. New York: Harcourt, Brace and World, 1958; London: Gollancz, 1961.
'Special Delivery.' Part of 'The Other Side of the Sky', *Infinity Science Fiction*, September 1957; in *The Other Side of the Sky*. New York: Harcourt, Brace and World, 1958; London: Gollancz, 1961; incorporated with 'Freedom of Space', as "'If You Gotta Message ...'", in *How the World Was One: Beyond the Global Village*. London: Gollancz, 1992.
'Take a Deep Breath.' Part of 'The Other Side of the Sky', *Infinity Science Fiction*, September 1957; in *The Other Side of the Sky*. New York: Harcourt, Brace and World, 1958; London: Gollancz, 1961.
'Let There Be Light.' *Dundee Sunday Telegraph*, 5 September 1957.
'Freedom of Space.' Part of 'The Other Side of the Sky', *Infinity Science Fiction*, October 1957; in *The Other Side of the Sky*. New York: Harcourt, Brace and World, 1958; London: Gollancz, 1961; incorporated with 'Special Delivery', as "'If You Gotta Message ...'" in *How the World Was One: Beyond the Global Village*, London: Gollancz, 1992.
'Passer-By.' Part of 'The Other Side of the Sky', *Infinity Science Fiction*, October 1957; in *The Other Side of the Sky*. New York: Harcourt, Brace and World, 1958; London: Gollancz, 1961.
'The Call of the Stars.' Incorporating 'The Other Side of the Sky', *Infinity Science Fiction*, October 1957; in *The Other Side of the Sky*. New York: Harcourt, Brace and World, 1958; London: Gollancz, 1961.
'The Other Side of the Sky.' Incorporating 'Feathered Friend', 'Special Delivery' and 'Take a Deep Breath', *Infinity Science Fiction*, September 1957 and 'Freedom of Space', 'Passer By' and 'The Call of the Stars', *Infinity Science*

Fiction, October 1957; in *The Other Side of the Sky*. New York: Harcourt, Brace and World, 1958; London: Gollancz, 1961.
'Out of the Sun.' *If*, February 1958.
'Cosmic Casanova.' *Venture*, May 1958.
'The Songs of Distant Earth.' *If*, June 1958.
'The Stroke of the Sun.' *Galaxy*, September 1958; as 'A Slight Case of Sunstroke', in *Tales of Ten Worlds*. Toronto: Longmans, 1962; New York: Harcourt, Brace and World, 1962.
'Who's There?' *This Week*, 11 May 1958; as 'The Haunted Space Suit', in Isaac Asimov and Groff Conklin (eds) *Fifty Short Science Fiction Tales*. New York: Collier Books, 1958.
'Out of the Cradle, Endlessly Orbiting ...' *Dude*, March 1959.
'Report on Planet Three', in *The Challenge of the Spaceship: Previews of Tomorrow's World*. New York: Harper, 1959; London: Frederick Muller, 1960.
'Vacation in Vacuum', in *The Challenge of the Spaceship: Previews of Tomorrow's World*. New York: Harper, 1959; London: Frederick Muller, 1960.
'Journey By Earthlight', in *The Challenge of the Spaceship: Previews of Tomorrow's World*. New York: Harper, 1959; London: Frederick Muller, 1960.
'I Remember Babylon.' *Playboy*, May 1960.
'The Hottest Piece of Real Estate in the Solar System.' *Vogue*, June 1960; as 'Summertime on Icarus', in Groff Conklin (ed.) *Great Science Fiction by Scientists*. New York: Collier Books, 1962; serialized as 'Incident on Icarus.' *Speed & Power*, 22 March 1974, 29 March 1974.
'Crime on Mars.' *Ellery Queen's Mystery Magazine*, July 1960; as 'Trouble with Time', in *Tales of Ten Worlds*. Toronto: Longmans, 1962; New York: Harcourt, Brace and World, 1962.
'Inside the Comet.' *The Magazine of Fantasy and Science Fiction*, October 1960; 'Into the Comet – Part One', *Speed & Power*, 5 April 1975, 'Into the Comet – Part Two', *Speed & Power*, 12 April 1975.
'Love That Universe.' *Escapade*, 1967.
'Saturn Rising.' *The Magazine of Fantasy and Science Fiction*, March 1961.
'Death and the Senator.' *Analog*, May 1961.
'Before Eden.' *Amazing*, June 1961.
'At the End of the Orbit.' *If*, November 1961; as 'Hate', in *Tales of Ten Worlds*. Toronto: Longmans, 1962; New York: Harcourt, Brace and World, 1962.
'Moon Dog.' *Galaxy*, April 1962; as 'Dog Star', in *Tales of Ten Worlds*. Toronto: Longmans, 1962; New York: Harcourt, Brace and World, 1962.
'An Ape About the House.' *Dude*, May 1962.

'The Secret of the Men on the Moon.' *This Week* 11 August 1963; as 'The Secret', in *The Wind from the Sun*. London: Gollancz, 1971; New York: Harcourt, Brace, Jovanovich, 1972.
'Sunjammer.' *Boys' Life*, March 1964; as 'The Wind from the Sun', in *The Wind from the Sun*. London: Gollancz, 1971; New York: Harcourt, Brace, Jovanovich, 1972.
'The Food of the Gods.' *Playboy*, May 1964.
'The Shining Ones.' *Playboy*, August 1964.
'Dial "F" for Frankenstein.' *Playboy*, January 1965.
'Maelstrom II.' *Playboy*, April 1965.
'The Last Command.' *Bizarre! Mystery Magazine*, November 1965.
'The Light of Darkness.' *Playboy*, June 1966.
'A Recursion in Metastories.' *Galaxy*, October 1966; as 'The Longest Science-Fiction Story Ever Told', in *The Wind from the Sun*. London: Gollancz, 1971; New York: Harcourt, Brace, Jovanovich, 1972.
'Playback.' *Playboy*, December 1966.
'The Cruel Sky.' *Boys' Life*, July 1967, August, 1967; in *The Wind from the Sun: Stories from the Space Age*. London: Gollancz, 1971; New York: Harcourt, Brace, Jovanovich, 1972.
'Crusade', in Joseph Elder (ed.) *The Farthest Reaches*. New York: Trident, August, 1968.
'Neutron Tide.' *Galaxy*, May 1970.
'Transit of Earth.' *Playboy*, January 1971.
'A Meeting with Medusa.' (*Playboy*, December 1971; in dos-à-dos format, with Kim Stanley Robinson, 'Green Mars'. New York: Tor, 1988.
'Reunion', in Robert Hoskins (ed.) *Infinity Two*. New York: Lancer 1971.
'Reunion', in *The Lost Worlds of 2001*. London: Sidgwick and Jackson, 1972; New York: Harper and Row, 1972; Boston: Gregg Press, 1979.
'View from the Year 2000', in *The Lost Worlds of 2001*. London: Sidgwick and Jackson, 1972; New York: Harper and Row, 1972; Boston: Gregg Press, 1979.
'When the Twerms Came', in *The Lost Worlds of 2001*. London: Sidgwick and Jackson, 1972; New York: Harper and Row, 1972; Boston: Gregg Press, 1979.
'Quarantine.' *Isaac Asimov's Science Fiction Magazine*, Spring 1977.
'The Songs of Distant Earth.' *Omni*, September 1981.
'On Golden Seas.' Newsletter of the Pentagon Defense Science Board, August 1986; *Omni*, May 1987.

'esisneG.' *The Wind from the Sun*, London: Gollancz, 1987; New York: Signet, 1987.
'The Steam-Powered Word Processor.' *Analog Science Fiction/Science Fact*, September 1986.
'Tales from the "White Hart"', 1990: 'The Jet-Propelled Time Machine', in Rob Meades and David B. Wake (eds) *Drabble II – Double Century*. Harold Wood, Essex: Beccon Publications, 1990.
'"If You Gotta Message ..."' (incorporates 'Special Delivery', part of 'The Other Side of the Sky', *Infinity Science Fiction*, September 1957 and 'Freedom of Space' part of 'The Other Side of the Sky', *Infinity Science Fiction*, October 1957, in *How the World Was One: Beyond the Global Village*. London: Gollancz, 1992.
'The Hammer of God.' *Time*, 28 September 1992.
'Improving the Neighbourhood.' *Nature*, 4 November 1999.

Novels

Against the Fall of Night. *Startling Stories*, 1948; New York: Gnome, 1953; revised as *The City and the Stars*. New York: Harcourt, Brace, 1956; London: Muller, 1956.

Earthlight. As 'History Lesson', *Startling Stories*, 1951; expanded New York: Ballantine, 1955, London: Muller, 1955.

Prelude to Space: A Compelling Realistic Novel of Interplanetary Flight. New York: World Editions, 1951; London: Sidgwick and Jackson, 1953.

The Sands of Mars. London: Sidgwick and Jackson, 1951; New York: Gnome, 1953; with introduction by Clarke, New York: Harcourt, Brace and World, 1967.

Islands in the Sky. Philadelphia: Winston, 1952; London: Sidgwick and Jackson, 1971; with introduction by Patrick Moore, Harmondsworth, Middlesex: Penguin, 1972; Boston: Gregg Press, 1979; with new introduction by Clarke, New York: Signet, 1987.

Childhood's End. As 'Guardian Angel', *New Worlds*, 1950, *Famous Fantastic Mysteries*, April 1950; expanded New York: Ballantine, 1953; London: Sidgwick and Jackson, 1954; with introduction and new first chapter London: Pan, 1990.

The City and the Stars. New York: Harcourt, Brace, 1956; London: Muller, 1956; revised from *Against the Fall of Night. Startling Stories,* 1948; New York: Gnome, 1953.

The Deep Range. As 'Deep Range', in Frederik Pohl (ed.) *Star Science Fiction Stories No. 3.* New York: Ballantine, 1954 and *Argosy,* February 1956; expanded into novel New York: Harcourt, Brace and World, 1957; London: Muller, 1957; with introduction, New York: Signet, 1987; London: Gollancz, 1988; New York: Bantam Spectra, 1991.

A Fall of Moondust. New York: Harcourt, Brace and World, 1961; London: Gollancz, 1961; with introduction, New York: Signet, 1987; New York: Bantam Spectra, 1991; London: Gollancz, 1995.

Dolphin Island: A Story of the People of the Sea. London: Gollancz, 1963; New York: Holt, Rinehart and Winston, 1963.

Glide Path. New York: Harcourt, Brace and World, 1963; London: Sidgwick and Jackson, 1969; with new introduction, New York: Signet, 1987; with both introductions, New York: Bantam Spectra, 1991.

2001: A Space Odyssey. London: Hutchinson, 1968; New York: NAL, 1968; with 2 short stories, London: Legend, 1990; Harmondsworth, Middlesex: Roc, 1992.

Rendezvous with Rama. London: Gollancz, 1973; New York: Harcourt, Brace and Jovanovich 1973; London: Pan, 1974; Boston: G.K. Hall, 1980.

Imperial Earth: A Fantasy of Love and Discord. London: Gollancz, 1975; expanded New York: Harcourt, Brace, Jovanovich, 1976; Boston: G.K. Hall, 1980.

The Fountains of Paradise. London: Gollancz, 1979; New York: Harcourt, Brace, Jovanovich, 1979; with afterword, London: Gollancz, 1989.

2010: Odyssey Two. Huntingdon Woods, Mich: Phantasia, 1982; New York: Ballantine, 1982; London: Granada, 1982.

The Songs of Distant Earth. London: Gollancz, 1986; New York: Ballantine, 1986.

2061: Odyssey Three. London: Grafton, 1987; New York: Ballantine, 1988.

The Ghost from the Grand Banks. New York: Ballantine, 1989; London: Gollancz, 1990.

The Hammer of God. London: Gollancz, 1993; New York: Bantam Spectra, 1993.

3001: The Final Odyssey. New York: Del Rey, 1997; London: Voyager, 1997.

Collections

Expedition to Earth. New York: Ballantine, 1953; London: Sidgwick and Jackson, 1954; New York: Harcourt, Brace and World, 1970.

Reach For Tomorrow. New York: Ballantine, 1956; London: Gollancz, 1962; New York: Harcourt, Brace and World, 1970.

Tales from the White Hart. New York: Ballantine, 1957; New York: Harcourt, Brace and World, 1970; London: Sidgwick and Jackson, 1972; adds collaboration with Stephen Baxter, 'Time Gentlemen Please', Hornsea, East Yorkshire: PS Publishing, 2007.

The Other Side of the Sky. New York: Harcourt, Brace and World, 1958; London: Gollancz, 1961; new introduction by Clarke, London: Gollancz, 1987.

Across the Sea of Stars. New York: Harcourt, Brace, 1959.

Tales of Ten Worlds. Toronto: Longmans, 1962; New York: Harcourt, Brace and World, 1962; London: Gollancz, 1963; New York: NAL, 1981.

The Nine Billion Names of God. New York: Harcourt, Brace and World, 1967.

The Lost Worlds of 2001. London: Sidgwick and Jackson, 1972; New York: Harper and Row, 1972; Boston: Gregg Press, 1979.

The Wind from the Sun: Stories from the Space Age. London: Gollancz, 1971; New York: Harcourt, Brace, Jovanovich, 1972; expanded, London: Gollancz, 1987; New York: Signet, 1987; 1972 version reprinted London: Gollancz, 1990.

Of Time and Stars. Introduced by J. B. Priestley, London: Gollancz, 1972; introduced by Clarke, London: Gollancz, 1984.

The Best of Arthur C. Clarke: 1937-1971. London: Sphere, 1973.

The Best of Arthur C. Clarke: 1937-1955. London: Sphere, 1976; London: Sidgwick and Jackson, 1977.

The Best of Arthur C. Clarke 1956-1972. London: Sphere, 1976; London: Sidgwick and Jackson, 1977.

The Sentinel. New York: Berkley, 1983; London: Grafton, 1985.

Tales from Planet Earth. London: Century, 1989; different contents and preface, New York: Bantam, 1990.

More Than One Universe: The Collected Stories of Arthur C. Clarke. New York: Bantam, 1991.

Childhood Ends: The Earliest Writings of Arthur C Clarke, edited by David Aronovitch. Rochester, MI: Portentous Press, 1996.

The Collected Stories of Arthur C. Clarke. London: Gollancz/Orion; New York: Tor, 2000.

The Collected Stories of Arthur C. Clarke: History Lesson, Volume I. New York: RosettaBooks, 2012.

The Collected Stories of Arthur C. Clarke: The Sentinel, Volume II. New York: RosettaBooks, 2012.

The Collected Stories of Arthur C. Clarke: The Star, Volume III. New York: RosettaBooks, 2012.

The Collected Stories of Arthur C. Clarke: A Meeting with Medusa, Volume IV. New York: RosettaBooks, 2012.

Omnibuses

From the Ocean, from the Stars. The Deep Range, The City and the Stars + 14 short stories. New York: Harcourt, Brace and World, 1962.

An Arthur C. Clarke Omnibus. [*Childhood's End, Prelude to Space, Expedition to Earth.*] London: Sidgwick and Jackson, 1965.

Prelude to Mars, Prelude to Space, The Sands of Man + 16 short stories. New York: Harcourt, Brace and World, 1965.

An Arthur C. Clarke Second Omnibus. [*A Fall of Moondust, Earthlight, The Sands of Mars.*] London: Sidgwick and Jackson, 1968.

The Lion of Comarre and Against the Fall of Night. New York: Harcourt, Brace and World, 1968, London: Gollancz, 1970; San Diego, CA: Harvest, 1986; New York: Harcourt, Brace, Jovanovich, 1986.

Four Great Sf Novels. [*The City and the Stars, The Deep Range, A Fall of Moondust, Rendezvous With Rama.*] London: Gollancz, 1978.

2001: A Space Odyssey; The City and the Stars; The Deep Range; A Fall of Moondust; Rendezvous with Rama. London: Heinemann/ Octopus, 1985.

As Editor

Time Probe: The Sciences in Science Fiction. New York: Delacorte, 1966.

The Coming of the Space Age: Famous Accounts of Man's Probing of the Universe. London: Gollancz, 1967; New York: Meredith, 1967.

Arthur C. Clarke's July 20, 2019: Life in the 21st Century. Writes introduction and epilogue only. New York: Macmillan, 1986; London: Grafton, 1987.

With David Brin

Project Solar Sail. New York: NAL/Roc 1990.

With Geo. W. Proctor

The Science Fiction Hall of Fame, Vol. 4. London: Gollancz, 1981; as *The Science Fiction Hall of Fame III: Nebula Winners, 1965–1969.* New York: Avon, 1982.

Nonfiction Collections

Interplanetary Flight. New York: Harper and Row, 1950.

The Exploration of Space. New York: Harper, 1951; London: Temple, 1951; revised, New York: Harper, 1959; new introduction, New York: Pocket Books, 1979.

The Exploration of the Moon. Illustrated by R. A. Smith; London: Muller, 1954; New York: Harper, 1954.

The Coast of Coral. New York: Harper, 1956.

The Young Traveller in Space. Illustrated by Edmund Louis Blandford. London: Phoenix House, 1954; as *Going into Space.* New York: Harper and Brothers, 1954; as *The Scottie Book of Space Travel.* London: Transworld/Scottie, 1957; with new text by Robert Silverberg, *Into Space: A Young Person's Guide to Space.* New York: Harper and Row, 1971.

The Making of a Moon: The Story of the Earth Satellite Programme. New York: Harper, 1957; London: Frederick Muller, 1957; revised, New York: Harper, 1958.

The Reefs of Taprobane: Underwater Adventures Around Ceylon. New York: Harper, 1957; London: Frederick Muller, 1957.

Voice Across the Sea. New York: Harper, 1958; revised, London: Luscombe, 1974; New York: Harper and Row, 1974; revised as *How the World Was One*, 1992, below.

The Challenge of the Spaceship: Previews of Tomorrow's World. New York: Harper, 1959; London: Frederick Muller, 1960; revised, New York: Ballantine, 1961.

The Challenge of the Sea. Introduced by Werner von Brown, New York: Holt, Rinehart and Winston, 1960; London: Frederick Muller, 1961.

Profiles of the Future: An Inquiry Into the Limits of the Possible. London: Gollancz, 1962; New York: Harper and Row, 1962; revised, London: Pan, 1973; New York: Harcourt, Brace, Jovanovich, 1973; revised, London: Gollancz, 1982; New York: Holt, Rinehart and Winston, 1984; London: Victor Gollancz, 2000.

Voices from the Sky: Previews of the Coming Space Age. New York: Harper and Row, 1965; London: Gollancz, 1966.

The Promise of Space. London: Hodder and Stoughton, 1968; New York: Harper and Row, 1968.

Report on Planet Three and Other Speculations. London: Gollancz, 1972; New York: Harper and Row, 1972.

The View from Serendip. New York: Random House, 1977; London: Gollancz, 1978.

1984: Spring / A Choice of Futures. London and New York: Granada, 1984; New York: Ballantine, 1984.

Ascent to Orbit: A Scientific Autobiography: The Technical Writings of Arthur C. Clarke. New York: Wiley, 1984.

Astounding Days: A Science Fictional Autobiography. London: Gollancz, 1989; New York: Ballantine, 1989.

The Fantastic Muse. Huddersfield: Hilltop Press, 1992.

How the World Was One: Beyond the Global Village. As *Voice Across the Sea.* New York: Harper, 1958; revised with new title, London: Gollancz, 1992; as *How the World Was One: Towards the Tele-Family of Man.* New York: Bantam, 1992; as *How the World Was One: The Turbulent History of Global Communication.* London: Gollancz, 1993.

By Space Possessed: Essays on the Exploration of Space. London: Gollancz, 1993.

The Snows of Olympus: A Garden on Mars. London: Gollancz, 1994.

Greetings, Carbon-Based Bipeds!: A Vision of the 20th Century As It Happened. London: Voyager, 1999; as *Greetings, Carbon-Based Bipeds!: Collected Essays 1934-1998.* New York: St Martin's, 1999.

Collaborations

With Stephen Baxter

'The Wire Continuum.' *Playboy,* January 1998.

'Hibernaculum 46.' Collector's Edition, London: Voyage, 2000.

The Light of Other Days. New York: Tor, 2000; London: Voyager, 2000.

Time's Eye. New York: Del Rey/Ballantine, 2003; London: Gollancz, 2004.

Sunstorm. New York: Del Rey/Ballantine, 2005; London: Gollancz, 2005.

'Time Gentlemen Please', in *Tales from the White Hart.* Hornsea, East Yorkshire: PS Publishing, 2007.

Firstborn. New York: Del Rey/Ballantine, 2007; London: Gollancz, 2008.

With Gregory Benford

Beyond the Fall of Night. New York: Ace, 1990; New York: Putnam, 1990; as *Against the Fall of Night and Beyond the Fall of Night.* London: Gollancz, 1991.

With Chesley Bonestell

Beyond Jupiter: The Worlds of Tomorrow. Boston: Little, Brown, 1972.

With Lord Dunsany

Arthur C. Clarke & Lord Dunsany: A Correspondence. Palo Alto, CA: Anamnesis Press, 1998.

With Peter Hyams

The Odyssey File. New York: Ballantine Books/Del Rey, 1985, London: Panther, 1985.

With Michael P. Kube-McDowell

The Trigger. HarperCollins Voyager, 1999; New York: Bantam Spectra, 1999.

With Gentry Lee

Cradle. London: Gollancz, 1988; New York: Bantam, 1988; New York: Warner, 1988.

Rama II. New York: Bantam, 1988; London: Gollancz, 1989.

The Garden of Rama. New York: Bantam 1991; London: Gollancz, 1991.

Rama Revealed. New York: Bantam 1993; London: Gollancz, 1993.

With C. S. Lewis

From Narnia to a Space Odyssey: The War of Letters Between Arthur C. Clarke and C. S. Lewis. New York: ibooks, 2003.

With Mike McQuay

Richter 10. London: Gollancz, 1996; New York: Bantam, 1996.

With Frederik Pohl

The Last Theorem. New York: Del Rey/Ballantine, 2008; London: HarperVoyager, 2008.

With Simon Welfare and John Fairley

Arthur C. Clarke's Mysterious World. London: Collins, 1980.

Arthur C. Clarke's World of Strange Powers. London: Collins; New York: Putnam, 1984.

Arthur C. Clarke's Chronicle of the Strange and Mysterious. London: Collins, 1987.

Arthur C. Clarke's A-Z of Mysteries: From Atlantis to Zombies. London: HarperCollins, 1993.

With Mike Wilson

Boy Beneath the Sea. New York: Harper, 1958.

The First Five Fathoms. New York: Harper, 1960.

Indian Ocean Adventure. New York: Harper, 1961; London: A. Barker, 1962.

Indian Ocean Treasure. New York: Harper and Row, 1964; London: Sidgwick and Jackson, 1972.

The Treasure of the Great Reef. New York: Harper and Row, 1964; New York: Ballantine, 1974.

With the Editors of *Time-Life*

Man and Space. New York: Time-Life, 1964.

Acknowledgement

Sources: An earlier version of this bibliography appeared in Vector 197. Information has been taken from:

Bodleian library catalogue, URL (accessed 3 May 2021): http://solo.bodleian.ox.ac.uk/

Clute, J. and Nichols, P. (eds) *The Encyclopedia of Science Fiction.* 2nd edn. London: Orbit, 1993.

Contento, W. G. *Index to Science Fiction Anthologies and Collections, Combined Edition,* URL (accessed 3 May 2021): http://www.philsp.com/resources/ISFAC/0start.htm

Contento, W. G. and Brown, C. N. *Science Fiction, Fantasy and Horror: 1984-1998,* URL (accessed 3 May 2021): http://www.locusmag.com/index/0start.htm

ISFDB.org Arthur C. Clarke entry, URL (accessed 3 May 2021): http://www.isfdb.org/cgi-bin/ea.cgi?17

Library of Congress catalogue, URL (accessed 3 May 2021): https://catalog.loc.gov/

National Library of Scotland catalogue, URL (accessed 3 May 2021): https://www.nls.uk/catalogues/

Nichols, P. and Clute, J. 'Clarke, Arthur C.', in Clute, J., Langford, D. and Sleight, G. *The Encyclopedia of Science Fiction*. 3rd edn, URL (accessed 3 May 2021): http://www.sf-encyclopedia.com/entry/clarke_arthur_c

Personal collections.

Introduction
Clarke's Mysterious Worlds

Andrew M. Butler and Paul March-Russell

Writing in *The Village Voice* in 1998, Jonathan Lethem offered a daydream of science fiction's 'squandered promise', an alternate history in which Thomas Pynchon's *Gravity's Rainbow* rather than Arthur C. Clarke's *Rendezvous with Rama*, won the Nebula Award in 1973. Sf, liberated from its genre ghetto by the experiments of the New Wave, re-joined the literary mainstream. Lethem's essay, even as it desires the dissolution of generic boundaries, insists upon them – Pynchon's experimental fiction is progressive whereas Clarke's is emblematic of 'a reactionary SF as artistically dire as it was comfortingly familiar' (Lethem, 1998). Such a blanket dismissal is contradicted, though, by Clarke's actual novel; a picaresque narrative in which very little happens, where nothing is revealed about the purpose of the Ramans, where the massive spacecraft remains a black box full of possibilities, and where – despite the financial and geopolitical crises that proceed Rama's entry into Earth's orbit – the Earthmen are of no more significance than in Clarke's earlier story 'The Star' (1955), his forebear H. G. Wells's *The War of the Worlds* (1898) or his near-contemporaries Arkady and Boris Strugatsky's *Roadside Picnic* (1972). The peculiarities of Clarke's narrative, overlooked by Lethem who can see no further than the conventionality of Clarke's prose, suggest a writer who deserves re-evaluation.

Although we have taken our title from Clarke's novel, the meaning of 'rendezvous' – like so much else to do with Clarke and his work – is not obvious. Colloquially, it refers to a secret assignation at a pre-arranged time and place but, in military terms, it can also mean the meeting of two agents, units or vessels. The word, taken from the French, means to present oneself but, etymologically, it comes from the older phrase *se rendre*, to surrender oneself. To 'rendezvous' with Clarke is not only to meet him in a specific location (as in a book such as this), but for each party to also present themselves or lay down their arms, to be honest and open with one another. Unlike Lethem, the writers assembled here do not prejudge Clarke but attempt to prise open the paradoxes within his work. Whether Clarke or his fiction could ever be so disarming is rather another matter.

It has become a cliché to refer to Clarke as one of science fiction's 'Big Three' alongside Isaac Asimov and Robert A. Heinlein, although this was a term that had been used to refer to Asimov, Heinlein, and A. E. van Vogt until Clarke eclipsed the latter in genre terms in the late 1940s (Glyer, 2017). All three appeared in John W. Campbell's *Astounding Science-Fiction* and magazines outside the genre. All three became bestsellers. Whilst Heinlein achieved cult status with *Stranger in a Strange Land* (1961), which protected him from being sidelined by the taboo-breaking and experimental tastes within the British and American New Waves of the 1960s, Asimov and Clarke became more visible in science columns of magazines than on the fiction pages.[1] The discourse around the British New Wave, both in the pages of *New Worlds* and in subsequent criticism, found it convenient to dismiss the work of Clarke, John Wyndham and John Christopher, as well as other writers from E. J. (Ted) Carnell's stable of writers such as Eric Frank Russell. Brian W. Aldiss damns Clarke with faint praise when he calls him 'faithful to a boyhood vision of science as saviour of mankind, and of mankind as a race of potential gods destined for the stars' (Aldiss, 1973: 260). The New Wave had parodied and undercut such notions of salvation, although they were hardly the first sf writers to do so. Aldiss (1973: 260) claims Clarke's 'literary abilities are traditional, and his prose workaday'. Even Clarke's celebrated ideas might not be as transcendent as could be claimed, with *Childhood's End*

(1953) expressing 'a rather banal philosophical idea' (Aldiss, 1973: 260). The New Wave wished to leave those platitudes behind and Aldiss, in assembling his history of science fiction, wanted to make grand claims for sf as literature.

However, in the past decades there have been important re-evaluations of Wyndham (Manlove, 1991; Wymer, 1992) and, more recently, of Asimov and Heinlein (Mendlesohn, 2019; Nevala-Lee, 2018; Patterson, 2010, 2014). There has been nothing comparable for Clarke. Gary Westfahl's 2018 book is a useful introduction but the approach, which emphasizes the plausibility and scientific rationality of Clarke's fiction, rehearses not only the argument of Westfahl's earlier study *Cosmic Engineers* (1996) but also Clarke's public persona as the space enthusiast, technocrat and futurologist – evidenced by our cover image taken from the set of *2001: A Space Odyssey* (dir. Stanley Kubrick, 1968). Westfahl aside, readers have to look further back to Robin Reid's selective critical companion from 1997 or Neil McAleer's authorized biography from 1992 (expanded 2017). In terms of articles and chapters, two works – *Childhood's End* and *2001* – tend to dominate, although Károly Pintér (2010) and Jeremy Withers (2021) have written on *The City and the Stars* (1956). Much of the critical work on *2001* – which took Clarke away from his own fiction for much of the 1960s as he worked on the various treatments – is more interested in Stanley Kubrick as auteur than in Clarke, and the sequel *2010: Odyssey Two* remains largely ignored, and there is little interest in Peter Hyams's *2010: The Year We Made Contact* (1984), despite that director's auteurist ambitions. Clarke's novels of the 1970s and 1980s may have gained large advances and been on best-seller charts – as was also the case with Asimov – but have received small critical attention. Clarke's knighthood in 2000 for services to literature confirmed him as an establishment figure,[2] in a way that Terry Pratchett did not seem to suffer in 2009.

So, that Big Three label has stuck as an historical term, but the lack of critical scholarship has also permitted Lethem's critique of Clarke to remain the norm. Like Asimov, Clarke remains one of science fiction's default voices – rational, technocratic, even nerdy – by which the genre is largely understood by the wider society. As with Asimov's

Three Laws of Robotics, Clarke's Third Law, in which 'any sufficiently advanced technology is indistinguishable from magic' (Clarke, 1962/2000: 2), has become commonplace, even amongst those with little knowledge of sf. Although Clarke's fiction no longer represents the genre's cutting-edge – just one of the dichotomies that surrounds the sf prize named after him and initially funded by Clarke himself – it continues to inspire authors such as Stephen Baxter, Lixin Ciu, Greg Egan, Paul McAuley, Alastair Reynolds and Kim Stanley Robinson. The enthusiasm that Clarke encapsulated at the height of the Space Race remains a touchstone for science communicators such as Maggie Aderin-Pocock, Brian Cox, Kevin Fong and Chris Lintott; for astronauts such as Chris Hadfield and Tim Peake; and, more contentiously, for would-be colonizers of space such as Jeff Bezos and Elon Musk. The packaging of sf novels, such as Chris Brookmyre's *Places in the Darkness* (2017), self-consciously emulates the iconography of *2001*, a film that, due to its technical detail, seemed to be an unrepeatable experiment but which has since influenced Oscar-winning movies such as *Arrival* (dir. Denis Villeneuve, 2016), *Gravity* (dir. Alfonso Cuarón, 2013) and – most clearly – *Interstellar* (dir. Christopher Nolan, 2014) and is a touchstone against which much sf film is measured. Clarke's optimism, so unlike the current vogue for dystopia, is echoed in Neal Stephenson's call for a new utopianism (Newitz, 2012), while Tim Berners-Lee took inspiration for the World Wide Web from Clarke's short story, 'Dial F for Frankenstein' (1964) (Wright, 2001). Besides giving succour for tech-utopians, Clarke's ecological concerns resonate with today's environmental movement. New audiences have been drawn to Clarke's fiction via the TV adaptation in 2015 of *Childhood's End*, a novel that continues to reverberate in pop culture from Led Zeppelin's *Houses of the Holy* (1973) to Boards of Canada's *Tomorrow's Harvest* (2013).[3]

The disparity between Clarke's popular influence and his critical status demands his reassessment. But the discrepancy also serves to obscure the man himself. Born in Minehead in December 1917, Clarke grew up in rural Somerset and was educated at Huish's Grammar School, Taunton. His brother Fred describes an almost idyllic childhood in which Clarke read voraciously, experimented wildly, gave impromptu lectures and played-out a folk idea of being a 'scientist' (F. Clarke, 1987: 9–14; Sleigh, 2018: 149–50). In his account, though, Fred omits that their father, who had plunged his army gratuity at the end of the First World War into buying a farm, died when Clarke was 13. Their mother was left to run the farm and raise four children single-handed. Any ambition Clarke might have had of going to university was denied by financial constraint. Instead, Clarke was emblematic of the 'working- and lower-middle-class young men' who constituted the first British science fiction fans (Sleigh and White, 2019: 178). As Charlotte Sleigh and Alice White (2019: 179) elaborate, these men had mostly been born in and around the World War One, and were young enough to be 'relatively untouched by the economic worries of the Great Depression'. Many, like Clarke, were wireless enthusiasts, a hobby encouraged by Hugo Gernsback, editor of *Amazing Stories* and the magazines that had preceded it. Clarke later recalled the impact that *Amazing Stories* had upon him when he first read it in 1929: 'the stories brimmed with ideas and amply evoked that sense of wonder that is, or should be, one of the goals of the best fiction' (Clarke, 1983). A child of the public libraries, Clarke was further enthused by Olaf Stapledon's *Last and First Men* (1930), a major influence on the British fans, and by David Lasser's work of popular science, *The Conquest of Space* (1931).

As Rob Hansen has demonstrated, British fandom grew from the correspondence columns in Gernsback's publications, which first put fans in touch with one another, followed by the formation of clubs in imitation of Gernsback's Science Fiction Leagues (Hansen, 1988–94). At the same time, and overlapping with the same networks that constituted early British fandom, the British Interplanetary Society (BIS) was formed in Liverpool in 1933 (Sleigh, 2016: 219–20). Clarke's membership of the BIS propelled him into the fan networks that resulted in the first British science fiction convention at Leeds in January 1937. In 1936, Clarke had moved to London, where he worked as a pensions auditor for the Board of Education, and flat-shared with another budding sf writer and member of the BIS, William F. Temple, best-known for 'Four-Sided Triangle' (1939). Following the Leeds convention, the activities of both British fandom and the BIS were increasingly focused around Clarke's flat in Gray's Inn Road and the fanzine *Terrae Novae*, edited by Carnell.

Despite Clarke's increasing prominence, he remained somewhat unworldly. Firstly, unlike the fans who had grown up in industrial centres such as Birmingham, Leeds, Liverpool and Manchester, Clarke had lived near to the coast in the West Country. Secondly, he was one of the younger fans, barely nineteen at the time of the Leeds convention. Thirdly, Clarke's social awkwardness could be attributed to his attempt to cultivate what he thought was a scientific demeanour, amounting to egotism. But lastly, and perhaps most importantly, Clarke was homosexual (despite a brief, six-month marriage to an American divorcee, Marilyn Mayfield, in 1953). Famously but also understandably reticent about discussing his private life, even after homosexuality was partially decriminalized in Britain in 1967, Clarke remained an enigma. In his obituary for Clarke, Michael Moorcock wrote that '[e]veryone knew he was gay. In the 1950s I'd go out drinking with his boyfriend' (Moorcock, 2008). Even if this was the case, 'everyone' could only mean the networks grouped around *New Worlds*, which had grown out of *Terrae Novae* to become Britain's leading sf magazine, and its sister title, *Science Fantasy* (also edited by Carnell). Furthermore, by the time Moorcock met Clarke, he was the preeminent science fiction writer and science communicator of his day, and while this did not give Clarke freedom from the law, he was undeniably in a more secure position than in the late 1930s.

Unlike his near-contemporary, the mathematician Alan Turing, Clarke did not work at Bletchley Park, but from 1941 to 1946 he served in the RAF as a radar specialist and flight instructor. As an ex-serviceman, Clarke gained a place at King's College London and, in 1948, graduated with first-class honours in mathematics and physics. Like another of his literary heroes, H. G. Wells, Clarke first established himself as a popular science writer, most notably with *The Exploration of Space* (1951). But it was an earlier article, published in *Wireless World* in October 1945, proposing the use of geostationary orbits for telecommunication satellites, that was to give him lasting fame.[4] Following the successful launch of Telstar in 1962, Clarke became a familiar figure on both British and American TV, commenting on the Moon landing in 1969 for CBS News. Alongside his non-fiction and media work, Clarke had published his first professional science fiction in 1946, 'Rescue Party' (*Astounding*). As Oliver Dunnett has argued, the so-called 'space trilogy' (*The Sands of Mars* [1951], *Islands in the Sky* [1954] and *Earthlight* [1955]) pursued the same purpose as the non-fiction by popularizing the assumption that humanity's place would be in outer space (Dunnett, 2012: 514–15). Clarke's role as technical advisor on 'Dan Dare, Pilot of the Future', the centrepiece of *The Eagle* comic launched in 1950, served a similar end (James, 1987: 43).

The more mature novels from this period though, *Childhood's End* and *The City and the Stars*, as well as the tales that would become *2001*, contextualize Clarke's historical determinism. Here, humanity is shown to be relatively unimportant, an object dependent upon impersonal, cosmic forces. These stories are full of sublime wonder, enhanced by the disproportionate scale between an insignificant human witness and a vastly complex, interstellar presence, but – as with other works of the sublime – they also rely upon the terror of the individual. Their cosmic horror echoes the residual influence of Charles Fort and H. P. Lovecraft, gleaned from Clarke's reading of *Astounding* and *Unknown* in the 1930s, as parodied by Clarke in 'At the Mountains of Murkiness, or Lovecraft into Leacock' (1940). While Clarke's non-fiction, early sf and carefully constructed media persona established him as a proselytizer for instrumental reason, his fascination with the paranormal – enhanced in 1980 by the TV series *Arthur C. Clarke's Mysterious World*, followed by *World of Strange Powers* (1985) and *Mysterious Universe* (1994) – positioned him as a sceptical investigator into occult beliefs.[5] For Roger Luckhurst, Clarke's use of such irrational ideas as parapsychology in his fiction places him in a lineage that extends back to the Society for Psychical Research (Luckhurst, 2005: 135–6) but also forwards to such institutions as the Fortean Society. To see Clarke's rational and irrational interests as mutually inclusive, rather than exclusive or contradictory, reinforces the impression of him as a *homo duplex*, a perpetually two-sided and enigmatic figure.

Clarke decided in 1956 to make his home in Ceylon (Sri Lanka), ostensibly to pursue his interest in scuba diving, but perhaps also to escape the sexual repression of Britain – in much the same way as other gay and bisexual authors and artists moved to Paris, Berlin, New York, San Francisco or North Africa. The move cemented an ecological concern in such novels as *The Deep Range* (1957) and *Dolphin Island* (1963). Clarke's pragmatism, as witnessed in his accommodation of irrational and Eastern (if not Western) religious thought, complemented the environmentalism of Rachel Carson and Buckminster Fuller, wherein humanity forms part of an intricate network of ecosystems. Although Clarke could be accused of Orientalizing the Sri Lankan people – his novel *The Songs of Distant Earth* (1986), based upon his 1958 short story of the same name, features a peace-loving, nature-worshipping, sexually liberated human species – he invested deeply in the country and was awarded its highest civilian honour (Sri Lankabhimanya) in 2005. Clarke's solutions to nationalism, capitalism and climate change were a mixture of a 1930s-style belief in world governance – which Wells had already advocated for – and a pre-Accelerationist belief in automation and Green technologies. Following his receipt of the UNESCO-Kalinga Prize for science communication in 1961, Clarke (again like Wells) increasingly consorted with statesmen, monarchs, newspaper barons and Nobel Prize-winning scientists.

Clarke's receipt, with Kubrick, of the 1969 Oscar for Best Screenplay for *2001* earned him an unprecedented three-book deal for a science fiction writer. His novels, *Rendezvous with Rama* (1973), *Imperial Earth* (1975) and *The Fountains of Paradise* (1979), won most of the genre's major prizes. Despite having proclaimed that *The Foundations of Paradise* would be his last novel, Clarke nevertheless continued to publish, but mostly (like Asimov in his later years) in the form of sequels to earlier works or collaborations. In 1986, the Science Fiction Writers of America appointed Clarke as its seventh Grand Master, after Heinlein in 1975 and a year before Asimov. For better or worse, Clarke's reputation was now established – in 1983, the Arthur C. Clarke Foundation was launched in Washington D. C. to promote science education; in 1987, the Arthur C. Clarke Award for best science fiction novel was first presented (controversially to Margaret Atwood for *The Handmaid's Tale*); and in 2005, the Sir Arthur C. Clarke Awards for space exploration were created. In 1988, Clarke's health began to decline due to the effects of the polio with which he had been diagnosed in 1962. He would live for another twenty years before dying on 19 March 2008. Clarke was buried in Colombo, alongside his close friend Leslie Ekanayake who had died in 1977, and to whom *The Fountains of Paradise* had been dedicated.

Clarke's odyssey, then, from a rural, lower-middle-class existence in Somerset to a genre-defining author and international celebrity is a quintessentially twentieth-century story about expanding social opportunities, buoyed both by the vision and reality of technological change. In February 1998, a month after the original announcement of Clarke's knighthood in the New Year's Honours List, the *Sunday Mirror* attempted to besmirch his reputation, but quickly withdrew and apologized for this. However, unsubstantiated rumours remain on the Internet, the mass communication network that (ironically) Clarke had predicted in 1964. More remarkable is how Clarke went from such humble origins to being more famous than any other science fiction writer, with the exception of Wells.

The following chapters do not pretend to answer how this was achieved but they describe the contours of this puzzle. Andy Sawyer begins by locating Clarke's sf and non-sf of the early 1950s within the rocket enthusiasm of the period. He compares Clarke's vision of space exploration with that of his near-contemporaries: Charles Chilton, Robert A. Heinlein and E. C. Tubb. Patrick Parrinder, beginning also with the early short stories of the 1940s and 1950s, looks at another aspect of Clarke's vision: the roles of archaeology, mysterious artefacts and his fascination with deep time. Thore Bjørnvig turns to the use of eschatology in *Childhood's End* and, in particular, examines the dialectic between apocalypse and transcendence, which he argues runs throughout Clarke's major fiction. Jim Clarke explores further the role of religion in the work of this apparently atheistic author by documenting Clarke's responses to Buddhism from such stories as 'The Nine Billion Names of God' (1953) through to *The Fountains of Paradise*.

Two chapters examine gender and sexuality in Clarke's fiction. Paul March-Russell focuses upon the queer, textual effects of *The City and the Stars* alongside the influence of Weird authors such as Lord Dunsany and H. P. Lovecraft. Later in the collection, Mike Stack explores the representation of sexuality in *Imperial Earth* in the wake of the partial decriminalization of homosexuality in 1967 and the Stonewall uprising. Meanwhile, Helen Rozwadowski examines a different form of attraction – Clarke's love affair with the ocean – contextualizing *The Deep Range* within other ventures of the 1950s and 1960s that attempted to stir interest in the ocean as an unexplored frontier, only to be superseded by the race into outer space. Andrew M. Butler compares the film adaptations of *2001* and *2010* with reference to the work of Marshall McLuhan, in particular, the tension between technology as an extension of human capabilities and as a replacement of the human altogether. Alexey Dodsworth-Magnavita analyses the original novels in terms of transhumanism and the ethics of transforming the body so as to terraform other worlds.

The final group of chapters examines Clarke's legacy. Lyu Guangzhao contrasts the optimism of *Childhood's End* and *2001* with the pessimism of Liu Cixin's *Three Body Problem* trilogy (2006–10). Whereas Clarke tends to view the universe as benign and is hopeful about first contact between humans and aliens, Liu sees the cosmos as filled with potential threats. In this struggle between self and other, both authors reflect upon the ethics and possible violence of real-world encounters between opposing forces. Joseph S. Norman meanwhile compares the 'big dumb object' in *Rendezvous with Rama* with that of Iain M. Banks's *Excession* (1996) in order to draw out the similarities and differences between these two key British writers of Old and New Space Opera. Nick Hubble turns to the history of the Clarke Award, and assesses both the extent to which the prize has sustained Clarke's legacy and the degree to which the annual shortlists have blurred the boundaries between sf and mainstream fiction, perhaps in ways that simultaneously disprove Lethem's thesis and vindicate his former hopes for the genre. Lastly, we are indebted to Stephen Baxter's afterword in which he reflects upon the significance of Clarke, and offers an insight into his friendship and collaboration with his great predecessor.

Notes

1. Clarke dedicated a collection of such columns, *Report on Planet Three*: 'In accordance with the terms of the Clarke-Asimov treaty, the second-best science writer dedicates this book to the second-best science-fiction writer' (Clarke, 1973: v).
2. Cf. Christopher Priest on Clarke's 'worldwide popularity': 'this is no doubt due to [...] a wholehearted, if facile, Englishness' (Priest, 1979: 196).
3. In addition, The Byrds' 'Space Odyssey' (1968), recorded and released whilst *2001* was in production, offers a musical retelling of the film's source text, Clarke's 'The Sentinel' (1951). The cover for Led Zeppelin's *Presence* (1975) by Peter Christopherson of the design group Hipgnosis – also of Throbbing Gristle and Coil – was inspired by *2001*'s monolith (pyramid in Clarke's story).
4. The typewriter on which Clarke wrote his essay is now housed as part of the Special Collections and Archives at the University of Liverpool, URL (accessed 9 March 2021): https://clarkesca.omeka.net/exhibits/show/arthur-c--clarke--architect-of/wireless-world--1945
5. Since Fort and Lovecraft were probably unreliable 'expert witnesses', Clarke would instead quote the biologist J. B. S. Haldane (1927: 286): 'the universe is not only queerer than we suppose, but queerer than we *can* suppose'.

Works Cited

Aldiss, B. W. (1973) *Billion Year Spree: The History of Science Fiction*. London: Weidenfeld and Nicolson.
Clarke, A. C. (1962/2000) *Profiles of the Future*. 3rd edn. London: Indigo.
Clarke, A. C. (1972/1973) *Report on Planet Three and Other Speculations*. London: Corgi.
Clarke, A. C. (1983) 'In the Beginning was Jupiter', *The New York Times*, 6 March, URL (accessed 4 March 2021): https://archive.nytimes.com/www.nytimes.com/books/97/03/09/reviews/clarke-jupiter.html
Clarke, F. (1987) 'Arthur C. Clarke: The Early Days', *Foundation* 41: 9–14.
Dunnett, O. (2012) 'Patrick Moore, Arthur C. Clarke and "British Outer Space" in the Mid 20th Century', *Cultural Geographies* 19(4): 505–22.

Glyer, M. (2017) 'The Big Three and a Lesson About Fixing Things Wrong.' *File 770* (9 January), URL (accessed 3 March 2021): http://file770.com/the-big-three-and-a-lesson-about-fixing-things-wrong/#:~:text=Clarke%20are%20often%20considered%20to,van%20Vogt.&text=Obviously%20at%20some%20later%20point,it%20on%20three%20sf%20writers

Haldane, J. B. S. (1927) *Possible Worlds and Other Essays*. London: Chatto and Windus.

Hansen, R. (1988–94) *Then*, URL (accessed 4 March 2021): https://ansible.uk/Then/then_1-1.html

James, E. (1987) 'The Future Viewed from Mid-Century Britain: Clarke, Hampson and the Festival of Britain.' *Foundation* 41: 42–51.

Lethem, J. (1998) 'The Squandered Promise of Science Fiction', URL (accessed 2 March 2021): https:// hipsterbookclub.livejournal.com/1147850.html

Luckhurst, R. (2005) *Science Fiction*. Cambridge: Polity.

Manlove, C. N. (1991) 'Everything Slipping Away: John Wyndham's *The Day of the Triffids*.' *Journal of the Fantastic in the Arts*. 4(1): 29–53.

McAleer, N. (1992) *Odyssey: The Authorized Biography of Arthur C. Clarke*. London: Gollancz.

McAleer, N. (2017) *Arthur C. Clarke: Odyssey of a Visionary*. London: Ashgrove.

Mendlesohn, F. (2019) *The Pleasant Profession of Robert A. Heinlein*. London: Unbound.

Moorcock, M. (2008) 'Brave New Worlds', *The Guardian*, 22 March, URL (accessed 4 March 2021): https:// www.theguardian.com/books/2008/mar/22/arthurcclarke

Nevala-Lee, A. (2018) *Astounding: John W. Campbell, Isaac Asimov, Robert A. Heinlein, L. Ron Hubbard, and the Golden Age of Science Fiction*. New York: Dey Street.

Newitz, A. (2012) 'Dear Science Fiction Writers: Stop Being So Pessimistic!' *Smithsonian Magazine*, April. https://www.smithsonianmag.com/science-nature/dear-science-fiction-writers-stop-being-so-pessimistic-127226686/ (accessed 4 March 2021).

Patterson, W. H. (2010) *Robert A. Heinlein: In Dialogue with His Century, Vol. 1*. New York: Tor.

Patterson, W. H. (2014) *Robert A. Heinlein: In Dialogue with His Century, Vol. 2*. New York: Tor.

Pintér, K. (2010) *The Anatomy of Utopia: Narration, Estrangement and Ambiguity in More, Wells, Huxley and Clarke*. Jefferson, NC: McFarland.

Priest, C. (1979) 'British Science Fiction', in P. Parrinder (ed.) *Science Fiction: A Critical Guide*, pp. 187–202. London: Longman.
Reid, R. A. (1997) *Arthur C. Clarke: A Critical Companion*. Westport, CT: Greenwood Press.
Sleigh, C. (2016) 'Science as Heterotopia: The British Interplanetary Society before the Second World War', in D. Leggett and C. Sleigh (eds) *Scientific Governance in Britain, 1914–79*, pp. 217–33. Manchester: Manchester University Press.
Sleigh, C. (2018) '"Come on you demented modernists, let's hear from you": Science Fans as Literary Critics in the 1930s', in R. Bud et al (eds) *Being Modern: The Cultural Impact of Science in the Early Twentieth Century*, pp. 147–65. London: UCL Press.
Sleigh, C. and A. White (2019) 'War and Peace in British Science Fiction Fandom.' *Osiris* 34(1): 177–97.
Westfahl, G. (1996) *Cosmic Engineers: A Study of Hard Science Fiction*. Westport, CT: Greenwood Press.
Westfahl, G. (2018) *Arthur C. Clarke*. Urbana: University of Illinois Press.
Withers, J. (2021) 'Better to Move by Foot or Slidewalk: Post-Automobile Environments in Asimov's *The Caves of Steel* and Clarke's *The City and the Stars*.' *Extrapolation* 62(2): 111–31.
Wright, R. (2001) 'The Man Who Invented the Web.' *Time*, 24 June, URL (accessed 4 March 2021): http://content.time.com/time/magazine/article/0,9171,137689,00.html
Wymer, R. (1992) 'How "Safe" is John Wyndham? A Closer Look at his Work, with Particular Reference to *The Chrysalids*', *Foundation* 55: 25–36.

1

'IT'S JUST MY JOB FIVE DAYS A WEEK'
'ROCKETMEN' OF THE 1950s

Andy Sawyer

From 1950 to 1951, Arthur C. Clarke was 'science and plot advisor' to the first Dan Dare comic strip in the *Eagle*, 'Voyage to Venus'. Dare's adventures, meticulously charted by artist Frank Hampson, saw the 'pilot of the future' in action against a number of foes, particularly the menacing Mekon and his plans for conquest. Following in the wake of Dan Dare, Charles Chilton's evocative *Journey into Space*, broadcast by the BBC Home Service from 1953 to 1956, created a new generation of science fiction fans. At the same time, in the US, the 'Rocketmen' TV serials, building upon the template of Flash Gordon in the 1930s, 'taught their young male fans to dream [...] to grow into leaders, thinkers, and Cold War heroes [...] drawn together by a shared belief that adventure awaited them in space' (Miller and Van Riper, 2012: 7, 9). This widespread fascination with the space-dominated future gave children of the 1950s the sense that space travel, as Clarke had been arguing since his pre-war days with the British Interplanetary Society (BIS), was a certainty rather than a speculation.

However, these works for children were deliberately simplistic propaganda. By contrast, heroes are scarce in more realistic representations of the 1950s space programme. Adult science fiction, especially that of Clarke, attempted to avoid the mythological heroism associated with such British adventurers as Robert Falcon Scott and the pioneers of the American West. Whereas US magazines, such as John W. Campbell's *Astounding*, often presented human expansion into the universe as a benign given at the expense of the views of other alien species, British science fiction was often ambivalent about the romance of what was to be dubbed the 'final frontier'. When we compare Clarke's writing of the early 1950s with Robert A. Heinlein's tie-in for *Destination Moon* (1950) and Russian science fiction such as Pavel Klushantsev's *Road to the Stars* (1957), we see the complexity and contradictions in the visions of the forthcoming space age. Some British writers, especially E. C. Tubb, even overshadowed Clarke in the implication that there was little romance to be seen at all in the enterprise.

The Dream of Space

Klushantsev's visionary documentary film *Doroga k zvezdam* (*Road to the Stars*), begun in 1954 and finished shortly after the Sputnik success of 4 October 1957, begins with a scene hailing the world's first artificial satellite before retracing its steps, first, with Konstantin Tsiolkovsky's principles of using rocket propulsion to escape Earth's gravity. Through Robert H. Goddard's first liquid fuel rocket (1926) and the first Russian rocket (1933), we are shown how this story culminates with Sputnik heralding an era of interplanetary travel. The film segues into the future, moving dramatically from relatively leaden documentary to detailed speculation built around a carefully visualized future.

A three-man crew prepares for the first space launch. There are carefully extrapolated scenes of take-off and free fall, and the first spacewalk. While the documentary style fails to allow any drama along the lines of contemporary US attempts to promote public enthusiasm for space, since nothing actually goes *wrong*, leaving no space for suspense and triumphant achievement, the effects are astonishing. We see a space station under construction and eventually operating with a crew of several dozen men and women carrying out scientific operations, monitoring Earth weather, broadcasting television programmes. The film ends with visions of the first moon landing and beyond; sealed cities, mining operations, and the conquest of the planets bringing new vistas of knowledge. As Tsiolkovsky himself averred, humanity's destiny lies not on Earth, and Klushantsev's narrative consolidates this claim.

The achievement of space travel began in comparative innocence with the amateur rocketry societies of the 1920s and 1930s in Germany, Russia, Britain, the US and elsewhere. Organizations such as the BIS, founded in 1933 by P. W. Cleator, were largely pressure groups involved with low-level experimentation and public-awareness work. They were made up of engineers or enthusiastic teenagers, such as the Manchester Interplanetary Society whose launch of a rocket in 1937 resulted in minor injury and an appearance before the local magistrate (Hansen, 2016: 34). However, the outbreak of war in 1939 turned idealistic hobbies into military potential: rockets could clearly be used as projectile weapons. The German rocketry enthusiast Willy Ley had already left Nazi Germany for the US, where he became a significant contributor to magazines such as *Astounding*, but his associate Wernher von Braun remained to head the missile programme at Peenemünde, developing the V1 and V2 rocket weapons. In 1945, von Braun surrendered to the Americans and came to work on NASA's space programme.

A teenage member of the BIS, Clarke volunteered for the RAF in 1941, and became a technical officer working on radar systems. Following his demobilization in 1946, Clarke enrolled at King's College London, graduating with First Class Honours in Mathematics and Physics. Before then, however, he had published perhaps his most prophetic work: the essay 'Extra-Terrestrial Relays' in the technical journal *Wireless World* (1945). Here, he suggested a system of satellites in geosynchronous orbits, from which signals could be bounced to blanket the Earth with a communications network.

During this period, Clarke was heavily involved with the BIS, promoting space travel with papers such as 'The Challenge of the

Spaceship' (1946). He served twice as chairman of the BIS in 1946–47 and 1950–3, at a time when many of his friends and colleagues, such as Val Cleaver, were developing rocket engines and other space-related technology. (Cleaver went on to work, in the 1960s, on British missile programmes such as Blue Streak and Black Arrow.) Clarke was also responsible for the address by Olaf Stapledon given as 'Interplanetary Man?' (1948); the title's question mark shows Stapledon's more sceptical stance towards the Society's objectives. The enthusiasm for space was, however, not confined to specialist propaganda societies like the BIS, or the readers of science fiction magazines. Although Clarke swiftly became a significant figure in promoting space among the wider Anglo-American public, he did not buy into – and sometimes actively opposed – the political and military objectives of the 'Space Race'.

While readers of American sf magazines like *Astounding* were certainly aware of the massive features appearing in 'slick' journals such as *Colliers* and *Life*, many of the readers of such articles would not necessarily have seen themselves as science fiction aficionados. It was here that science fiction and the 'mainstream' collided in a creative, collective passion for space ably overseen by the military authorities. The images of space created by the artist Chesley Bonestell in his contributions to *Colliers*, *Life* and the *Illustrated London News* reached an audience far removed from the readers of *Astounding* and *Galaxy*, for which he provided cover art. *Colliers*, for instance, published seven issues from March 1952 to April 1954 on the space programme beginning emphatically with 'Man will Conquer Space Soon', featuring articles by Ley, Von Braun and Fred Whipple with dramatic illustrations by Bonestell. Subsequent issues featured space suits, survival in space and life on Mars 'at a time when Congress was trying to convince itself to invest several billion dollars of taxpayer's money in a space program' (Miller and Durant, 2001: 77).

The culmination of the pre-Sputnik US dream of space was probably the film *Destination Moon* (1950), produced by George Pal and directed by Irving Pichel, and the Disney animated TV programmes, *Man in Space*, *Man and the Moon* (both 1955) and *Mars and Beyond* (1957). In the first of several science fiction collaborations, which included Byron Haskin's adaptation of *The War of the Worlds* (1953), Pal hired Bonestell to produce matte paintings for the space and lunar scenes of *Destination Moon*, itself based in part on Heinlein's *Rocket Ship Galileo* (1947), 'the first mature and coherent vision of a potential American future in space' (Kilgore, 2003: 87). The film also shares affinities with Heinlein's novella, 'The Man Who Sold the Moon' (1950), written prior to his work on the screenplay for *Destination Moon*.

Heinlein's story argues the case for a specifically commercial, private-enterprise exploitation of the Moon and against nationalist and military motives. His businessman hero, Harriman, prefigures the Antarctic Treaty of 1959 which 'generated a then-new type of legal space on Earth's landmasses: a land that was owned by no one, but which was not a *terra nullus* available for possession' (Collis, 2016: 274), the 1962 Convention on the High Seas which affirmed that the seas were 'open to all nations' (Collis, 2016: 276), and the 1967 Outer Space Treaty in which 'Space was clearly defined as *res communis*, in which there is freedom of movement and use, and freedom from state appropriation' (Collis, 2016: 280). Harriman argues that possession of the Moon may be 'the greatest real-estate venture since the Pope carved up the New World', but that it cannot 'be owned by a single country [...] nationalism should stop at the stratosphere' (Heinlein, 1978: 133). Instead, Harriman argues that *political* ownership of the Moon will enflame national tensions:

> The other nations – quite rightfully – will be scared to death of the United States. They will be able to look up in the sky any night and see the main atom-bomb rocket base of the United States staring down the backs of their necks. (Heinlein, 1978: 147)

Destination Moon, and Heinlein's own tie-in published in *Short Story* (1950), argue differently. The importance of private industry, as the force in capitalist society that gets things *done*, is still stressed. However, after Jim Barnes's avowal of adventure ('What's the payoff? – it's *research*, it's *pioneering*'), and the inspiring Woody Woodpecker cartoon played to the industrialists who are being asked to fund the venture, General Thayer gets to the point: 'The first country that can use the moon for the launching of missiles will control the Earth.' Once the expedition has landed, Doc Cargraves claims the Moon 'on behalf of and for the benefit of all mankind.' This is later glossed by Barnes as emphasizing the role of the United States.

In Heinlein's story, names are changed (Cargraves and Thayer are now Corley and Bowles; Sweeney is Traub) and there is more emphasis upon the need to establish that the fate of the country is at stake. The possible deaths of the crew as they struggle to lighten the ship in order to be able to use their remaining fuel stocks to return to Earth are nothing compared to the importance of getting the message back that the Moon has been reached: and by Americans. Whatever the idealism of the engineers and pilots, visionary-capitalist military *Realpolitik* dictates that the first moon-base must be the USA's. In Britain, the BIS council was invited to a preview of the film. Reviewing it for the society's journal, A. V. Cleaver praises its realism, although criticizing some technical points; but concludes 'we should have preferred a little less emphasis on the 'He-who-controls-the-moon-controls-the-Earth' theme' (Cleaver, 1950: 244). The story ends ambiguously:

> 'Are we really going to make it?' Traub asks.
> Barnes decided to be truthful. 'Probably not.' He glanced at Bowles; the Admiral's features were sunken; his false-teeth had gone with the rest. Barnes grinned warmly. 'But we're sure going to give it a try!' (Heinlein, 1979: 176)

The self-sacrifice of *Luna*'s crew offers the story a heroic tinge, but the way Heinlein pulls back from *showing* them as tragic heroic pioneers (although necessitated by the ending of the film) is perhaps significant if we consider the way *Destination Moon* was part of the build-up to the space programme. The Disney comics and films brought fact and hard speculation to the imaginations of children stimulated by the cheaply made 'rocketmen' tv serials such as *Tom Corbett, Space Cadet* and *Space Patrol* (both 1950–5). But, partly because they were aimed at children, partly because there *were* no role models in real life, they presented the conquest of space as reassuring fantasy, focusing upon the fascination of knowledge rather than the political or human issues. In *Man in Space*, for instance, Heinz Haber introduces a section on dealing with the hostile environment of space by presenting a cartoon 'common man [...] a man just like you and me' through which questions like the crushing pressure of acceleration during take-off are illustrated. Our 'common man' blacks out and reels about the screen while illustrating concepts like weightlessness in space, turning green with nausea. In a comic sequence when he is surrounded by cigar-smoke (apparently, the idea of smoking inside a spaceship is not *itself* to be rejected), we learn that astronauts may be in danger of being suffocated by their own exhalations unless an air-circulation system is installed. But this is the ultimately safe grotesquery of the children's cartoon. If any *living* trainee astronauts were injured or killed during the research that these programmes illustrate, we are not told.

Failure could only be envisaged if it was eventually overcome. Heinlein ends his tie-in with a vague reference to those who fell in achieving the goal of spaceflight, but if those fallen are heroic, they are only heroes in the jingoistic sense that those sacrificed for a greater good are deemed heroes by those who directed them and are in safe and secure possession of what they 'fell' for. This is, perhaps, to be expected. The arguments presented in 1959 over the legal ownership of Antarctica are the dry and detailed disputes of lawyers and diplomats, a world away from the heroic and often tragic explorations of Shackleton, Scott and Amundsen. The conquest of space is the utopian dream opposing the nightmare of nuclear annihilation, even though the technology that would bring about both is very much the same. For example, to ensure that Kurt Neumann's *Rocketship X-M* (1950) reached cinemas earlier than the more expensive *Destination Moon*, stock footage of the actual German V2 rockets dropped on London were used in the take-off scenes.

From Dream to 'Blueprint'

The apparently gravity-defying Skylon structure, designed by Hidalgo Moya, Philip Powell and Felix Samuely for the 1951 Festival of Britain, was not necessarily meant to symbolize a rocket but its needle-like structure would have subliminally suggested 'spaceship' to the young Dan Dare fans who saw in it (James, 1987). The once eccentric ideas of the pre-war rocket societies were now ripe with promise. Clarke, whose involvement with them and scientific training gave him a unique perspective, was positioned to fuse science fiction's dreams with space technology's blueprints.

His first book, *Interplanetary Flight* (1950), its successor *The Exploration of Space* (1951) and a novel he had written in 1947, *Prelude to Space* (1951), were visionary propaganda for the forthcoming Space Age. Here, Clarke is not arguing that humanity *will* move into space but that it *should*. It is through the opportunities offered by space that international co-operation and human betterment will be developed. Neil McAleer calls *Interplanetary Flight* 'the first book in the English language to present the basic theory of space flight with any technical detail' (McAleer, 1992: 74). Its selection as a Book of the Month Club choice in the US boosted its sales, and Clarke was in the position of arguing the case for space through non-fiction as well as fiction.

Prelude is in some ways a fiction parallel to *Interplanetary Flight*. Set in 1978, it is told from the viewpoint of an American historian (Dirk Alexson) engaged to record the first Moon landing while it happens. Interplanetary, the international (though British-dominated) body that has long argued for space travel and is now putting its arguments into practice, is modelled upon non-military organizations such as the BIS. Space as a focus for *national* rivalries is absent from *Prelude* which, apart from a vague reference to the 'unsettled 1950s', overlooks the Cold War. The *Prometheus* lifts off to the comforting, nostalgic tones of Big Ben, which affirm for Clarke's contemporary readers a British presence in the Space Race.

For Clarke, though, the lunar project is a single step in a greater mission: the long voyage of understanding the universe. In one of those visionary flashes which make Clarke's chapter-endings verge upon genuine poetry, Alexson reflects on the moon's isolation. His interior monologue segues into the narrator's 'And now at last, after all these ages, its loneliness was coming to an end' (Clarke, 1951a: 132).

This 'lunar' loneliness can only, for both Alexon and the project's charismatic Director-General, Derwent, be a reflection of human loneliness. In the following chapter, Derwent, reading Swinburne, reflects upon the inevitability of 'eternal night'. Can humanity, he wonders, stand against the unavoidable end by achieving knowledge? Clarke's stoic utopianism is hardly geared to give cosy answers to that question, but it identifies it as one worth answering. An epilogue thirty years later justifies the venture. Alexson himself is shown as one of thousands saved from the consequences of heart conditions by the Moon's low gravity.

The Sands of Mars (1951) presents a very similar observer's-eye view of the camaraderie of the spaceways; and is in many ways a reworking of the themes of *Prelude*. The protagonist, Martin Gibson, is a science fiction writer who chooses to remain on Mars when his task of writing about the new colony is over. The somewhat maudlin sub-plot in which Gibson discovers that the youngest member of the crew of the *Ares* is his son by a failed relationship counterpoints the cosmic theme with personal loneliness. Its awkwardness lies partly in the sense that Clarke, writing at a time when notice of his own sexuality would have been unwelcome and lead to criminal proceedings, might well have been attempting to express a different kind of relationship between the two men, and a different kind of loneliness. The discovery of Martian life, and revelation of a terraforming project emphasizes that this personal quest is verging on what C. S. Lewis was to call, with reference to *Childhood's End* (1953), 'eschatological fiction' (Lewis, 2000: 455).

These books and others brought Clarke success, not only among the British and American science fiction readership but also the general public. Clarke's clear explanations of factual science and the way he calmly inserted his visions for space into his fiction made him popular with the mainstream press. 'Venture to the Moon' (1956) was written as a series of six interlinked stories for the *Evening Standard*. Here, British, American and Russian teams, each with their own ship, vie for the acclaim of first reaching the Moon. The narrator is the captain of the British ship. This is Clarke in the humorous mode of *Tales From the White Hart* (1957), in which he spoofs his own profession through a series of tall tales told by a hanger-on, but there is a serious undertone in the way he rewrites the Space Race. The first story begins with the astronauts in training aboard the orbiting space station. They are meant to set off and land together, but the narrator is persuaded by his authorities into leaving Earth orbit 95 minutes early only to find, somewhat to his relief, that the others have done the same. The final story has the British crew volunteering to remain on the Moon so that the larger American ship can take more of the crew of the damaged Russian craft. Those who return first will be lucratively rewarded for their memoirs and TV appearances, but one of the British crew has worked out that having spent over half the financial year on the Moon, they are not liable for tax on their earnings.

The success of the stories led to 'The Other Side of the Sky', published as 'Six Stories of the Space Stations' in *Infinity Science Fiction* just as Sputnik was launched. The first three stories were introduced in *Infinity* by a short essay linking them to 'International Geophysical Year': 'The launching of the first artificial Earth satellite is, of course only one of many IGY projects' (Clarke, 1957a: 5). Vignettes with the characteristic Clarke 'twist', rather than short stories, they nevertheless display several different effects, and are loosely linked as the reminiscences of a pioneer. 'Special Delivery' describes the 'rugged life' of the constructors of the space stations that are going to provide a global communications network, and ends with a typically Clarkeian sense of awe (mixed here with wry humour) as the narrator realizes that the misdirected supply rocket with the team's long-awaited 'needle-jet shower baths' will not in fact be wholly lost, as its new orbit will bring it back in A. D. 15,862. A more overt comedy, 'Feathered Friend' has one of the space-station's crew smuggle in a pet – a canary which, it turns out, safeguards them in the way canaries detected a loss of breathable air in mines (linking their work in space to a more traditional kind of manual labour). 'Take a Deep Breath' is Clarke in scientific mode, showing that it *is* theoretically possible to survive exposure to vacuum.

The second trio of stories commences with 'Freedom of Space', in which an African-American radio anchor-man decides that space is a more congenial environment than the stress-ridden and polluted

Earth. 'Passer By', perhaps, most closely approaches the cosmic awe of 'The Sentinel' (1951), although again the setting offers humour and pathos (or even bathos): the narrator's glimpse of what may be an alien ship, 'utterly alien and [...] very, very old' (Clarke, 1957b: 62) cannot be reported because he observes it from a supply shuttle on the way back from an illicit visit to his girlfriend on another station. Would he, he ruefully observes, have risked their careers had he known that eventually Julie would marry someone else? By the time of 'Call of the Stars', the project has been long finished and, indeed, a new project, the first expedition to Mars, is about to set out in another chapter of humanity's expansion into space.

Clarke, though, was overtaken by events. 'Special Delivery' opens with 'I can still remember the excitement, back in 1957 (or was it 1958?) when the United States of America launched the first artificial satellites and managed to hang a few pounds of instruments up here above the atmosphere' (Clarke, 1957a: 5). The 1958 collected version reads 'back in 1957, when Russia launched the first artificial satellites' (Clarke, 2000: 631). Although laced with humour, the sequence looks back at the poignancy of the novels, and there is an elegiac farewell in 'Call of the Stars', set in the closing hours of the twentieth century, as the narrator looks down from space recalling the conflict with his father who was against his going into space and their final meeting before his father's death. Remembering his father's pain, the narrator goes to make his last farewell to his son, who is himself heading for the stars. The scene is reminiscent of Judith Merril's 1952 novella 'Daughters of Earth', although Merril's text did not achieve wider recognition until it was reprinted in New Worlds in 1967.

Like Heinlein, Clarke depicts a shift in human achievement brought about by human endeavour, but the epical quality is undermined by the pervasive humour. In fact, the moments of awe at the scale of the universe have no room for epic: heroism has no place here. In 'Passer By', the scale of the proof that humanity is not alone in the universe makes no difference whether our narrator is a pathetically lovelorn chancer misusing resources to obtain some sex on the side, or a pioneer in the greatest human endeavour ever (which is why the logical flaws in the story – would the unauthorized use of a shuttle have not been *noticed?* – do not in the end matter). In 'Feathered Friend', we know that Sven is expert in assembling space-stations in free-fall, but the story is not about the achievement of his task against heroic odds: it is about the advantages of having a canary in space. Sven and his team are as good as construction workers on skyscrapers back on Earth (with the added advantage that they can step back and admire their work without plummeting to the ground). But the cartoon-like joke implies neither the sense that construction workers on Earth are particularly heroic, nor that the conditions under which space-workers work give *them* a particular claim upon the term. Even in *A Fall of Moondust* (1961), in which dust-cruiser crew Pat Harris and Sue Wilkins and their passengers bravely overcome potential catastrophe, there is little sense of pioneer heroics. They are ordinary people doing ordinary jobs who, when called upon, prove up to the task. It is their very mundanity that allows Clarke to highlight the sublimity of their surroundings.

The influence both of Clarke and Heinlein appears in *Journey into Space*. Centred around the unquestioned assumption that there would be a major British presence in space so colourfully presented by Dan Dare in the *Eagle* (for which Charles Chilton also wrote), the first of the three stories, *Operation Luna* (1953–4), begins in the early 1960s when 'Doc' Matthews, an American working on a space programme mothballed by Washington, receives a call from his British friend 'Jet' Morgan, who tells him about the atomic rocket motors an Australian engineer (Mitch) has been developing and invites him to join the crew of the first expedition to the Moon.

Chilton cleverly links his narrative to the body of British science fiction by making Morgan bring, as the one personal item each crew member is allowed, a copy of H. G. Wells's *The First Men in the Moon* (1901). It is clear, also, that Heinlein and *Destination Moon* are somewhere in the background. Joe Sweeney, the Brooklyn comic relief in *Destination Moon* who panics at the effects of take-off, plays about when they are floating in free-fall, and has to have everything explained to him is akin to *Journey into Space*'s Lemmy. They even both play the harmonica. (Another character is nicknamed 'Doc' and the ship, of course, is *Luna*). Heinlein's influence appears more strongly in the third adventure, *The World in Peril* (1955–6), when the song 'The Green Hills of Earth' composed by the poet Rhysling in Heinlein's 1947 story of that name, is sung by 'conditioned' Earthmen making up a Martian invading force and again after the closing credits.

The awe and terror of alien encounter creates tension, as do the scenes of the bickering crew, trapped on the Moon with no obvious escape (another possible echo of *Destination Moon*, although Chilton credited the scene as an attempt to prove that there were things radio could do that the emerging technology of television could not: the entire episode is played of course in pitch darkness). We have a neat balance here between stiff-upper-lip Britishness and complete desolation. There is also very little overt Cold War anxiety. Perhaps because the primary audience for the programme was children and young teenagers, there is no rivalry with the Russians, no politics at all except for a minor piece of triumphalism when it is revealed that the programme is 'the greatest Commonwealth co-operative effort even undertaken in peacetime.' The Australian base for the project is, like that in *Prelude to Space*, Luna City where, we are told, 'every race and tongue of the British Commonwealth of Nations was to be seen and heard.' What we actually hear (mostly Australian or Canadian) is much more limited.

Heinlein's conclusion to his tie-in of *Destination Moon* is certainly tinged with heroic language:

> The monument where the proud Luna once stood is pictured in every schoolroom. Many trips followed, some tragic, some not, before space transportation reached its present safe operation. The spaceways are paved with the bodies and glorious hopes of pioneers. With accomplishment of their dream some of the romance has gone out of space. (Heinlein, 1979: 176)

But as remarked above, this is ambiguous. As a propagandist, Heinlein lauds 'the bodies and glorious hopes of pioneers', but as an essentially realist writer, attempting to suggest what life after the dream might be like for those living it, he is at pains to stress the nostalgia and the way 'romance has gone out of space'. This is, he seems to be saying, how things are; what happens after major projects have been fulfilled.

Heinlein is, of course, the writer who told his readers at the 1941 World Science Fiction Convention that there will not 'always be an England' and that the essence of science fiction is *change* (Heinlein, 1941: 3–4).

The Dream ... Fulfilled?

Both Heinlein and Clarke fictionalized the conquest of space as something entirely positive. Their work can be seen in the context of the wider post-war enthusiasm for space; partly a cover for the use of rockets to deliver weapons of mass destruction, partly a Great Power rivalry where the stakes were national prestige, and partly a shorthand for a vision of a transformed, even utopian future. While Ley and Bonestell in *The Conquest of Space* (1949) 'convinced an entire generation of post-World War II readers that spaceflight was possible in their lifetime' (Miller and Durant, 2001: 57), and Clarke in *Interplanetary Flight* suggested *how* this might be achieved, it was the fiction in which *people* were presented in space that offered a realistic scenario. Clarke echoed Heinlein's pioneering spirit, but as a post-imperial Briton, his depictions of humans in space skirted uneasily around the issues of militarism, national rivalry and colonialism. The British captain in 'Venture to the Moon' feels shocked about being asked to double-cross his American and Soviet colleagues but does not think to actively refuse. The joke by which his fellow-captains have obviously received the same 'suggestion' and fallen into the same trap of complicity with ideas of 'national prestige' only confirms the story's implication that they think of themselves as good friends and 'all in this together' (Clarke, 2000: 532).

A markedly different tone appears in E. C. Tubb, one of the most prolific contributors to the British science fiction paperback imprints and magazines of the 1950s and 1960s. Tubb was not an idealist. He presented space not as a Clarkeian paradigm shift in human evolution or a Heinleinian necessity for economic or military survival, and certainly not the 'boys-own' romance of Dan Dare or the dramatic events of *Journey into Space*, but a drab, workaday, unromantic, even squalid environment that could drive people to madness. If in Heinlein's post-pioneer future 'some of the romance has gone out of space', it is hard to find any suggestion in many of Tubb's stories that romance and 'the glorious hopes of pioneers' were ever there in the first place.

In 'Blow the Man Down' (1955), published as by Julian Carey, an aging spaceman is on his last trip home before enforced retirement. His fellow crew jeer at him, and he looks forward to the low status of being grounded with trepidation, but he reflects, what is he losing? 'Boredom, monotony, the endless waiting from takeoff to planetfall and with it the inevitable spite and nastiness of men forced to live too close together for too long' (Tubb, 1955: 80). In 'The Beatific Smile' (1958), the narrator shares a cramped, odorous cabin with a drug-addled captain he hates while waiting for rescue, while in 'Bitter Sweet' (1954) a derelict spaceship and the man who flew her round the Moon are long forgotten. Harrigan tries to interest a space-mad young boy in his story but he would rather go and watch a serial. The pioneering romance has long faded: 'Ships go to the Moon every day and to the planets twice a week' (Tubb, 1954: 33).

Tubb also presented a more domestic sense of a future in space. In 'The Letter' (1956), as by Alice Beecham, a young boy waits desperately to hear about his application to the Space Academy. His mother, a spaceman's widow, has to deal with the heavy-handed sympathy of her friend who advises her not to let Peter go, as well as her own feelings about the loneliness she would feel without him. Another Alice Beecham story, 'Like a Diamond' (1956), focuses upon a little girl's coping strategy for her anxiety about her father, who works on the space station she sees in the sky each night as she goes to sleep. There is a touch of sentimentality in these stories, and Tubb's choice of a female pseudonym for them probably reflects a sense that domesticity equals a 'feminine approach', but their focus upon the human rather than the technological reminds us there are other ways of approaching space. The only other text to approximate Tubb's fiction is *Road to the Stars* where, in a charming domestic scene, a woman takes her cat onboard ship. The editorial tag-line for 'Like a Diamond' (written by Tubb himself, as editor of *Authentic* during that period) is telling: 'The romance of space is wonderful – for those who can actually participate. But what of those who cannot?' (Tubb, 1956a: 97). It is Tubb, more than any other science fiction writer of the period, who imagines aspects of the coming Space Age that do not fit into the model of science fiction as received by the fans of *Rocket Ship Galileo* or the colourful future depicted in the *Eagle*. While the wonders of the universe will be laid open for us, and life will be utterly transformed in ways that we cannot dream of, there will be those who are damaged by the new age, those who are unable to reap the benefits of it, the drifters and inadequates who, like Curt Gregson in 'The Troublemaker' (1953), are the victims of an economic system which is stacked against them.

The Individual in Space

Tubb, although far less of a visionary writer than Clarke or Heinlein, offers an interesting counter-perspective on the paradigm of space as an emblem of the utopian future, an emblem that had been part of Anglo-American science fiction since before the days of the early pulps. In presenting movement beyond Earth into space as a goal to be achieved, space travel's propagandists – from the military-industrial complex to the writers competing for the attention of an audience of enthusiasts – had to present convincing reasons. For the writers, this meant experiencing the awesomeness of the paradigm-shift through characters who could be imagined as living in this new environment. In advocating space as both possible and desirable, writers like Clarke and Heinlein were also faced with the problem of how to create a plausible environment. While knowing that their audience contained a large proportion of young enthusiasts who wanted to share in the heroics of bursting into the new frontier, they were also (particularly Clarke) in direct communication with the engineers and technicians engaged in bringing about this reality. For this kind of writing, therefore, the simple hero is not enough. While character is, perhaps necessarily, subordinate to setting when the setting itself is so dramatically important, it becomes increasingly the case that the characters reflect how the author sees the nature of the goal to be reached.

Clarke's characters, then, are scientists and technocrats with the camaraderie of the shared group, almost certainly drawing upon his school and military service; and the playful anarchy of fandom. He evokes the working atmosphere of his construction workers in 'The Other Side of the Sky', particularly in the original versions published in *Infinity*:

> It's only fair to say that we were being paid about a thousand dollars a week to endure these temporary discomforts, but after a month in space any one of us would have exchanged the money for a nice hot tub or a room that wasn't shared with six other men who all snored in different keys. (Clarke, 1957a: 8)

But we note these are privileged workers on 'a thousand dollars a week', and although the strain leads to fights, the conflict is deflated by humour: 'Luckily no great harm was done, because it's very difficult for weightless fighters to damage each other' (Clarke, 1957a: 8). Heinlein's characters are entrepreneurs and technicians, fired in their enthusiasm to make money by an ideology of patriotism. They, and Clarke's protagonists (as well as the Russian cosmonauts of *Road to the Stars*), have a greater social goal in mind than individual heroics. The crew in *Destination Moon* are even prepared to sacrifice themselves for the greater national good. To that extent, perhaps, they are heroes. Certainly, Heinlein's novella inscribes heroism upon the pioneers of the spaceways. But Tubb's characters explicitly disavow heroics even in this limited sense. They are from a lower social class. They are working people and hustlers, who whenever they express an opinion are cynical about self-sacrifice and national or international interests.

Despite the idea of space as a leap into the unknown, there are few explorers in this kind of science fiction. The nearest such character in Heinlein, and one of his actual *heroes*, is the balladeer Rhysling, whose self-imposed task is to create heroic myths (becoming, ironically, a hero himself). The children's literature of the early space programme certainly spawned heroes: the Jet Morgans, Dan Dares, Space Kingleys and Captain Condors of the British comics and radio serials were, like their names suggest, dramatic action figures, like Captain

Future or Tom Corbett, Space Cadet of the US TV serials. The later space programme, once it involved human individuals, produced personalities – Yuri Gagarin, John Glenn, Valentina Tereshkova and, later, Neil Armstrong – but rarely heroes on the scale of the Antarctic explorers of the early twentieth century. Such heroes, like Scott, are linked to tragic failure whereas the *Realpolitik* of the Space Race necessitated heroes more like the fictional Dan Dare or Jet Morgan. On both sides of the Iron Curtain, failures were hushed up in case they turned public opinion against the project. By contrast, Clarke's distrust of imperial ventures made him suspicious of heroics: 'It is not easy to see how the more extreme forms of nationalism can long survive when men begin to see the Earth in its true perspective' (Clarke, 1946: 72) and 'Empires, like atomic bombs, are self-liquidating assets' (Clarke, 1946: 76). In *Prelude to Space*, Clarke was determined that 'We will take no frontiers into space' (Clarke, 1951a: 94). Heinlein's anti-Communism, on the other hand, made success too important to entertain the possibility of failure.

But it is Tubb who gives space a living (if depressing) economy. To say that Clarke and Heinlein are writing propaganda may sound dismissive of their achievements; both men firmly believed (in their different ways) in the value of space travel and wrote, in great part, to persuade their readers that the future was in space. But neither were writing (to use Heinlein's preferred term) truly *speculative* fiction, in the sense that they were attempting to create a fully rounded picture of what this new era would be. Perhaps, in a sense, neither was Tubb, the most generically standard writer of the three. But, in contrast to them, Tubb is not propagandizing a transformation. The achievement of space travel is not a paradigm shift. Space travel is an industry and, like all industries, it depends on unwilling grunt labour to turn the wheels. Tubb's spacemen are like Rudyard Kipling's soldiers in the poem 'Tommy' (1890) without even the consolation of being 'thin red lines of `eroes' (line 22). Instead, it's lonely out in space, they miss their wives and kids, it's just their job five days a week, and all they want is a good pay-cheque and the chance to go home.

Works Cited

Chilton, C. (1953–4/2006) *Journey into Space: Operation Luna*. BBC Worldwide. [CD]
Chilton, C. (1955–6/2007) *Journey into Space: The World in Peril*. BBC Worldwide. [CD]
Clarke, A. C. (1946) 'The Challenge of the Spaceship.' *Journal of the British Interplanetary Society* 6(3): 66–81.
Clarke, A. C. (1951a) *Prelude to Space*. New York: World Editions.
Clarke, A. C. (1951b) *The Sands of Mars*. London: Sidgwick and Jackson.
Clarke, A. C. (1957a) 'The Other Side of the Sky' (Part 1). *Infinity Science Fiction* 2(5): 5–17.
Clarke, A. C. (1957b) 'The Other Side of the Sky' (Part 2). *Infinity Science Fiction* 2(6): 55–66.
Clarke, A. C. (2010) *The Collected Stories of Arthur C. Clarke*. London: Gollancz.
Cleaver, A. V. (1950) 'Destination Moon [Review]', *Journal of the British Interplanetary Society* 9(5): 241–4.
Collis, C. (2016) 'Res Communis?: A Critical Legal Geography of Outer Space, Antarctica, and the Deep Seabed', in P. Dickens and J. S. Ormrod (eds) *The Palgrave Handbook of Society, Culture and Outer Space*, pp. 270–91. Basingstoke: Palgrave Macmillan.
Doroga k zvezdam [Road to the Stars] (1957) dir. P. Klushantsev, URL (accessed 22 April 2020): https://www.youtube.com/watch?v=9CX0oSjwLqI [Film]
Hansen, R. (2016) *Then: Science Fiction Fandom in the UK 1930–1980*. Reading: Ansible Editions.
Heinlein, R. A. (1941) *The Discovery of the Future*. Los Angeles: Novacious.
Heinlein, R. A. (1978) *The Past Through Tomorrow, Vol. 1*. London: New English Library.
Heinlein, R. A. (1979) *Destination Moon*. Boston MA: Gregg Press.
James, E. (1987) 'The Future Viewed from Mid-century Britain: Clarke, Hampson and the Festival of Britain', *Foundation* 41: 42–51.
Kilgore, D. W. D. (2003) *Astrofuturism: Science, Race, and Visions of Utopia in Space*. Philadelphia: University of Pennsylvania Press.
Kipling, R. (1890) 'Tommy', URL (accessed 22 April 2020): http://www.kiplingsociety.co.uk/poems_tommy.htm
Lewis, C. S. (2000) *Essay Collection and Other Short Pieces*, ed. L. Walmsley. London: HarperCollins.

McAleer, N. (1992) *Odyssey: The Authorised Biography of Arthur C. Clarke*. London: Gollancz.

Man in Space (1955) dir. W. Kimball, URL (accessed 3 November 2019): https://www.youtube.com/watch?v=WFXza9RH7-E [Film]

Merril, J. (1952/1967) 'Daughters of Earth.' *New Worlds* 172: 6–76.

Miller, C. J. and A. B. Van Riper (2012) *1950s 'Rocketman' TV series and Their Fans*. Basingstoke: Palgrave Macmillan.

Miller, R. and F. Durant III (2001) *The Art of Chesley Bonestell*. London: Paper Tiger.

Tubb, E. C. (1953) 'The Troublemaker.' *Nebula* 5: 73–118.

Tubb, E. C. (1954) 'Bitter Sweet.' *Science Fantasy* 4(10): 31–38

Tubb, E. C. ['Julian Carey'] (1955) 'Blow the Man Down.' *Authentic* 62: 72–80.

Tubb, E. C. ['Alice Beecham'] (1956a) 'Like a Diamond.' *Authentic* 70: 97–105.

Tubb, E. C. ['Alice Beecham'] (1956b) 'The Letter.' *Authentic* 68: 121–29.

Tubb, E. C. (1958) 'The Beatific Smile.' *Nebula* 31: 27–35.

2

CLARKAEOLOGY
ARTHUR C. CLARKE'S TIME CAPSULES

Patrick Parrinder

During his lifetime, Arthur C. Clarke was rightly regarded as one of the world's leading futurologists. Many of his book titles – *The Exploration of Space, Prelude to Space* (both 1951), *Childhood's End* (1953), *Reach for Tomorrow* (1956), *2001: A Space Odyssey* (1968) and its sequels – are strikingly forward-looking. It is true that his non-fiction collection *Profiles of the Future* (1962), dedicated to his 'Colleagues in the Institute for Twenty-first Century Studies', begins with the observation that 'It is impossible to predict the future' (Clarke, 1962: 9). But the book ends with a time-chart (which Clarke says is not to be taken too seriously) culminating with the achievement of immortality and our first meeting with extra-terrestrials in the year 2100. This, for Clarke, as for his predecessor Olaf Stapledon (whose *Last and First Men* (1930) also contains a series of elaborate time-charts), is only the end of the beginning of the human story. After all, as Clarke tells us, 'the one fact about the Future of which we can be certain is that it will be utterly fantastic' (Clarke, 1962: 12). It seems paradoxical, then, to argue that the idea of belatedness rather than prematurity is one of the keys to reading Arthur C. Clarke.

If we look more closely at the author's description of his futurological aims in *Profiles of the Future*, we find that he compares the ages stretching ahead of us to an 'unmapped and unexplored country'. His aim is to 'survey its frontiers and to get some idea of its extent. The detailed geography of the interior must remain unknown – until we reach it' (Clarke, 1962: 9). In fact, as a novelist, Clarke is not just a surveyor and geographer of his imagined futures, but also a digger – someone whose concern is to examine the soil of these futures for traces of their (and, very often, our) forgotten past. With the exception of his late-career *Time Odyssey* series co-written with Stephen Baxter, his protagonists are almost invariably space travellers, not time travellers, which means that they are citizens of the future rather than Wellsian explorers stumbling into it as an unknown country. Their aim is not to travel further forward but to get to know their country and its history more fully; and in much of Clarke's fiction this history is (sometimes literally) buried.

Tales of Fieldwork

When, in *Childhood's End*, Jan Rodricks finds himself in the main city of the Overlords' planet, he is naturally taken to visit their museum. One of its great rooms contains the exhibit for Earth, containing everything from television receivers to palaeolithic axes (Clarke, 1953/1990: 179). This is just one of the large number of museums in Clarke's novels and stories, each with its knowledgeable curator or guide. Academics, too, throng in his fictions. Most are professors of physical science, but a few are specialists in rediscovering the past. Two of his short stories are directly concerned with archaeological and geological fieldwork, and it is notable that the first of these, 'Time's Arrow' (1950), is, most unusually for Clarke, a time-travel story. Professor Fowler and his two assistants are palaeontologists excavating a petrified mud-flat in which they have found footprints of a giant dinosaur hitherto unknown to science. Nearby is a top-secret laboratory in which two physicists are developing a means of time travel, but with the aim of exploring the past rather than the future.

After all, as one of them tells Fowler and his team, 'It would save you a lot of trouble, wouldn't it, if you could actually *see* what took place in the past', thus taking the labour and guesswork out of archaeology (Clarke, 2000: 230). But their attempt at time travel (with Fowler as passenger) apparently comes to a swift and nasty end, as the assistants realize when they come across a jeep's tyre-tracks almost obliterated by a dinosaur footprint in the 50 million-year-old mud deposit. Professor Fowler and his assistants closely resemble Professor Forster and his two graduate students in Clarke's second fieldwork story, 'Jupiter Five' (1953). Here, sometime in the early 2040s, the three archaeologists are part of the seven-man crew of the first human mission to land on the fifth moon of Jupiter. While there are other main characters in Clarke's fiction who see themselves as amateurs of archaeology, it is in the story of Forster and his students that the pattern of what I will call 'Clarkaeology' is set.

Professor Forster is an adherent of the controversial and now discredited archaeological theory known as 'hyperdiffusionism'. He is attempting to prove his 'diffusion theory of extraterrestrial culture' by finding further traces on Jupiter V of an ancient, reptilian civilization that has already been located on Mercury and Mars (Clarke, 2000: 438). To Forster, the fact that the remains of similar civilizations (known as Culture X) have been discovered on two different planets indicates that they possessed the means of space travel and have a single, presumably interstellar origin. They left behind works of art with astronomical motifs, including a 'rather well-preserved bas-relief of the Solar System' found on Mercury and pinpointing Jupiter V (Clarke, 2000: 440). What Forster and his students discover on the Jovian moon goes far beyond simply vindicating the Professor's diffusion theory. It is, we are told, 'the greatest archaeological find in all history' (Clarke, 2000: 443), since the moon turns out to be none other than an artificial satellite built of metal. Once they have found an opening in the moon's surface, Clarke's archaeologists are ready to explore the original spaceship which brought the Culture X 'reptile-people' to the solar system from somewhere else in the galaxy five million years ago (Clarke, 2000: 445–6).

It will be evident that 'Jupiter Five' is a precursor to *Rendezvous with Rama* (1973), where Commander Norton of the *Endeavour* also explores the interior of an interstellar spaceship that has entered the solar system. Norton is a professional rocket engineer, but early in the novel we see how his expedition is planned on Earth by a committee that includes an astronomer, an exobiologist, a historian of science, an anthropologist and the archaeologist Dr Thelma Price, known for her excavations in the now dried-out bed of the Mediterranean. It is Dr Price's expertise that seems most relevant to Norton when he first penetrates the interior of Rama. Norton, who has never forgotten the 'course of industrial archaeology' (Clarke, 1973/1978: 73) that he once took during a summer vacation in England, several times compares his mission to one of the most famous moments of archaeological discovery, Howard Carter's excavation of the tomb of Tutankhamen (Clarke, 1973/1978: 34–5, 36). *Rendezvous with Rama* was eventually followed by a number of sequels co-written with Gentry Lee, which will not be considered here; but 'Jupiter Five' is more than just a foreshadowing of the *Rama* series. It contains crucial motifs that can also be tracked in Clarke's other major works, notably *The City and the Stars* (1956), *Childhood's End* and *2001*. Crystallized in this story are the three main aspects of Clarkaeology to be discussed below: the 'diffusion theory of extraterrestrial culture', the peculiarity of Clarke's aliens, and the characteristic Clarkian device of the time capsule.

Hyperdiffusionism

Given how much of science fiction (and especially that of Clarke and writers influenced by him) speaks of vast aeons of time, of lost civilizations, and of the discovery of cultures which are either long dead or have long ago departed, it is striking how little attention students of the genre have paid to archaeological science.[1] But if we were to single out one archaeological theory that crops up time and again in twentieth-century sf it would undoubtedly be hyperdiffusionism, or the hypothesis that crucial historical technologies and ideas must have originated with a single people or civilization before being communicated to other cultures. For the hyperdiffusionists, the source of civilization was normally located in ancient Egypt, and the task of archaeology was to piece together the unified story of the migration of civilized peoples and cultures across the globe: the wheel, for example, could only have been invented once. Hyperdiffusionist theory, though always contested, flourished mainly in the 1920s and 1930s due to the advocacy of scholars such as Grafton Elliot Smith and W. J. Perry. It relied on highly speculative chronologies, many of which would later be disproved by the advent of radiocarbon dating (Shaw and Jameson, 1999: 200). With hindsight we could say that Professor Forster, a cutting-edge archaeologist still wedded to diffusionism in the 2040s, is almost a hundred years out of date.

In 'Jupiter Five', Clarke is careful to specify that Jack, his narrator, was initially unconvinced by Professor Forster's theories: 'After all, the evidence was so slight and the conclusions so revolutionary that one could hardly help being sceptical' (Clarke, 2000: 439). But Jack has to change his mind, at least as far as extraterrestrials are concerned. Whether or not Clarke himself was a hyperdiffusionist in the 1950s, its attraction to sf writers was that extraterrestrials could be neatly invoked in the place of the ancient Egyptians. (It should be noted, however, that in 'Jupiter Five' human beings have independently discovered the means of space travel within the solar system, although not outside it; and there is no hint of hyperdiffusionism in *Rendezvous with Rama*.) The principal examples in Clarke's work of the 'diffusion theory of extraterrestrial culture' are the remnants of the lost Galactic Empire in *Against the Fall of Night* (1949) and its revision, *The City and the Stars*, and the series of three-million-year-old monoliths or interstellar signalling devices discovered by explorers and archaeologists in *2001* and its successors. What seems particularly relevant to Clarke's monoliths is that some of the main evidence for the hypothesis that all human civilizations had a single origin had been found in the distribution and supposed spread of megalithic monuments across the world (Smith, 1915: 5–6, 133).

As is well known, the first of Clarke's monoliths appears in his short story 'The Sentinel' (1951). Here the narrator, Wilson, is a geologist (strictly speaking, he tells us, a selenologist) who knows 'a little of archaeology' – mainly Egyptian archaeology, as it turns out (Clarke, 2000: 306). Wilson is one of the explorers who stumble across the 'crystal pyramid' on the Moon and realize that it is a beacon waiting to be triggered by its first human visitors. Judging by the 'thickness of the meteoric dust' on the lunar plateau, it is millions of years old and has been placed there 'before life had emerged from the seas of Earth' (Clarke, 2000: 307). In *2001* this lunar monolith reappears, but now it is buried under the meteoric dust and has to be excavated. In the definitive book version, David Bowman then locates a second monolith ('big brother' to the first) on Japetus, one of the moons of Saturn, and this turns out to be the 'Star Gate' (Clarke, 1968/1999b: 198). In Clarke's earlier drafts, however, the Star Gate was to have been located on Jupiter V (Clarke, 1974: 168–73), and in Stanley Kubrick's film it is also in orbit around Jupiter. What we might call the third monolith is described as the 'New Rock' in the opening 'Primeval Night' section of *2001*, but curiously enough it is not discovered until the year 2513 when, as revealed in *3001: The Final Odyssey* (1997), it is excavated by archaeologists at Olduvai Gorge (Clarke, 1997b: 56–8). How on Earth had they missed it until then?[2] By this time – as we discover in Clarke's various sequels – the monoliths have proliferated to the point where they no longer have a single defined shape. In *3001*, if not earlier, we find Clarke using the word 'Monolith' to describe not a physical object of any kind, but rather the alien intelligence behind all the different manifestations that have been identified: an unseen but protean intelligence which pervades the solar system and, it is assumed, the universe beyond.

Vividly represented in Kubrick's film, the physical monolith rapidly became one of science fiction's favourite icons, attracting at least one deliberate spoof in Kim Stanley Robinson's 1984 novel *Icehenge*. Here a series of archaeological expeditions in the twenty-sixth century culminate in the discovery of a mysterious megalith on Pluto, the Icehenge. It transpires that this is both a modern human construct and, quite possibly, a deliberate hoax designed to fool the archaeologists. But in *2001* and its successors we never doubt that the monoliths are linked to one another and that they provide evidence of a single, highly complex monitoring and signalling system directed from interstellar space. A different version of hyperdiffusionism is found in *Against the Fall of Night* and *The City and the Stars*, where the obelisk and other remains discovered in a remote star system are attributed to an earlier and long-vanished human or quasi-human civilization. Here, once again, Clarke is outlining a galactic history stretching back over millions of years.

In *Against the Fall of Night*, Alvin and Theon arrive on a deserted planet which, we are told, was once the 'centre of the universe'. It contains a marble amphitheatre with a huge pillar or column of white stone that may have marked the 'zero point of all astronomical measurements' (Clarke, 1992: 125–6). *Against the Fall of Night* was one of Clarke's earliest works of fiction, originally drafted between 1936 and 1940, and when he revised and expanded it as *The City and the Stars* he removed the suggestion that Alvin and his companion (now named Hilvar) have reached the one-time centre of the universe. Instead, the white obelisk is simply located on the first planet that they happen to visit on their interstellar voyage. Nevertheless, they conclude that it has been a place of pilgrimage, possibly visited by 'billions of human beings' in the past (Clarke, 1956/1979: 201). Alvin and Hilvar quickly leave this planet since, as Clarke finds it necessary to specify, they 'were trying to contact intelligence, not to carry out archaeological research' (Clarke, 1956/1979: 203). And this brings us to the second aspect of Clarkaeology: Clarke's aliens, who are not really aliens at all.

Greetings, Carbon-Based Bipeds!

Clarke affirmed in a 1989 foreword to *Childhood's End* that 'I have little doubt that the Universe is teeming with life' (Clarke, 1953/1990: n.p.). While he did as much as any writer or scientist to popularize the idea that there must be other kinds of intelligence in outer space, it is tempting to say that he 'doesn't do' aliens in his fiction, since they are all basically humanoid, both in mental disposition and, not infrequently, in bodily shape. For all his reverence for H. G. Wells, there is nothing truly Gothic or flesh-creeping about his aliens, and he has no equivalent to the Martians of *The War of the Worlds* (1898). In part, this may reflect a general deficiency of characterization in Clarke's fiction, though it also results from the fact that, in sharp contrast to Wells, his main scientific interests were in astrophysics and space engineering rather than biology. (There is, as it happens, rather more archaeology than biology in his novels and stories.) It is true that some of his aliens have reptilian (as in 'Jupiter Five') or insectile bodies (as in his 1946 story 'Rescue Party'). The reptilians of 'Jupiter Five' are endowed with 'long, powerful tail[s]', reminding us of terrestrial dinosaurs and also echoing the Overlords of *Childhood's End* who are seen to resemble traditional folkloric images of demons and devils. But Professor Forster's verdict on the Jovian reptiles is that they are 'Not human – but humane', which suggests that in everything that really matters their nature is akin to ours (Clarke, 2000: 447). The same is true of the demonic Overlords, who announce as soon as they arrive on Earth that they have come in the name of 'reason and science' (Clarke, 1953/1990: 13). As for *Rendezvous with Rama*, although we never actually get to see the Ramans we learn that they are upright beings with three arms and legs, not two: tripeds not bipeds.

Although the definitive collection of Clarke's non-fictional journalism published in 1999 has the title *Greetings, Carbon-Based Bipeds!*, very few of its contents are concerned with extraterrestrial intelligence, and the title-essay itself is a very brief piece commissioned by *Life* magazine in 1992. Here Clarke writes that, even though humanoid bipeds 'may well occur frequently on Earth-type planets', 'most ETs may well be stranger in appearance than an octopus, a mantis, or a dinosaur' (Clarke, 1999a: 480). His fiction hardly reflects this. In some comments on the writing of *2001*, Clarke implied that he had little faith in our ability to imagine modes of being or intelligence completely different to our own: 'A writer who sets out to describe a civilization superior to his own is obviously attempting the impossible' (Clarke, 1974: 188). In other contexts, such as science or engineering, Clarke would have had little compunction about attempting the impossible, but here he desisted. *The Lost Worlds of 2001* (1972) reprints three abandoned versions of the first human encounter with the alien world entered through the Star Gate, and it is interesting to follow these, since they show that Clarke did originally intend to give a physical shape to the extraterrestrial intelligence that, in the completed book and film, is never actually seen.

Version 1 reintroduces the humanoid Clindar, one of the 'scientists of the Galactic Survey' (Clarke, 2000: 460), who were shown observing primeval humanity in Clarke's 1953 story 'Encounter in the Dawn'. Now we learn that Clindar's three-million-year-old body has been 'remoulded into many strange forms, for unusual missions, but always it had reverted to the basic humanoid design' (Clarke, 1974: 192). If, as Clindar reflects, the human visitors from the spaceship *Discovery* are expecting to meet the 'fantastic creatures of an alien evolution', they are in for a disappointment; however, 'they would have their full of strangeness in due course'. That is, what they see will be new and strange *to them*. For Clindar himself, 'After a thousand worlds, nothing alien was inhuman to him' (Clarke, 1974: 195). What is most striking about this neat reversal of Terence's famous aphorism is the slippage from Clindar's 'humanoid design' to the idea of humanity, as if there were no real difference between the two concepts. To be humanoid is also to be human. Something very similar is implied in versions 2 and 3, in which the encounter is seen from Bowman's, not the alien's, point of view. In version 2, Bowman's initial impression is of a 'tall, extremely elongated human being' (Clarke, 1974: 208), and we may presumably expect that the differences from terrestrial humanity, however marked they may appear, will all be eventually assimilated into a single, enlarged conception of what it is to be human. In version 3, Bowman reflects on the arguments of unnamed exobiologists that the hominid shape is likely to be widespread, if not universal, among intelligent beings. At first he is inclined to doubt this, but soon he finds himself confronting a creature with 'two arms, two legs, a vertical torso supporting an ovoid head, and two eyes; almost all the main ingredients of the human body were there, and in approximately the right places. Yet the total result was completely alien, and for the first time Bowman realized how many variations were possible on the basic human design' (Clarke, 1974: 229–30). Clarke goes on to detail just why it is that the 'total result' is 'alien' despite its humanoid design, yet once again the impression left by this passage is of the ultimate unity, not the discontinuity, of universal intelligent life. In contrast to a writer such as Stanisław Lem, it could be said that Clarke does not really believe in alienness. Yet, if his aliens fail to seize the imagination, what he can do very powerfully is to dramatize the idea of the universe itself as unfathomable and strange.

Clarke's conclusion in his essay 'Greetings, Carbon-Based Bipeds!' is that the possibility that 'we are alone in the universe' is 'the most awesome possibility of all' (Clarke, 1999a: 481). This, of course, is an exact reversal both of the idea of a universe teeming with life and of one of the classic, awe-inspiring sentences to be found in his fiction, both in *Childhood's End* and, in a modified form, in *Rendezvous with Rama*: 'The human race was no longer alone' (Clarke, 1953/1990: 3).³ Although we learn that the Ramans are tripeds, the mystery of Rama is never solved, and we are told of Commander Norton and his crew that 'the more they discovered about it, the less they understood' (Clarke, 1973/1978: 176). There is, in other words, a crucial contrast in Clarke's fiction between the cosmic revelation that the human race is not alone, and the paradoxical human experience that we are never more alone than when we realize we are 'not alone'. Moreover, Clarke's sense of ultimate mystery suggests the extent to which his novels finally go beyond archaeology, and beyond the Overlords' 'reason and science', by embarking upon a journey – like that of the whole post-human race in *Childhood's End* – away from familiar human landmarks and into the unknown. But there is a characteristic Clarkian device that links archaeology and the recovery of the past to the unknown future: the time capsule.

The Ambassador

On at least one occasion, Clarke used the word 'time-capsule' to mean a project of archaeological restoration. In *Imperial Earth* (1975), Duncan Makenzie visits the Earth from his home on Titan and is given a guided tour of the *Titanic*, which has been salvaged and made into a tourist attraction in New York Harbour. Everything has been restored just as it was before the encounter with the iceberg, making the *Titanic* a 'time-capsule', 'a cross-section of an entire society, at the unique moment before it started to dissolve' (Clarke, 1975/1977: 156). The idea of the 'time-capsule' as a resurrection of the past is echoed in Duncan himself, who is an exact clone of his father and grandfather, and in the thoughts of Sir Mortimer Keynes, the surgeon who presided over Duncan's creation; Keynes finds a precedent for his handiwork in the Egyptian Pharaohs, who tried to replicate themselves through incest (Clarke, 1975/1977: 160). The problem with this use of the term 'time capsule', however, is that the phrase was originally coined to mean not an archaeological restoration but an object or collection of objects designed to serve as a means of communication with the future: an encapsulation of the present, not of a moment of past time. It is a message to future archaeologists. One of the best-known early time capsules (including, among much else, microfilm of the October 1938 edition of *Amazing Stories*) was put on display at the New York World's Fair in 1939 before being buried in Flushing Meadows Park, where it still lies. The monoliths in *2001* appear to be both surveillance beacons and time capsules in this original sense, while the most remarkable of the various objects that Clarke's archaeologists discover in 'Jupiter Five' is another time capsule.

Early in *Rendezvous with Rama*, when Norton strikes a flare and gazes into the vast interior of the spaceship that has entered the solar system, he reflects that he is the 'first of all mankind to gaze upon the works of an alien civilization' (Clarke, 1974: 39). The word 'works' here reminds us of P. B. Shelley's 'Ozymandias' (1818): "'Look on my works, ye mighty, and despair!'" (Shelley, 1967: 550). Here the ancient King of Kings speaks to us directly through the inscription on the pedestal of his shattered statue. Yet, although Rama is hundreds of thousands of years old, it is not a ruin like Shelley's imagined statue, nor is it a tomb like Tutankhamen's. Instead, Norton is amazed to find that 'Everything was bright and clean, as if the builders had left only yesterday' (Clarke, 1974: 71). And then, suddenly, the lights go on, and mysterious biotic robots begin to appear. In 'Jupiter Five' there are no lights or cyborgs, but once again the archaeologists are puzzled to find that inside Jupiter's artificial moon 'everything still seemed intact' (Clarke, 2000: 446). Could this be more than an archaeological monument – could it be an edifice whose purpose has yet to be fulfilled? As he explores the moon's interior, Jack, Clarke's graduate-student narrator, comes across what he takes to be a lifelike statue of one of the Jovians, which he calls 'a great work of art', a work as powerful and disturbing as a masterpiece by Leonardo da Vinci: 'The slender, reptilian head was looking straight toward me, the sightless eyes staring into mine' (Clarke, 2000: 447). Jack concludes that the statue 'was set here to bridge time and to greet whatever beings might one day stand in the footsteps of its makers', and his name for it is 'The Ambassador' (Clarke, 2000: 449). Jack, at least, is convinced that the statue is a time capsule bringing a message from a long-dead civilization whose members 'must have guessed that the future belonged to Earth or Venus' (Clarke, 2000: 447).

Perhaps the earliest time capsule in Clarke's fiction is the cryonically preserved body of a controversial cult leader known as 'the Master' in the very brief short story 'The Awakening' (1942, rev. 1952). The Master has been put to sleep and buried in a metal sphere on Mount Everest, until his long-forgotten corpse is discovered and brought back to life by scientists millions of years later. But he comes back to consciousness only to die from shock as he realizes that these future scientists are insects, not men (Clarke, 2000: 24–6). Another heavily ironic treatment of the time-capsule theme is 'History Lesson' (1949), where a spaceship from Venus arrives on Earth sometime in the far future, attracted by a dying radio signal. Underneath a 'cairn of grey stones' (Clarke, 2000: 95), the Venusians find the buried transmitter together with a jumble of other items – old books, coins, electrical parts, and a film canister – that are meant to tell the 'story of a civilization that had passed beyond recall' (Clarke, 2000: 93). But the Venusians cannot understand the terrestrial language, and still less can their historians and psychologists make sense of the film, which is hardly surprising since (as Clarke finally reveals) it is a Walt Disney cartoon. These wryly humorous stories form a background to the more serious presentation of the time capsules in Clarke's major novels and in *2001*.

While the time capsule has been defined as a message from the present to the future, Clarke is aware that in certain circumstances it might also constitute a message to the past. The monoliths of *2001* speak unambiguously to the future, since they are lying in wait for a civilization on Earth (or elsewhere in the solar system) to develop the capacity for space travel. However, in 'Encounter in the Dawn' which inspired the opening sequence of *2001*, Clarke shows an interstellar crew in the 'last days of the Empire' visiting the Earth and coming upon a group of Neolithic humans (Clarke, 2000: 460). Bertrond, the alien anthropologist, tells these primitive human beings that 'One day, perhaps, your ships will go searching among the stars as we have done and they may come upon the ruins of our worlds and wonder who we were'. To encourage their emergence from barbarism he gives them a set of tools, including a metal knife and what seems to be a battery-operated electric torch, saying that 'They are your world's greatest treasures' (Clarke, 2000: 468). Yaan, the Neolithic hunter who accepts these gifts, seems to agree with him.

In *The City and the Stars*, the galactic empire has long disappeared but what is left behind is not barbarism but a quasi-utopian city, Diaspar, existing in a timeless post-historical interregnum. Diaspar is a near-anagram of Paradise, suggesting Clarke's recurrent theme of the insufferable boredom of utopia, although as Gregory Benford has noted it also suggests 'Despair' (Clarke, 1992: 171). Clarke's hero, Alvin, is a rebel against utopian boredom who in the course of the novel 'uncovers the truth of Earth's history' (James, 2005: 439), both literally as well as metaphorically. First Alvin discovers a long-forgotten underground railway in immaculate working order – a tube train lying in wait for the once-in-a-millennium passenger who wants to get away from Diaspar. The railway takes him to Lys, a pastoral Elysium or utopian community where he meets Hilvar, a similarly discontented spirit. Alvin then returns to Diaspar and locates the buried spaceship in which he and Hilvar are to explore the galaxy. At the climax of their space voyage they find the ultimate time capsule in the shape, or rather the shapelessness, of Vanamonde, the unformed galactic mind through whom Alvin will learn to access the true nature of human and galactic history. In Vanamonde, whose name suggests the avant-garde of a new world, there is also a prospect of the Arthurian second coming of the once and future galactic empire; but this prospect, typically for Clarke, remains remote and is left unrealized. In *Rendezvous with Rama*, too, the resurrection promised by the time capsule is ultimately thwarted. The most important archaeological discovery on Rama is that of a vast digital store of holograms, including the hologram of a spacesuit that could presumably be manufactured again by the technique that we would now call 3D printing. But of the Ramans themselves there is no sight, and their entry into the solar system apparently had no reference to humanity at all; it was simply a refuelling stop on an unknown mission.

Childhood's End concludes with a similar disappointment, as the knowledge promised by the time capsule once again gives place to the eternally unknowable. Here the Earth is invaded by the Overlords, super-intelligent beings who come, we are told, from a 'totally alien evolutionary tree', being 'neither mammals, insects, nor reptiles' (Clarke, 1953/1990: 70). Yet when these imperial masters eventually reveal themselves, their 'leathery wings', 'little horns' and 'barbed tail' make them instantly recognizable to humanity (Clarke, 1953/1990: 56). They come from the past known to mythography rather than archaeology, having haunted – or so Clarke confidently asserts – 'the childhood of every race of man' (Clarke, 1953/1990: 53). It is not until the end of the novel, however, that we learn what the Overlords really represent. Far from being a memory of the primitive past, they are time capsules in the reverse sense also found in 'Encounter in the Dawn'. Just as the Biblical Satan appears in Revelation but not in the Book of Genesis, the Overlords speak to humanity not of our beginnings but of our apocalyptic future.

The Overlords' true nature becomes known only to Rodricks, the student who smuggles himself aboard one of their cargo ships going through the star gate to their native planet. He returns after a few months to an Earth that, thanks to the 'Relativity time-dilation effect', is now eighty years older (Clarke, 1953/1990: 183). Rodricks thinks of himself as a time capsule, surviving beyond the period of his normal terrestrial lifespan and bringing back essential information, since 'of one thing he was certain – men would want to hear his story, and to know what he had glimpsed of the civilization of the Overlords' (Clarke, 1953/1990: 173). But he is too late, since human civilization has collapsed during his eighty-year absence. Facing up to his situation as the 'Last Man' (Clarke, 1953/1990: 190), Rodricks speculates that 'Perhaps, lost in one of the still-intact cities, was the manuscript of some latter-day Gibbon, recording the last days of the human race'; but, if so, there would be nobody to read it (Clarke, 1953/1990: 191).

Not only do the Overlords show Rodricks a video representation of the new post-human species (leading him to reflect that 'the Overlords themselves were more human than this' [Clarke, 1953/1990: 185]), but they are now at liberty to tell him that their apparent ubiquity in humanity's mythological past was the result of a deliberately implanted false memory. The reason why they have become the 'symbol of fear and evil' is that they foreshadow humanity's eventual disappearance and replacement by a new species. They are 'not a memory, but a premonition' (Clarke, 1953/1990: 189–90). The Overlords themselves fall far short of the potential of the post-human species, which is directed by a universal Overmind of which the Overlords know little more than we do. When Rodricks is shown the terrestrial exhibit in the museum on the Overlords' home planet, he wonders if, 'for all their superb mental gifts, [they] could really grasp the complete pattern of human culture' (Clarke, 1953/1990: 179). But even if they do grasp it – since, apparently, they can foresee human history before it happens – in Clarke's universe such knowledge is never enough. Faced with 'the unimaginable complexity of a galaxy of a hundred thousand million suns, and a cosmos of a hundred thousand million galaxies', it seems to Rodricks that the Overlords' mental power 'made no difference in the final reckoning' (Clarke, 1953/1990: 188).

Bloomsbury or South Kensington?

Science fiction for Clarke, Brian Aldiss once wrote, is 'the literature of the gods' (Aldiss, 1973: 260); but these gods have either not yet revealed themselves or have long disappeared from the universe. Their time capsules are the most that we can know them by. Similarly, far from discovering the future, Clarke's characters tend to live in the future, with a strong and melancholy sense of their own belatedness. At most, they might hope to have left a sufficient impression on the universe for others to one day read the signs they have left behind. In this they are like the long-disappeared Jovians of 'Jupiter Five', whose prime memorial is the statue known as 'The Ambassador'. Clarke's story turns into a melodramatic struggle between Professor Forster and his archaeologists on the one hand, and the journalist and entrepreneur Randolph Mays on the other, for possession of the statue. Forster wins, since he and his fellow-archaeologists represent the true interests of science. And the destination of the statue? At the end of *The War of the Worlds*, Wells had put an almost completely preserved specimen of the Martian invaders on display in that great temple of biology, the Natural History Museum in London; and in the opening paragraph of his first adult story 'Travel by Wire!' (1937), Clarke transported his readers to its next-door neighbour in South Kensington, the Science Museum (Clarke, 2000: 1). But in 'Jupiter Five' the Jovian ambassador, being an artistic representation and not a corpse, finds its appropriate resting-place not in South Kensington but in Bloomsbury, in a new gallery in that temple of archaeology, the British Museum (Clarke, 2000: 459).

Notes

1 One recent exception is Shawn Malley (2018). Disappointingly, Fredric Jameson's much-cited *Archaeologies of the Future* (2005) lacks any reference to archaeology beyond the title-page. For Jameson, it seems, 'archaeology' is a grand metaphor and no more.

2 Clarke, in fact, gives this monolith the number 0, not 3 (Clarke, 1997a: 53).

3 In *Rendezvous with Rama* Dr Perera comments that 'we are not alone. The stars will never again be the same to us' (Clarke, 1973/1978: 46).

Works Cited

Aldiss, B. W. (1973) *Billion Year Spree: The History of Science Fiction*. London: Weidenfeld & Nicolson.

Clarke, A. C. (1953/1990) *Childhood's End*. Revised edn. London: Pan.

Clarke, A. C. (1956/1979) *The City and the Stars*. London: Corgi.

Clarke, A. C. (1962) *Profiles of the Future: An Enquiry into the Limits of the Possible*. London: Gollancz.
Clarke, A. C. (1973/1978) *Rendezvous with Rama*. London: Pan.
Clarke, A. C. (1974) *The Lost Worlds of 2001*. 2nd edn. London: Sidgwick & Jackson.
Clarke, A. C. (1977) *Imperial Earth: A Fantasy of Love and Discord*. London: Pan.
Clarke, A. C. (1992) *Against the Fall of Night*, with *Beyond the Fall of Night* by G. Benford. London: Orbit.
Clarke, A. C. (1997a) *2061: Odyssey Three*. London: HarperCollins.
Clarke, A. C. (1997b) *3001: The Final Odyssey*. London: HarperCollins.
Clarke, A. C. (1999a) *Greetings, Carbon-Based Bipeds!: A Vision of the 20th century As It Happened*, ed. I. T. Macauley. London: HarperCollins.
Clarke, A. C. (1999b) *2001: A Space Odyssey*. London: Orbit.
Clarke, A. C. (2000) *The Collected Stories*. London: Gollancz.
James, E. (2005) 'Arthur C. Clarke', in D. Seed (ed.) *A Companion to Science Fiction*, pp. 431–40. Oxford: Blackwell.
Jameson, F. (2005) *Archaeologies of the Future: The Desire Called Utopia and Other Science Fictions*. London: Verso.
Malley, S. (2018) *Excavating the Future: Archaeology and Geopolitics in Contemporary North American Science Fiction Film and Television*. Liverpool: Liverpool University Press.
Robinson, K. S. (1984) *Icehenge*. London: HarperCollins.
Shaw, I. and Jameson, R. (eds) (1999) *A Dictionary of Archaeology*. Oxford: Blackwell.
Shelley, P. B. (1967) *Poetical Works*, ed. T. Hutchinson. London: Oxford University Press.
Smith, G. E. (1915) *The Migrations of Early Culture: A Study of the Significance of the Geographical Distribution of the Practice of Mummification as Evidence of the Migrations of Peoples and the Spread of certain Customs and Beliefs*. Manchester and London: Manchester University Press and Longmans, Green.

3

LEAVING THE CRADLE
APOCALYPSE, TRANSCENDENCE AND *CHILDHOOD'S END*

Thore Bjørnvig

Although the science fiction genre often praises and endorses science and a materialistic worldview, nevertheless it often displays mythological and religious themes. A good example of this is Arthur C. Clarke's *Childhood's End* (1953). Clarke believed in progress and saw technology as a necessary, though not sufficient, stage of development towards transcendence (Huntington, 1974: 156), and believed that science fiction played a crucial role in preparing humanity for spaceflight (Berger, 1978: 101–2; Poole, 2012: 257–8). As 'prophet of the space age' (Reddy, 1969), Clarke propagated the view that human progress would, and should, lead to the stars, stating 'that we are in the grip of some mysterious force or *Zeitgeist* that is driving us out to the planets' (Clarke, 1965/1969: 14–15). Indeed, outer space was often described by Clarke as a place of salvation and transcendence: 'The very phrase "heavenly being" implies a freedom from gravity [...] One could argue [...] that the familiar levitation dream is not a memory form the past, but a premonition of the future' (Clarke, 1962/1983a: 58).

Yet, Clarke was also critical of religion, describing, for example, the Sunday school of his childhood as 'nonsense' (Clarke, 2001). Consequently, Clarke would also describe the conquest of outer space as a movement away from religion, mysticism and superstition. In *Childhood's End* religion is portrayed as a kind of children's disease, or a psychological problem, which the Overlords cure (Clarke, 1953/1990: 65). As a result, humanity enters a 'completely secular age' in which 'only a form of purified Buddhism' survives. Indeed, all 'creeds that had been based upon miracles and revelations' collapse 'utterly' (Clarke, 1953/1990: 66). All former religious revelations are annulled by the penultimate secular revelation of the Overlords (Clarke, 1953/1990: 66).

This may lead the reader to think that *Childhood's End* is a treaty against religion and agree with Elizabeth Hull's criticism of David Samuelson's assessment of Clarke as a religious writer:

> [The] insistence that Clarke is religious [...] reminds me of the patient who accused the psychologist administering a Rorschach test of showing him dirty pictures. Clarke does employ whatever religious material seems useful, both from Eastern and Western traditions, because it makes his tale reverberate in an interesting way. But he makes his religious cynicism perfectly clear. (Hull, 1983: 20)

John Huntington by contrast, in his reading of *Childhood's End*, argues that the novel follows a two-step pattern in which rational, technological progress is followed – and superseded – by irrational, transcendent revelation (Huntington, 1974: 155). In this chapter, I will take a middle course between Hull and Samuelson. Following Peter Pels's identification of sf as a 'secular religion' (Pels, 2012), not only can *Childhood's End* be read as a secular apocalyptic myth, contrary to Hull's reading, but the theme of transcendence can also be seen as underwriting much of Clarke's fiction whereas Samuelson (1973) regards *Childhood's End* and a few other works as exceptions. Although the presence of apocalyptic thought in Clarke's novel has been examined before, I will be looking at the millennial promise of the Overlords' Golden Age in greater detail.

Science Fiction and Apocalypse

Many scholars have argued that the connections between science fiction on the one hand, and myth and religion on the other, are intimate, and some have also argued for similar connections between popular science and religion and mythology. For example, James Herrick speaks of 'scientific mythologies' which 'over the past three centuries' in 'popular works of science fiction, speculative science, and the documents of certain religious movements' have developed and propagated 'transcendent narratives addressing ultimate questions' (Herrick, 2008: loc. 3142). Likewise, the pro-space movement has been analysed as a religion (Bjørnvig, 2013a). That the pro-space movement and science fiction support similar religious belief structures should come as no surprise since many pro-spacers have been science fiction authors (Poole, 2012: 257–8).

Many world religions (but especially Judaism and Christianity) feature a notion of apocalypse that also surfaces as a recurring trope in science fiction. One definition of apocalypse is 'a genre of revelatory literature with a narrative framework, in which a revelation is mediated by an otherworldly being to a human recipient, disclosing a transcendent reality which is both temporal insofar as it envisages eschatological salvation, and spatial insofar as it involves another, supernatural world' (Collins, 1979: 9). In *New Worlds for Old* (1974), David Ketterer argues that 'the apocalyptic imagination [...] finds its purest outlet in science fiction' (Ketterer, 1974: 15). James Blish says that science fiction is 'the modern Apocalyptic literature' which is 'overlaid with the mythologies of scientific humanism' (cited in Kreuziger, 1982: 54). According to Frederick Kreuziger, science fiction must be seen as a kind of modern secular apocalypse. Kreuziger observes several parallels between science fiction and biblical apocalyptic and points out that science fiction 'looks for salvation and deliverance from something or someone beyond present reality (of which it despairs), whether in terms simply of the future (through chance), or in terms of extra-terrestrial life' (Kreuziger, 1982: 50).

According to Kreuziger, there is in the science fiction genre an expectation about the promise of the future, which cannot be reduced to extrapolation from current science and technology alone. Moving from the logos of science and into the realm of mythos, science fiction promises deliverance by 'future history', which may encompass the end of the cosmos, and the promise that 'we are not alone', that is, that there is other intelligent life in the universe besides us (Kreuziger, 1982: 96–7). Thus, science fiction 'provides its readership with a rich source of meaning that, just as in the case of religion in general, has salvational potential'. Science fiction can shape perceptions and expectations and thus influence political decision making. One way in which it does that is to function for the reader *as* revelation: 'Science fiction is not just *about* (apocalyptic) revelation but is *in itself* revelation' (Kreuziger, 1982: 79–80).

Another important part of apocalyptic narrative is judgment of humanity and its history from a non-human vantage point (Kreuziger, 1982: 80). In science fiction, the traditional apocalyptic role of God as judge of human actions is taken by extraterrestrial intelligence as judge of present humanity. As Kreuziger explains, 'History is fulfilled and creation consummated when the possibility exists to determine what is good and what is evil, once and for all' (Kreuziger, 1982: 82). All of this is relevant to *Childhood's End*.

Clarke and Apocalypse

The mythic structure underlying much of Clarke's fictional writing, as well as his popular science works, is apocalyptic, which has been noted by several scholars (Bjørnvig, 2012; Levy, 1974; McMillen, 2004: 157). Not in the broadly used sense, where the word merely denotes a catastrophic end to the world, but in a narrower sense, derived from the New Testament.

The worldview that formed many of the writings of the New Testament – especially the Pauline letters and the Apocalypse of John – was a millenarian apocalypticism characterized by specific eschatological expectations. The overarching mythological narrative had the following basic structure: first was Paradise, in which humankind in the form of Adam and Eve lived in a sinless, painless, careless way.

Then came the Fall through the temptation of the serpent, which led to the expulsion from Paradise into mundane existence. This period under the yoke of Original Sin is characterized by suffering. Only when the 'Second Adam', in the form of Jesus Christ, sacrifices himself is Original Sin dispelled. And in the early Christian congregation, there was a real expectation that this meant that death and suffering would end, the living would live forever, and the dead would be resurrected (Breengaard, 1992: 12–22).

These eschatological ideas, however, were not realized and disillusionment, in tandem with Roman persecution of fellow Christians, prompted the writing of the Apocalypse of John, or The Book of Revelation ('apocalypse' means 'revelation' in Greek [Collins, 1979: 2]). In Revelation it is revealed what is in store for humanity: Christ will return to Earth and subdue Satan, and a thousand-year reign will be instigated, in which the souls of the faithful will reside with Christ in the New Jerusalem. This narrative structure plays a pivotal role as a mythological sounding board for Clarke's arguments for space exploration. It is not just clever metaphors and erudite literary allusions, making his writings 'reverberate in an interesting way'. Clarke projected the early Christian apocalyptic narrative onto the development of technology and humanity's journey in the cosmos, creating a myth where gravity took the place of Original Sin, and which may be rendered as follows.

Life started out in the oceans, where the buoyancy of salt water made sure that the pull of gravity had little effect on the creatures living there. The movement of animal life onto the dry surface of the Earth was a fall into the clutches and devastating effects of gravity. Since that time, humans have dreamt of escaping gravity once again, by entering the heavens. The movement into space is an evolutionary leap that mirrors the moment when the first amphibian chose to leave the ocean. In space – or in the meeting with alien intelligence in, or from, space – all humanity's troubles will be over. War, hunger, injustice, pain and suffering will cease, and a completely new kind of existence will begin, which breaks away completely from the old, gravity-ruled existence. We can represent this four-step movement diagrammatically (Table 1).

Table 1. Arthur C. Clarke's apocalyptic narrative

Physical stage	Life in sea	Fish on land	Human existence on land	Colonization of space/ meeting with ETI
Significance	Weightless-ness	Evolutionary leap	Gravity-ruled existence	Evolutionary leap Weightless-ness
Mythological counterpart	Paradise/ First Adam	Temptation	Mundane life	Ascension and return of Christ/Second Adam
Religious meaning	Sinlessness	The Fall	Existence ruled by Original Sin	Liberation from Original Sin Sinlessness

Thus, Clarke plugged into a powerful narrative that has permeated Western civilization for millennia. Projecting it onto the utopian promise of space exploration, he created a modern apocalyptic mythology, which multitudes have been exposed to, not least through the film version of *2001: A Space Odyssey* (1968). *Childhood's End* is among those of his works that most clearly demonstrates this.

Apocalypse and *Childhood's End*

In *New Worlds for Old*, Ketterer states that the 'various facets of the apocalyptic imagination' analysed in his book come together in *Childhood's End* (Ketterer, 1974: 265). More recently, Gabriel McKee has noticed Clarke's use of the word 'apotheosis' (deification) to describe the New Children's transformation into the Overmind and concludes that this identifies the Overmind as a form of God (McKee, 2007: 241). McKee also points out that the old world order is replaced not only once but twice, first by the temporary utopia established by the Overlords, and then by the Overmind's destruction of Earth: 'This scheme echoes the Book of Revelation, in which the New Jerusalem is preceded by the millennium – a thousand-year reign of Christ before the forces of evil are set free on the world a final time' (McKee, 2007: 242). In this scheme 'the Overmind of *Childhood's End* becomes the New Jerusalem of Revelation, and the apotheosis the coming of the kingdom of God' (McKee, 2007: 243). Thus, the initial revelation of the Apocalypse of John corresponds to the arrival of the Overlords in the first part of *Childhood's End*, the thousand year reign to the middle section, and the arrival of a New Jerusalem and the passing away of the old Earth to the final section.

However, in order to gain a fuller understanding of precisely how and why *Childhood's End* is an almost emblematic apocalyptic science fiction story, we need to delve deeper. I will do this by sorting the apocalyptic contents of *Childhood's End* under themes, which each in their own way serve as focal lenses for Clarke's apocalyptic imagination: transcendence; gravity; time; unity; the view from above; and childhood.

1. *Transcendence*

Clarke's fiction echoes the famous remark of Konstantin Tsiolkovsky that humanity's destiny is to leave the cradle of Earth. It is the leaving of the cradle that constitutes transcendence in Clarke's work. In *Childhood's End*, however, Clarke operates from the premise that this route has been closed: 'The stars are not for man' (Clarke, 1953/1990: 128–30, 206). Despite Clarke's disclaimer that 'The opinions expressed in this book are not those of the author', *Childhood's End* is still preoccupied with the same desire for transcendence expressed in Clarke's space-oriented fiction. Ultimately, humanity's destiny does lie with the stars: the only difference is the means by which that transcendence occurs.

This dichotomy of means is pictured in *Childhood's End* as a road 'forked in two directions', one leading to the Overlords and the other to the Overmind. Neither lead 'to a goal that [takes] any account of human hopes and fears' (199), which is not really true, since Clarke and his circle of space enthusiasts fantasized of reaching the space-faring capabilities similar to those of the Overlords, a dream of transcending earthly existence prefigured by Apocalyptic and Gnostic writings since at least the middle centuries of the first millennium BCE (Bellah, 2011: 265–82). Clarke himself admits to this when he writes of the Overmind: 'Now it had drawn into its being all that the human race had ever achieved. This was not tragedy, but fulfilment. The billions of transient sparks of consciousness that had made up humanity would flicker no more like fireflies against the night' (Clarke, 1953/1990: 199). Here, Clarke not only portrays humanity's merger with the Overmind as 'fulfilment', which resonates with his usage of 'apotheosis' (200), but he also likens human consciousness to 'sparks' and 'fireflies', which is reminiscent of the Gnostic Manichean idea of divine light particles captured in the material world (Giversen, 1999: 37). Indeed, at the end of *Childhood's End*, Earth itself transforms into light (Clarke, 1953/1990: 210).

Whereas transcendence in Clarke's works is usually brought about by science and technology, for example in the form of rocketry, transcendence in *Childhood's End* is realized by occult means. Telepathy and telekinesis play a central role in the narrative. Although it may seem strange that Clarke chooses an occult avenue to the stars, rather than a technological one, a closer look at the historical roots of the belief in telepathy makes the presence of these themes in *Childhood's End* understandable, including also the focus upon children.

Despite its anti-scientism, in his book *Scientific Mythologies* (2008), Herrick exposes many different kinds of myths that are valuable tools in the analysis of *Childhood's End*. One of these is the 'Myth of the New Humanity' which 'represents a secular hope for individual and societal salvation' (Herrick, 2008: loc. 1183). The myth originated in the nineteenth century and developed into a story depicting a human race that 'evolves progressively upward toward spiritual as well as physical transformation, or toward absorption into something even grander – a Cosmic Mind, a Conscious Universe, The One. Our evolutionary path takes us off our home planet and out toward the stars' (loc. 1187–88). In this schema, 'telepathy supposedly demonstrated that humanity was evolving spiritually, becoming increasingly attuned to a pantheistic cosmic force actively at work in all things. Science, it was thought, could assist such spiritual progress' (loc. 1384–86). This kind of thinking has also been in science fiction, perhaps nowhere so clearly as in the works of Olaf Stapledon:

> In 1930 [aged 13], I came under the spell of a considerably more literate influence, when I discovered W. Olaf Stapledon's just-published *Last and First Men* in the Minehead Public Library. No book before or since ever had such an impact on my imagination; the Stapledonian vistas of millions and hundreds of millions of years, the rise and fall of civilizations and entire races of men, changed my whole outlook on the universe and has influenced much of my writing ever since. (Clarke, 1962/1983b)

On Earth, the Overmind manifests as occult phenomena in which the Overlords take a keen interest, exemplified, for instance, by their concern about the occult library of Rupen. When a group of people gathered at a party in Rupen's house play a game of ouija-board, they establish contact with an entity which presents itself as 'IAMALL'. This is later considered a kind of first contact with the Overmind by the Overlords. It is here that Jean, as an involuntary medium, discloses the precise location of the Overlords' home-world by having 'tapped a hitherto unknown source of knowledge' (Clarke, 1953/1990: 102) originating 'in the unknown darkness, just beyond the little circle of light cast by the lamp of science' (Clarke, 1953/1990: 144–5).

When evaluating the contents of Rupen's library, the Overlords conclude that there are 'eleven clear cases of partial breakthrough, and twenty-seven probables', but that 'the evidence is confused with mysticism – perhaps the prime aberration of the human mind' (Clarke, 1953/1990: 95). What comes about, when the Overmind 'arrives' at Earth, however, is 'Total breakthrough'. This moment also signals the breakdown of time as we know it: 'All through history there have been people with inexplicable powers which seemed to transcend space and time'. That is, powers such as telepathy which in its highest form 'is not subject to the usual limitations of time and space' (Clarke, 1953/1990: 168). Even though the Overlords arrive by spaceship – and thus represent transcendence by technological means – they are only an intermediate state between earthly, physical existence and the transcendent state of the Overmind.

As Robert Poole notes, both the stories 'Guardian Angel' and 'The Sentinel', which became the respective bases for *Childhood's End* and *2001*, were written in the same year – 1948 (Poole, 2012: 256). Both the occult transcendence of the former and the technological transcendence of the latter ultimately lead to the same result: transcendence of matter and gravity-ruled existence. On a symbolic level, the affinity between the two texts becomes even clearer when Stormgren goes to meet the Overlord Karellen who hides behind a 'vision screen': 'behind that rectangle of darkness lay utter mystery. Yet there also lay power and wisdom – and perhaps, most of all, an immense and humorous affection for the little creatures crawling on the planet beneath' (Clarke, 1953/1990: 13). In *2001* there is another 'rectangle of darkness', namely the monolith. Both veil the mysteries of the stars – and the disclosure of the mystery behind the rectangles signifies an apocalyptic (unveiling) moment.

In both works (and many others by Clarke), transcendence is not only transcendence from earthbound gravity but also from material and physical existence. In *Childhood's End*, only the mind, not the body, is of importance to the Overlords (Clarke, 1953/1990: 22). The Overmind has left the 'tyranny of matter' behind. Indeed, the transition to the state of the Overmind will be 'a transformation of the mind, not of the body' (Clarke, 1953/1990: 177). For the children about to transfer into the Overmind, physical existence becomes less and less important. As Karellen states: 'One day, we believe, they may find the material world equally distracting' (Clarke, 1953/1990: 198). And of the children who finally join the Overmind, 'Their probation is ended: they're leaving the last remnants of matter behind' (Clarke, 1953/1990: 208). The very moment of transcendence is simultaneously a dismantling of the material world: 'in an instant all the trees and grass, all the living creatures that had inhabited this land, flickered out of existence and were gone' (Clarke, 1953/1990: 210).

As Robert M. Geraci argues, the dualistic urge to transcend matter and earthly existence underlines apocalyptic thinking, and has helped to popularize the ideas of transhumanists and developers of artificial intelligence. Geraci calls this modern religious myth 'Apocalyptic AI' and posits that it 'integrates the religious categories of Jewish and Christian apocalyptic traditions with scientific predictions based upon current technological developments' (Geraci, 2010: 9). Furthermore, the desire to resolve this dualism will only come about through the destruction of the current world and the arrival of a new and perfected one (Geraci, 2010: 14). Both ancient and transhumanist apocalypses are characterized by a profound dislike of the physical body, and in Apocalyptic AI, the Gnostic tendency leads into outer space. Ultimately, the universe itself will be animated with intelligence spread by the technological Singularity's 'Mind Fire' (Geraci, 2010: 32–5).

Though Geraci mentions Clarke, he does not discuss *Childhood's End*. Perhaps this is because the novel's apocalyptic transcendence does not come about by means of technology, a basic tenet of Apocalyptic AI. He does, however, mention *2001* as an example of how Clarke promoted transhumanist ideas, and quotes Clarke's ultimate vision of the destiny of intelligent life in the Galaxy: 'They could become creatures of radiation, free at last from the tyranny of matter' (qtd Geraci, 2010: 55). The recurrent phrase 'tyranny of matter' again links both *2001* and *Childhood's End*. One of Clarke's early influences was J. D. Bernal's *The World, the Flesh and the Devil* (1929), which offered a premonition of transhumanist thought alongside the dream of conquering outer space (Herrick, 2008: loc. 979–82). Despite the lack of a technological gateway to the Overmind, *Childhood's End* clearly expounds a vision that share many affinities with Apocalyptic AI. And just as science fiction works such as *2001* may inspire real-life scientists working to create artificial intelligence (Geraci, 2010: 51–6), so may of course *Childhood's End*. Indeed, in the very transhumanist narrative, the boundaries between science and science fiction are blurred (Masson, 2014: 446).

2. Gravity

In *Childhood's End*, Clarke refers directly to gravity in five places. The first time occurs when, as in a 'miracle', Karellen reveals his true identity to two children who ascend the gangway into his ship: 'their bodies were tilted at right angles [...]. It possessed a private gravity of its own, one which could ignore that of Earth' (Clarke, 1953/1990: 60). The second time we are told that humanity has not yet discovered anti-gravity – only the Overlords possess this 'ultimate secret' (Clarke, 1953/1990: 66). The third is when Jan visits the world of the Overlords where they have 'no fear of gravity' (Clarke, 1953/1990: 186). The fourth time is when the Earth is being ripped apart and Jan notices that his weight is decreasing and exclaims: 'Something's happened to gravity!' (Clarke, 1953/1990: 209). And the fifth and final time is when we are told:

> In a soundless concussion of light, Earth's core gave up its hoarded energies. For a little while the gravitational waves crossed and re-crossed the Solar System, disturbing ever so slightly the orbits of the planets. Then the Sun's remaining children pursued their ancient paths once more, as corks floating on a placid lake ride out the tiny ripples set in motion by a falling stone. (Clarke, 1953/1990: 210–11)

In Clarke's work, gravity is the great enemy of humankind and its annulment signals the moment of apocalyptic transcendence. The Overlords can both fly and manipulate gravity. Though they do not possess the potential for apotheosis, nevertheless they are sufficiently high up on what Mary Midgley (2002: 33–9) has called the evolutionary 'escalator' to manipulate gravity. But only at the very moment when Earth itself is dismantled, when their very cradle is annihilated, is the gravitational pull of the birthplace of humankind once and for all destroyed. This signals the ultimate apocalyptic moment where gravity and, in Clarke's secular apocalypse, Original Sin are abolished, and final transcendence is achieved.

3. Time

In *Childhood's End* time is treated on two different, yet related, levels. On one level, various portrayals of time dramatize the momentousness of the Overlords' appearance above Earth. In the prologue, in which an astronaut sees her dreams of conquering space disrupted by the appearance of the Overlord's space ships, we are told that 'history as men had known it had come to an end' (Clarke, 1953/1990: 4) and that 'This was the moment when history held its breath, and the present sheared asunder from the past as an iceberg splits form its parent cliffs, and goes sailing out to sea in lonely pride' (Clarke, 1953/1990: 5).

What happens with the appearance of the Overlords is a disruption of the normal flow of time. All of a sudden, the anticipated and promised future clashes with the present of mankind and creates the first of several apocalyptic moments: 'the gleaming, silent shapes hanging over every land were the symbol of a science man could not hope to match for centuries' (Clarke, 1953/1990: 10). What has arrived is the very future towards which humanity has been aspiring. And when, finally, Jan is confronted with the world of the Overlords, he realizes 'that a man from the Stone Age, lost in a modern city or building, might be equally helpless' (Clarke, 1953/1990: 186).

Yet, in a sense, it is not only the future that has arrived but also the past, since the Overlords have knowledge of both. They can access the past and the 'pattern of the future is clear enough' to them (Clarke, 1953/1990: 51). They can even, in a sense, control the flow of time as it happens during the rescue of Stormgren from his kidnappers (Clarke, 1953/1990: 37). When the Overlords are revealed 'the human race will experience what can only be called a psychological discontinuity' (Clarke, 1953/1990: 52), which is also simultaneously a discontinuity of time. Thus, the appearance of the Overlords marks the end of history and the linear flow of time, thus marking a truly apocalyptic moment.

Yet, Clarke does not hesitate to use the concepts of 'time' and 'history' in seemingly self-contradictory ways. For example, when he says of the two children, who greet Karellen in his true, demonic form, they do so by moving 'into history' (Clarke, 1953/1990: 60) in the sense of taking part in a really significant event of linear time. Consequently, time functions on two levels in the novel. One that conforms both with linear time and apocalyptic temporal narrative in the form of the evolutionary escalator, 'A century before, man had set foot upon the ladder that could lead him to the stars' (Clarke, 1953/1990: 85). The other is linked to the vertical aspect of apocalypse that puts the concept of linear time into doubt: 'Time is very much stranger than you think' (Clarke, 1953/1990: 168) and 'time is more complex than your science ever imagined' (Clarke, 1953/1990: 201).

An example of the disruption of time is the fact that the Overlords resemble earthly images of devils, or demons. At first, it is merely assumed that humanity has actually met some former representatives of the Overlords in the past and that images of the devil is a kind of racial memory (Clarke, 1953/1990: 55, 63). At the close of the book, however, an even more fantastic truth is revealed, namely that humanity's visual conception of the devil is (was) a result of a premonition, a memory of the future. What originally created the visual concept of the devil was a foreboding of the arrival of the Overlords in modern times, which again was associated with the demise of the human race: 'There must be such a thing as racial memory, and that memory was somehow independent of time. To it, the future and the past were one' (Clarke, 1953/1990: 201).

What is, then, disclosed by the revelation of *Childhood's End* is that time is 'block time', that is, all time is somehow concurrent – which again leads to the conclusion that what happens is inevitable – and good. The final merging of the children with the Overmind is described as 'achievement' and 'fulfilment' (Clarke, 1953/1990: 210), while Jan thinks of the final apocalypse as 'fitting: it had the sublime inevitability of a great work of art' (Clarke, 1953/1990: 198). To the Overlords, both past and future are known – and thus, nothing, in their perspective, happens by accident. All is already lain out as an inevitable story, just as the story of apocalypse is inevitable.

4. Unity

Throughout *Childhood's End* unification is portrayed as having salvatory power and transcendental potential. Unification takes place on two levels: that of the nation-state and that of the individual. As discrete, separate entities, nation-states and individuals are both portrayed negatively. In contrast, the unification of all nation-states into one world-state brings peace and justice for all; the unification of all children under the age of ten brings final transcendence to the human race.

As soon as they arrive, the Overlords start completing what humanity had already begun with the European Federation, namely the creation of a world-state (Clarke, 1953/1990: 8). By doing this, the Overlords bring 'security, peace and prosperity to the world' (Clarke, 1953/1990: 9). One nation attacks an Overlord spaceship but to no avail (Clarke, 1953/1990: 11), and South Africa is forced to abandon apartheid when the Overlords turn the sunlight off above the capital (Clarke, 1953/1990: 12). Since the power of the Overlords seems to be without limit, soon all national strife ceases:

> Ignorance, disease, poverty, and fear had virtually ceased to exist. The memory of war was fading into the past as a nightmare vanishes with the dawn; soon it would lie outside the experience of all living men. With the energies of mankind directed into constructive channels, the face of the world had been remade. It was, almost literally, a new world. (Clarke, 1953/1990: 64)

The Overlords (or perhaps rather the Overmind) have judged humanity and found that it needs firm guidance in order both to survive the threat of nuclear war and prevent it from spreading its telepathic cancer to the rest of the universe: 'When we arrived, you were on the point of destroying yourselves with the powers that science had rashly given you. Without our intervention, the Earth today would be a radioactive wilderness' (Clarke, 1953/1990: 129).

At the end of the book, all the children of the Earth finally unite spiritually and telepathically in order to join the Overmind which itself already consists of several races (Clarke, 1953/1990: 168). The gradual merger with the Overmind erases individuals and spreads like an epidemic (Clarke, 1953/1990: 172). The unification with the Overmind also means the end of loneliness (Clarke, 1953/1990: 180), and when all the children have joined, they have as little identity as cells have in a human body, yet together are something much greater than individual man could ever be (Clarke, 1953/1990: 196–7). Thus, the world-state is only a step towards the novel's final and greater revelation and the moment of unification signals an apocalyptic moment of destruction and renewal.

5. The View from Above

The transfigurative effects of seeing Earth from the elevated point of outer space is one of the core tenets of what I have termed 'Outer Space Religion' (Bjørnvig, 2013a, b). By entering and dwelling in the realm traditionally reserved for divine beings, the initiate gains access to special insights and celestial character traits such as increased objectivity, altruism, morality and purity – as is often seen in apocalyptic narratives. Though the older generations of humanity in *Childhood's End* never gain direct access to outer space, some heavenly secrets are still bestowed on them through the meetings between Stormgren and Karellen.

The sacredness of outer space, and the beings who dwell there, is expressed in *Childhood's End* in several places, such as when Karrellen's small ship hovers above the ground 'as if it feared contamination with Earth' (Clarke, 1953/1990: 13). Like Stormgren in his UN building, the Overlords' view of Earth is so elevated that they can be detached and thus objective: a 'presence of illimitable power' (Clarke, 1953/1990: 34) with 'wise and sympathetic eyes' (Clarke, 1953/1990: 171). Though man is still 'a prisoner on his own planet', it has become a much better place due to the interference of the godlike Overlords who have 'abolished war and hunger and disease' (Clarke, 1953/1990: 85).

When Karellen looks down on Earth from his celestial abode he sees 'the people that had been given into his reluctant keeping', and he is able to behold the future 'and what this world would be only a dozen years from now' (Clarke, 1953/1990: 130). Likewise, from his elevated point of view where Karellen is able to see both past and future simultaneously, he can also disclose that humanity stands at the 'the crossroads of nuclear power' (Clarke, 1953/1990: 174). It is from the Overlords that humans learn of 'the hierarchy of the universe. As we are above you, so there is something above us, using us for its own purposes' (Clarke, 1953/1990: 177). It is a central constituent of apocalypse that the receiver of the revelation is transported into heavenly regions and there gains special powers and insights. This idea may be rooted in ancient shamanistic beliefs of ascension, but it is the specifically apocalyptic version of heavenly sojourn that has fed into modern day speculations on the meaning and importance of space exploration and the search for extraterrestrial intelligence (Bjørnvig, 2013a).

6. Childhood

On one level, the development stage of childhood is used in *Childhood's End* to designate all of humanity. To the Overlords the task of managing Earth and humanity is like raising children (Clarke, 1953/1990: 154). Simultaneously, they keep humanity 'in the nursery' (Clarke, 1953/1990: 115) and prevent them from taking the natural step beyond the planet because they fear that they might contaminate the universe. At the same time, the isolation is also a state in which humanity is 'like children amusing themselves in some secluded playground, protected from the fierce realities of the outer world' (Clarke, 1953/1990: 144).

On another level, however, childhood designates the new generation of children who are receptacles of the Overmind. As it turns out, it is the emergence of *these* children that the Overlords have been watching all along, and as such they have been 'midwives attending a difficult birth' (Clarke, 1953/1990: 168). The Overlords have overseen the transition of other races into the Overmind and it always begins with a child. These children will belong to a new humanity who will look at their parents' 'greatest achievements as childish toys' (Clarke, 1953/1990: 178), a strange, new breed with spectacular, paranormal abilities, and with hopes and desires utterly alien to their parents. Yet, their transformation also comes at the expense of their own individuality as they become one with the Overmind.

Thus, the end of childhood is to be understood in a double sense: the arrival of the Overmind ends the childhood of humanity, the maturing of which into a new breed of super-children constitutes an evolutionary leap that is so radical as to be inherently discontinuous. However, the childhood of the new human breed ends even more abruptly, as they are possessed by the Overmind. Whichever way one looks at it, it is the end of the human race and the childhood it signifies, and a birth into true maturity which is the Overmind when humanity has reached 'fulfilment' and 'finished playing with their toys' (Clarke, 1953/1990: 210).

The conclusion reverberates with St Paul's apocalyptic words: 'When I was a child, I spake as a child, I understood as a child, I thought as a child: but when I became a man, I put away childish things. For now we see through a glass, darkly; but then face to face: now I know in part; but then shall I know even as also I am known' (1 Corinthians 13:11–12). To see 'face to face' can only be done through revelation, an unveiling, and the metaphoric projections between individual development, species evolution and apocalyptic transcendence are both rhetorically effectual and cognitively powerful. It resonates with the culturally entrenched apocalyptic belief system, is naturalized through the invocation of biological development, and is further invigorated by drawing on the myth of the evolutionary escalator, leading straight from gravity-bound, earthly existence to sinless rapture among the stars.

Conclusion

Childhood's End abounds with religious, and more specifically, apocalyptic ideas, which, though draped in a seemingly secular ideology posed against superstition and religion, offer themselves as a new kind of religion to the reader. Reading the works of Clarke, and in this case *Childhood's End*, without taking heed of their religious message, will not produce a complete picture of their contents, nor what motivated Clarke to popularize – and fantasize about – space exploration and humanity's destiny among the stars. The seemingly depressing (to space enthusiasts) message of *Childhood's End*, that the stars are not for man, is only depressing at its surface. The deeper message of the book is that the manifest destiny of humanity is transcendence in outer space. As such, *Childhood's End* feeds into the apocalyptic myth of Outer Space Religion, which not only presents itself as a religious belief system, but also motivates real-life space exploration.

Works Cited

Bellah, R.N. (2011) *Religion in Human Evolution: From the Paleolithic to the Axial Age.* Cambridge MA: The Belknap Press of Harvard University Press.

Berger, A.I. (1978) 'Science-Fiction Critiques of the American Space Program, 1945-1958', *Science Fiction Studies* 5(2): 99-109.

Bjørnvig, T. (2012) 'Transcendence of Gravity: Arthur C. Clarke and the Apocalypse of Weightlessness', in A. Geppert (ed.) *Imagining Outer Space: European Astroculture in the Twentieth Century,* pp. 127-46. Basingstoke: Palgrave Macmillan.

Bjørnvig, T. (2013a) 'Outer Space Religion and the Overview Effect: A Critical Inquiry into a Classic of the Pro-Space Movement.' *Astropolitics* 11(1-2): 4-24.

Bjørnvig, T. (2013b) 'Outer Space Religion and the Ambigious Nature of *Avatar's* Pandora', in B. Taylor, ed., *Avatar and Nature Spirituality,* pp. 37-58. Waterloo: Wilfrid Laurier University Press.

Breengaard, C. (1992) *Kristenforfølgelser og kristendom.* Copenhagen: Forlaget ANIS.

Clarke, A.C. (1953/1990) *Childhood's End.* New York: Random House.

Clarke, A.C. (1962/1983a) *Profiles of the Future.* London: Pan.

Clarke, A.C. (1962/1983b) 'In the Beginning was Jupiter,' *The New York Times,* 6 March, URL (accessed 12 February 2021): https://archive.nytimes.com/www.nytimes.com/books/97/03/09/reviews/clarke-jupiter.html

Clarke, A.C. (1965/1969) *Voices From the Sky.* London: Mayflower Books.

Clarke, A. C. (2001) 'Arthur C. Clarke's Credo.' *The Skeptical Inquirer* 25(5): 61–2.
Collins, J. (1979) 'Introduction: Towards the Morphology of a Genre.' *Semeia* 14: 1–19.
Geraci, R. (2010) *Apocalyptic AI: Visions of Heaven in Robotics, Artificial Intelligence, and Virtual Reality*. New York: Oxford University Press.
Giversen, S. (1999) Introduction to Mani, *Jeg, Mani – Jesu Kristi apostel*. 19–46. Copenhagen: Museum Tusculanums Forlag.
Herrick, J. (2008) *Scientific Mythologies: How Science and Science Fiction Forge New Religious Beliefs*. Downers Grove IL: InterVarsity Press. Kindle Edition.
Hull, E. (1983) 'Fire and Ice: The Ironic Imagery of Arthur C. Clarke's *Childhood's End*', *Extrapolation* 24(1): 13–32.
Huntington, J. (1974) 'The Unity of *Childhood's End*.' *Science Fiction Studies* 1(3): 154–64.
Ketterer, D. (1974) *New Worlds for Old: The Apocalyptic Imagination, Science Fiction, and American Literature*. Bloomington: Indiana University Press.
King James Bible Online, URL (accessed 13 April 2020): https://www.kingjamesbibleonline.org/
Kreuziger, F. (1982) *Apocalypse and Science Fiction: A Dialectic of Religious and Secular Soteriologies*. Chico CA: Scholars Press.
Levy, M. (1974) *Apocalypse and Apotheosis in the Fiction of Arthur C. Clarke*. Unpublished MA thesis. Ohio State University.
Masson, O. (2014) 'Turning into Gods: Transhumanist Insight on Tomorrow's Religiosity', *Implicit Religion* 17(4): 443–58.
McKee, G. (2007) *The Gospel According to Science Fiction: From the Twilight Zone to the Final Frontier*. Louisville: Westminster John Know Press.
McMillen, R. (2004) *Space Rapture: Extraterrestrial Millennialism and the Cultural Construction of Space Colonization*. Unpublished PhD Thesis. University of Texas, Austin.
Midgley, M. (1985/2002) *Evolution as a Religion: Strange Hopes and Stranger Fears*. London: Routledge.
Pels, P. (2012) 'Amazing Stories: How Science Fiction Sacralizes the Secular', in J. Stolow (ed.) *Deus In Machina: Religion, Technology and the Things in Between*, pp. 213–38. New York: Fordham University Press.
Poole, R. (2012) 'The Challenge of the Spaceship: Arthur C. Clarke and the History of the Future, 1930–1970', *History and Technology* 28(3): 255–80.
Reddy, J. (1969) 'Arthur Clarke: Prophet of the Space Age', *Reader's Digest* 94(564): 134–40.

Samuelson, D. (1973) 'Childhood's End: A Median Stage in Adolescence?', Science Fiction Studies 1(1): 4–17.

4

A SPACE BODHI TREE
THE 'CRYPTO-BUDDHISM' OF ARTHUR C. CLARKE

Jim Clarke

What did Arthur C. Clarke believe? Generally perceived as an atheist (Feeley, 1990: 60; Samuelson, 1982; Westfahl, 2018), or at least as implacably opposed to religious faith, Clarke nevertheless accommodated Buddhism within his fiction. This accommodation unfolds like a recurring pattern, wherein a particular form of Buddhism which eschews deities but has a wary curiosity or even rapprochement with scientific endeavour, is consistently spared from eradication in the aftermath of alien encounter. Was Clarke, as he claimed, a 'crypto-Buddhist' (Brandreth, 2000; Cherry, 1999)? Is his exposure to Buddhism the means by which he 'strove for a rapprochement between the scientism of American sf and a need for transcendence beyond the technological sublime' (J. Clarke, 2019: 59)? This chapter will examine iterations of Buddhist characters and concepts from his early short stories to *The Fountains of Paradise* (1979), alongside his own, often playful, statements on religion, to explore the role Buddhism plays in his work and thought.

Parsing Clarke's Credo

In the introduction to his essay on Willy Ley, Clarke reminisced about that period in his life, some half a century earlier, when he had initially decided to become a writer. Having rummaged in his extensive archive, he unearthed what he described as the 'disintegrating remains' of a notebook from 1944, wherein he had written 'What I believe', a thousand word long 'statement of philosophy' published that year in the *Probe* newsletter. As Clarke himself sadly notes, 'I have no idea what profundities this long-lost piece contained. It would be interesting to compare it with the – I hope – more mature *Credo* written a half-century later' (Clarke, 1999: 11–14).

Though this early manifesto has not survived, it is significant that he remained faithful to the 'Credo' he wrote in 1991. In this essay, he described his beliefs as those of a 'logical positivist', a position he had assumed 'at about the age of ten' (Clarke, 1999: 359). Logical positivism was a philosophical movement, popular in Clarke's youth in the 1920s and 1930s, centred on schools in Berlin and Vienna, which insisted that the only possible cognitively meaningful statements were those that could be independently verified. Within philosophical circles, this challenged the validity of religious beliefs but also metaphysics, ontology and even aspects of ethics. For Clarke, with his burgeoning interest in science, it was a framework that facilitated his worldview, one that was consistently rational and empirical, even despite his future fame as a writer of speculative fiction.

Clarke insisted that he had remained loyal to this position despite 'half a century of reading, travel and contact with other faiths', but accepted wryly the witty critique from the geneticist J. B. S. Haldane that he ought to have been awarded 'a prize for theology' due to the numerous theological perspectives which can be identified in his fiction (Clarke, 1999: 359). In an attempt to dispense with notions of God in a logically positivist manner, Clarke reiterates the bifurcation of deity he described in *The Songs of Distant Earth* (1986), in which he distinguishes two aspects of God – 'Alpha', the Old Testament figure who monitors behaviour and rewards and punishes accordingly, and 'Omega', 'the Creator of Everything' who Clarke concedes is 'not so easily dismissed.' In search for a resolution to this problem, Clarke notes that while it may not be possible to empirically argue away such a creator deity yet, it is equally irrational to assume that such an experiment may not be possible at some future date. Furthermore, he argues, such a question 'and many of the questions we ask of the universe may turn out to be completely meaningless' (Clarke, 1999: 361).

This suggests that Clarke may have been open to a Deist position, which he seems to have accommodated in a live interview he did on CNN on New Year's Eve 1999, wherein he was asked if he felt people should do more to recognize God's hand in the creation of all things in the natural world. Clarke responded that he did not believe God controls or creates things, except at the very beginning of the universe. This can be read as Deism, but equally, it could be read as a kind attempt to accommodate the religious or as simply the sort of error one makes during live broadcasting. However, he addressed the Deist argument directly in *The Fountains of Paradise*, wherein he suggests that 'the hypothesis' of God, 'though not disprovable by logic alone, is unnecessary for the following reason':

> If you assume that the universe can be quote explained unquote as the creation of an entity known as God, he must obviously be of a higher degree of organization than his product. Thus you have *more* than doubled the size of the original problem, and have taken the first step on a diverging infinite regress. William of Ockham pointed out as recently as your fourteenth century that entities should not be multiplied unnecessarily. I cannot therefore understand why this debate continues. (Clarke, 1979/1980: 95)

Further evidence for an accommodation of Deism may potentially be found in his statement that 'Any path to knowledge is a path to God – or Reality, whichever word one prefers to use' (cited in Mintowt-Czyz, 2008). This apparent conflation is notably qualified by reference to the audience's preferred term. This can be read either as a generous attempt to communicate with those of a religious bent, or equally as a slightly mischievous and flippant merger of two concepts which he kept very separate in his own mind.

With similar flippancy, Clarke also regularly referred to God as female. In the same interview with CNN, he replied, 'I do not believe in God, but I do not disbelieve in Her either.' This feminization of the traditional gendering of deity was something he often repeated. On other occasions, he noted that 'I don't believe in God but I'm very interested in Her' (cited in Fleetham, 2006: 84). Clarke's usage matches that of the Abrahamic religions, none of which doctrinally attribute a gender to God, despite scriptural language's tendency to favour a masculine pronoun. From the fourth century's Gregory of Nazianzus to the current Roman Catholic catechism, gendered terms like 'God the Father' are identified as strictly metaphorical (Bordwell, 2002). Similarly, neither Judaism nor Islam (whose fundamental concept of *tawhid* identifies a Monist oneness of the deity) attribute a doctrinal gender to God (Kaplan, 1983: 144).

If Clarke's occasional apparent espousal of Deism or the femininity of God are explainable by a mischievous and playful use of language, his wartime espousal of pantheism is somewhat more difficult to explain. Pantheism is the belief that everything can be considered a manifestation of divinity and contains within the immanent divine figure. In the Western tradition it was popularized via Baruch Spinoza in his *Ethics, Demonstrated in Geometrical Order* (1677), and has remained present in Western culture since, enjoying a particular revival among the New Age movement of the 1980s and 1990s. Robin Reid has noted that when Clarke joined his RAF station he insisted that his religion be listed as 'pantheism' on his dog-tags, and extrapolates that pantheism may account for some of the religiosity in his atheism (Reid, 1997: 5). However, little of Clarke's works explore pantheism in any significant manner. While transcendence and the sublime may often be encountered in his fiction, there is no sense in which inherent deity is revealed in his characters or their exploits. In an interview with Gyles Brandreth in 2000, Clarke retold the incident: 'When I joined the RAF they put me down as C of E. I got hold of the man handling the paperwork and made them change it to "pantheist". Now I say I'm a crypto-Buddhist, but I'm anti-mysticism and I have a long-standing bias against organized religion. I don't believe in God or an afterlife' (Brandreth, 2000).

Despite the presence of religious ideas in his fiction from as early as 1948, Clarke is remarkably consistent in insisting on his atheism, or to be specific, his logical positivism. However, this self-description as a 'crypto-Buddhist' requires some glossing, and is not as easily explained away as are other, more throwaway remarks, primarily because he reiterated it on a number of occasions. In interview with Matt Cherry in 1999, Clarke clarified his understanding of Buddhism in a manner which sought to render it compatible with the non-theist position he espoused: 'Though I sometimes call myself a crypto-Buddhist, Buddhism is not a religion' (Cherry, 1999: 37).

Neil McAleer similarly notes 'a dialogue on man and his world' which Clarke held with the philosopher and theologian Alan Watts, whose interests in both Buddhism and sf also influenced the work of Frank Herbert. At the beginning of a three-day conversation, Clarke explained how many people 'confuse religion with a belief in God.' According to Clarke, 'Buddhists don't necessarily believe in a god or a supreme being at all, whereas one could easily believe in a supreme being and not have any religion' (McAleer, 1992: 236–37). This proposes a particular understanding of Buddhism at significant odds with the faith as it is most commonly practised, at least in its Mahayana forms which often feature worship of Buddhas and Bodhisattvas, and hence emulate the significant pantheons derived from Hinduism or other indigenous belief systems. This somewhat austere iteration of Buddhism more closely evokes the precepts of Theravada Buddhism, and has an intriguing lineage that is worth exploring, though its impact on Clarke's fiction should not be overstated.

Clarke moved to Sri Lanka (then Ceylon) in 1956 ostensibly to enjoy his pastime of scuba diving, living initially on the south coast of the island before moving to the capital Colombo, where he lived until his death in 2008. Sri Lanka's official religion is Theravada Buddhism, practised by around seventy per cent of the population, though Clarke claimed that 'I suppose I didn't even know this was a Buddhist country, when I first came here' (Robinson, 1997). What is worth noting is that his personal encounter with Theravada Buddhist culture came after the religion, or hints of it, had featured in a number of earlier works, including 'The Sentinel' (1951), 'The Nine Billion Names of

God' and *Childhood's End* (both 1953). Therefore, it is not possible to extrapolate from those fictions any understanding of Buddhism that is entirely reliant on his experience of living in a Buddhist country.

Buddhism in Clarke's Early Fiction

In 'The Sentinel', lunar explorers encounter evidence of extra-terrestrial sentience in the form of 'a glittering roughly pyramidal structure, twice as high as a man, that was set in the rock like a gigantic many-faceted jewel' (Clarke, 2000: 305). This pyramid is, the explorers establish, a sentinel intended to inform the alien species that left it there that a civilization has arisen on Earth capable of extra-terrestrial travel. The narrator identifies that 'this was not a building, but a machine, protecting itself with forces that had challenged Eternity' (Clarke, 2000: 306). However, in order to come to this conclusion, the lunar expedition force had been forced to dismantle it:

> It has taken us twenty years to crack that invisible shield and to reach the machine inside those crystal walls. What we could not understand, we broke at last with the savage might of atomic power and now I have seen the fragments of the lovely, glittering thing I found up there on the mountain.
>
> They are meaningless. The mechanisms – if indeed they are mechanisms – of the pyramid belong to a technology that lies far beyond our horizon, perhaps to the technology of paraphysical forces. (Clarke, 2000: 307)

The Sentinel must be destroyed to be understood, and once destroyed, it initiates a different paradigm of reality. In other words, its destruction is a necessary part of the process required to achieve a fuller understanding of the universe and humanity's place within it. The Sentinel can, therefore, be understood as a metaphor for Maya in Mahayana Buddhism, which denotes the illusion of reality, how we suffer from believing that objects and people have intrinsic reality divorced from circumstances and contexts, including the self. (In Theravada Buddhism, by contrast, Maya is the name of the Buddha's mother.) Though not intended as a parable of Buddhist thinking by any means, this early significant story by Clarke – it would inspire the more substantial *2001: A Space Odyssey* (1968) and resulting novels – is nevertheless open to Buddhist interpretation. Recognizing this, it is possible to identify a first stage of Clarke's 'crypto-Buddhism', a stage in which Buddhist thought can be detected in Clarke's work independent of overt reference or authorial intentionality.

This is not the case with 'The Nine Billion Names of God'. The short story, much anthologized since its first appearance, details the commissioning of two engineers who have been requested to set up and program a computer in a remote monastery in Tibet. Having attempted manually to record the nine billion names for God, a task set to take 15,000 years, the monks intend to digitize the task in order to perform it much more efficiently. Their faith that creation itself will conclude when the task is completed is vindicated when the computer finishes its run and the engineers, *en route* from the monastery, witness that the stars are extinguishing in the sky above.

Despite featuring a Buddhist milieu and characters, the story is notable for its *lack* of informed engagement with Buddhist beliefs. Though it is set in and around a Tibetan lamasery, there is little evidence of Tibetan Buddhist faith present. Unlike more austere forms of Theravada Buddhism, the Tibetan form of Buddhism features many divinity figures rather than merely one creator, which is more a feature of the Abrahamic religions. Most prominent are the eight Dharmapalas who defend Buddhism against demons but there is also a full pantheon of wrathful deities, the Herukas and Dakinis, who are wrathful in opposition to ignorance. However, Tibet had been invaded by China in 1950, and so was current in the media at the time of writing. Additionally, it had long been an exotic backdrop for adventure and sf writing in the US pulp magazines. Far from being an authentic component of Tibetan Buddhist belief, this narrative's depicted obsession with naming God is more appropriate to Judaism, in particular the Kabbalistic mystical tradition.

Clarke's introduction to the story states simply that it 'triggered a charming response from the highest possible authority – His holiness the Dalai Lama' (Clarke, 2000: 417.) This letter is preserved with the Clarke papers in the archives of the Smithsonian National Air and

Space Museum. It states simply: 'Dear Mr. Clarke, Thank you very much for sending me copies of your two books: 1984: SPRING – A Choice of Futures and THE NINE BILLION NAMES OF GOD. Mr. Jeff Greenwald was kind enough to bring these to me. Your short story titled "The Nine Billion Names of God" was particularly amusing. Once again, thank you for your thoughtful gesture. With prayers and good wishes.' There is clearly no formal endorsement of the depiction of Buddhism therein, however neither is there condemnation thereof.

One way in which Clarke's narrative (and its misunderstanding of Buddhist philosophy) may be interpreted alongside the Dalai Lama's gnomic response emerges from an extrapolated reading of the story's dénouement of the story. Tibetan monks, though adhering in general to a complex pantheon of deities, do not accept the principle of a creator God in the Abrahamic sense. Therefore, they have no need to Kabbalistically examine the names of God, and indeed would find such a pursuit meaningless on multiple levels. So what is being extinguished when their task is completed? Clarke's espoused atheism would suggest that perhaps this is a narrative of technology rendering belief in an Abrahamic God pointless. His estimable astronomical knowledge surely would have informed him that for stars to extinguish simultaneously as perceived on Earth, they would have to have been extinguished at very different times in their own local vicinity. Perhaps what is being extinguished by the non-Deist monks and the technology they have harnessed is the need to believe in such a God. This point of contact between Clarke's atheism and Buddhist theology is one which he reiterates many times.

However, the question arises as to whether this is indeed a legitimate reading of Buddhist theology, given the prevalence of deity figures in various iterations of Buddhism, especially in the Mahayana tradition. A number of verses in the *Dhammapada*, a key early Buddhist text in the Pali canon, are often used to support such a reading. Verse 165, in Acharya Buddharakkhita's translation (*Dhammapada*, 1985: 48), stresses the issue of personal responsibility: 'By oneself is evil done; by oneself is one defiled. By oneself is evil left undone; by oneself is one made pure. Purity and impurity depended on oneself; no one can purify another.' This is also reinforced in verse 380, which insists: 'One is one's own protector, one is one's own refuge. Therefore one should control oneself, even as a trader controls a noble steed' (*Dhammapada*, 1985: 81).

The *Dhammapada* also contains a verse which links organized religion, in the Hindu form from which Buddhism originally emerged, to fear. Verse 188 notes what Buddhism sees as the detrimental nature of such organized practice: 'Driven only by fear, do men go for refuge to many places – to hills, woods, groves, trees and shrines' (*Dhammapada*, 1985: 52). This sits uneasily alongside the occasionally baroque hierarchies and pantheons extant in some forms of Buddhism, but it is worth recalling that the Theravada form prevalent in Sri Lanka is not only the earliest of the three main Buddhist traditions, but also the one with the least accretion of divinities. Though the *Dhammapada* does not preclude the involvement of divinities overtly, it does highlight that such things are not necessary in Buddhist theology. This is the Buddhist tradition which Clarke was to encounter when he moved to Sri Lanka in 1956, but it is evident from his fiction written before that date that Theravada Buddhism, rather than Mahayana or Vijrayana Buddhism, was the form he was more familiar with prior to that date.

Buddhist Exceptionalism in *Childhood's End*

This perhaps explains the curious exemption of Buddhism from the eradication of religion that takes place in *Childhood's End* (1953). In the novel, belief in religion is swiftly destroyed following human encounter with the alien Overlords, who present humanity with the ability to empirically examine the origins of the world's major religions. In the novel, the aliens acquiesce to human curiosity. Humanity wishes to understand 'the true beginnings of all the world's great faiths'. It transpires that 'most of them were noble and inspiring – but that was not enough. Within a few days, all mankind's multitudinous messiahs had lost their divinity. Beneath the fierce and passionless light of truth, faiths that had sustained millions for twice a thousand years vanished like morning dew' (Clarke, 1953/1994: 54).

What results from this distinctly non-divine intervention is 'a completely secular age. Of the faiths that had existed before the coming of the Overlords, only a form of purified Buddhism – perhaps the most austere of all religions – still survived' (Clarke, 1953/1994: 53). This characterization of Buddhism as 'austere' and 'secular' is curious, and suggests a particularly non-theist Theravadic form is what Clarke has in mind rather than, for example, something more elaborate and potentially pantheistic, such as some Tibetan variants of the faith.

Edward James has noted how the Overlords 'lead humanity to what appears to be a Utopia; but Utopia is only a stage towards the actual goal, which is to prepare a proportion of the human race for evolution into a state of pure mind – a godlike state which is humanity's true end, and which reveals all humanity's past to have been merely the childhood of the species' (James, 2005: 438). This phase of human evolution functions as a dynamic utopia, dynamic because it is transient. Humanity is destined to evolve into a godlike group-mind which will in turn merge with the Overmind which guides Karellen and his Overlord colleagues. In order for this to occur, however, most of mankind must be destroyed, so that their children, now displaying unusual mental powers, can evolve into the Overmind.

In a sense, then, Gary Westfahl is only partly correct when he asserts that 'all *Childhood's End* argues is that humanity and all its beliefs are destined to end, and a new species will emerge with beliefs we cannot understand' (Westfahl, 2018: 91). Clarke has clarified specifically that a non-theist form of Buddhism survives into this temporary Utopia. Specifically, *Childhood's End* states that 'Humanity had lost its ancient gods: now it was old enough to have no need for new ones' (Clarke, 1953/1994: 54). It may be possible to read this in two ways as an illustration of the second noble truth of Buddhism, the concept of Samudāya, which considers the origin of suffering as arising from desire, or attachment. It is humanity's relinquishing of theist faiths that allows it to enter the utopian phase of its development in *Childhood's End*. Similarly, however, it is the adults' attachment to the past, and to their children, which leads to their suffering and destruction. In such a reading, Karellen and the Overlords function as Bodhisattvas who lead others to enlightenment.

Additionally, the evolution of humanity's children into the Overmind could be read, not in the deist terms so often favoured by Clarke's critics, but more properly as Nirvana, the supramundane state of eternal happiness that transcends attachment to the self. Like Nirvana, the Overmind is apparently infinite, totalizing, involves the dissolution of all individuality, and is unimaginable yet achievable. This may well be overreading Buddhism into the novel. Nevertheless, the persistence of a non-theist Buddhist faith in *Childhood's End* stands as further evidence that Clarke was prepared to exempt at least one form of Buddhism from his habitual rejection of religion. Notably, he did this more than once.

Buddhism in *The Deep Range*

In *The Deep Range* (1957), Buddhism again is the sole religious faith to survive seismic social upheaval and evolution of human thinking. In the face of 'catastrophic political and social changes', all the major religions bar Buddhism have been fatally harmed:

> Christianity, which had never fully recovered from the shattering blow given it by Darwin and Freud, had finally and unexpectedly succumbed before the archaeological discoveries of the late twentieth century. The Hindu religion, with its fantastic pantheon of gods and goddesses, had failed to survive in an age of scientific rationalism. And the Mohammedan faith, weakened by the same forces, had suffered additional loss of prestige when the rising Star of David had outshone the pale crescent of the Prophet. (Clarke, 1957/1991: 174)

The result is that 'with the failure or weakening of its three great rivals, Buddhism was now the only religion that still possessed any real power over the minds of men (Clarke, 1957/1991: 173–4). Indeed, unlike in *Childhood's End*, Buddhism not merely survives but thrives:

> Only the teachings of the Buddha had maintained and even increased their influence, as they filled the vacuum left by other faiths. Being a philosophy and not a religion, and relying on no revelations vulnerable to the archaeologist's hammer, Buddhism had been largely

unaffected by the shocks that had destroyed the other giants. (Clarke, 1957/1991: 174)

By the time he wrote *The Deep Range*, Clarke had moved to Sri Lanka, a mostly Theravada Buddhist nation. This direct encounter with Buddhism is likely to have been the inspiration for the prominence of Buddhism within the novel. In addition to being (again) the only religion to survive the trials of empiricism, Buddhism also manifests in terms of the sacred mountain, Adam's Peak, which is a key location in the novel, and in the figure of the Mahanayake Thero of Anuradhapura, a leading Buddhist figure who is also a Westerner.

The Maha Thero, described as 'the most influential man in the East' (Clarke, 1957/1991: 173), transpires to be a Scottish convert to Buddhism, a sixty-year old *bhikku* (monk), born Alexander Boyce. Having risen to the top of Buddhism, the Thero counts 'at least a billion' sympathizers among his followers. His path to prominence has involved the purification, or 'spring-cleaning' of Buddhism (Clarke, 1957/1991: 175) to remove Hindu accretions, a process of initiating a conservative austerity within the religion. This unusual character, who functions in part as an antagonist in the novel, appears initially to be based on the historic figure of Sīlacāra (Jack F. McKechnie), an English-born Scotsman who converted to Buddhism in his twenties and moved to Rangoon in Burma to pursue his interest in Buddhism. He was ordained sometime around 1906, and spent much of his subsequent career in Burma and Sikkim, translating Buddhist texts into English before returning to Britain in later life due to health complications. Elizabeth Harris notes that he 'stressed only the rationality of Buddhism' in his extensive writings (Harris, 2006: 217), and speculates that he may have visited Sri Lanka during his time in Asia.

However, an additional potential source for the Maha Thero is a Western convert to Buddhism who Clarke himself was to later meet in 1959. Cambridge graduate Harold Musson was one of two demobbed soldiers who became interested in Buddhism in the post-war period and decided to relocate to Ceylon to become Buddhist monks. In 1949, Musson along with his friend Osbert Moore, were ordained as novices and then as *bhikkus* a year later. Moore was given the monastic name of Ñāṇamoli and Musson that of Ñāṇavīra. He then spent most of his life secluded in a single room brick hut in a remote part of the south-eastern coast of Sri Lanka, where he dedicated himself to writing about Buddhism.

His early writings indicate an interest in Western philosophy, especially Existentialism and science, most notably quantum mechanics, and his letters to his good friend Ñāṇamoli are littered with mathematics equations. His later work, especially *Notes on Dhamma* (1960–5), are an attempt to clarify the meaning of the Pali *suttas* from an intellectual basis, which he himself accepted was unlikely to meet with general approval from Buddhists. This austere form of Buddhism, imbricated with Western ideas, has remained controversial in Buddhist theological circles ever since.

Ñāṇavīra was living in his remote hut in mid-April 1959 and corresponding about science with his friend Ñāṇamoli, when he encountered two scuba divers on a nearby beach, one of whom indubitably was Clarke. On 18 April, he wrote to Ñāṇamoli to describe the encounter:

> I also met (while bathing in the field) two Englishmen who have been in Ceylon doing underwater photography and writing books about it. (Seeing me, they stopped their car and got out.) One of them is interested in space-travel, but since he is now getting too old for travelling in space (but I thought it made you younger) he has turned to underwater photography (what is the connexion?). Apart from the Ven. C. Thera, he is the first such enthusiast I have met, but is doubtless typical of millions of others in the world today.
>
> I was asked what the Buddha had to say about space-travel, and I managed to remember Rohitassa Devaputta (in A.IV and elsewhere) who space-travelled for a hundred years without coming to the end of the world. The Buddha told him that it is not by going that one comes to the end of the world, as doubtless you will remember. This rather fascinated them; but I fear that the Buddha's 'end of the world' remained a mystery. The would-be-space-traveller is also, it seems, a bit of a philosopher – he has even written a book of philosophical essays, now in the press. What is his philosophy? Answer: we only have to wait another hundred thousand years before we shall have met (through space-travel) beings far, far more intelligent than any

we know of, who will tell us all the answers. What faith in Science! What hopes for the future! What confidence that by going the end of the world will be reached! After the encounter I felt rather as if I had read all the scientific articles in fifty London Observers. (Ñāṇavīra, 2014: 285–6)

It may be that the Thero is a composite of McKechnie and Musson, or simply derived from Musson. Certainly, though the Scottishness of the Thero suggests McKechnie, the austerity of the Buddhism depicted much more closely evokes Ñāṇavīra, whom Clarke had likely heard about from locals prior to their meeting two years after the publication of *The Deep Range*. The very circumstances of their meeting also suggest this, since Clarke's reason for being in that particularly remote part of Sri Lanka – to dive – is not really justified by the sites available in that location. It is speculative, though likely, that Clarke had heard of Musson, and fictionalized his character, prior to hunting out the reclusive monk for the conversation recorded in Ñāṇavīra's letter.

The 'Buddhist Philosophy' of *The Fountains of Paradise*

A similar character, bridging Western thinking and Sri Lankan Buddhism, can be found in *The Fountains of Paradise* (1979), which tellingly is dedicated to his friend Leslie Ekanayake, with the text 'Nirvana Prapto Bhuyat' ('He has attained Nirvana'). With such a dedication, it is unsurprising that Sri Lanka and Buddhism permeate the entire novel, which shifts in time between the eras of two immense engineering feats, those of the long-dead second century King Kalidasa and of the Australian Vannevar Morgan, Chief Engineer (Land) of the Terran Construction Corporation.

The King of Taprobane (a thinly fictionalized Sri Lanka relocated to the equator, some 550 miles to the south) battles with Buddhist clergy to erect his palace on top of Yakkagala, the demon rock. Clarke adapted this narrative thread from the story of the fifth century usurper king, Kashyapa I of Anuradhapura, who built a citadel and new capital city around Sigirya, the Lion Rock, upon which he placed his palace. This narrative is contrasted with the similar resistance Morgan faces as he attempts to construct a space elevator, which must be anchored to Earth on the equator, and hence only one location is suitable – the sacred mountain of Sri Kanda, which Clarke acknowledged was based on the local Sri Lankan holy mountain of Adam's Peak, which is sacred to Christians, Muslims, Hindus and Buddhists.

In the novel Morgan encounters another Maha Thero, who is accompanied by his private secretary, the Venerable Parakarma, a Westerner who had previously been an astrophysicist called Choam Goldberg. He abandoned his scientific career following first contact with a craft from an alien species, the Starglider, announcing: 'Now that the Starglider has effectively destroyed all traditional religions, we can at last pay serious attention to the concept of God' (Clarke, 1979/1980: 76). Parakarma/Goldberg again evokes the figure of Ñāṇavīra, whose interests in scientific inquiry is well attested in his many letters. Morgan is quick to identify the Parakarma as the real threat to his project, given his ability to scientifically argue against Morgan's reassurances that the orbital tower for the elevator will not disturb the monastery.

The tensions between Morgan and the Parakarma are carefully constructed (and resolved) by Clarke to reiterate his consistent position that, though alien intervention might well render most terrestrial religions redundant, Buddhism in its austere, non-Deist, Sri Lankan Theravadan form is to be considered an exception. Though they disagree on the construction of the tower, Morgan and the Parakarma are not depicted as ideological opponents. Just as the Parakarma converts to Buddhism to better understand the impact of the Starglider's arrival, and then later leaves his vocation to pursue science once more as a meteorologist, so too is Morgan presented as an open-minded engineer, inclined not only towards the technological sublime, as expressed by his celebrated Gibraltar Bridge, but also towards a Buddhist-tinged numinous. Staring at a statue of the Buddha in the Maha Thero's office, Morgan notes that:

> Here was a work of art that, like the Mona Lisa, both mirrored the emotions of the observer and imposed its own authority upon them.

> La Gioconda's eyes were open, however, though what they were looking at no one would ever know. The eyes of the Buddha were completely blank – empty pools in which a man might lose his soul, or discover a universe. (Clarke, 1979/1980: 81)

The Parakarma attempts to manipulate the weather in order to disrupt testing of the elevator, but succeeds only in blowing a swarm of golden butterflies to the summit of the sacred mountain. This fulfils an ancient prophecy from the time of King Kalidasa, which means that the monks must leave the mountain, thereby permitting construction of the elevator in earnest. The Parakarma's intervention is a scientific failure which allows the elevator to proceed, and become, as we discover in the novel's coda, a great scientific success. In an ironic sense therefore, he lives up to his title, suffering a sort of karmic retribution for his attempt at sabotage. This playful resolution of Morgan's quandary may be rooted in superstition and entail the symbolic defeat of the Buddhist *bhikkus*, but it is ultimately based on their own acquiescence to leave. It is also a tentative accommodation between the visions of science and Buddhism, as expressed in the figure of the Parakarma, whose interests naturally seem to migrate between both, and in terms of the mutual respect depicted between Morgan and his religious counterparts.

Conclusion

A decade in the making, Clarke at the time of publication considered *The Fountains of Paradise* to be his crowning achievement in fiction. Peter Perakos, in *Cinefantastique*, reported that it would be his last novel (Perakos, 1979: 35) while Clarke told journalist Martin Walker that it was his magnum opus: 'Everything is in it: Buddhist philosophy, ancient history, the ultimate space transport system' (Walker, 1978: 75). Clarke's self-assessment proved somewhat inaccurate: he is better known among the general public for his collaboration with Stanley Kubrick on *2001*. However even here, where his vision had initially been circumscribed by Kubrick, Clarke ultimately offered a rapprochement to people of faith. For Buddhist writer Philip Purves,

2001 raises questions 'about the trajectory of human evolution and its ultimate destiny, and about how metaphysical and even transcendental questions are addressed. Parallels with Buddhist thought and the philosophy of Nietzsche emerge' (Purves, 2018: 46).

In *3001: The Final Odyssey* (1997), Clarke's carefully hedged antipathy to religion, especially theist beliefs, is expressed via the character Theodore Khan, who attacks 'the psychopathology known as religion' (Clarke, 1997: 132). Yet the same novel contains a curious coda directed to his religious friends:

> Finally, I would like to assure my many Buddhist, Christian, Hindu, Jewish, and Muslim friends that I am sincerely happy that the religion which Chance has given you has contributed to your peace of mind (and often, as Western medical science now reluctantly admits, to your physical well-being). Perhaps it is better to be un-sane and happy, than sane and un-happy. But it is the best of all to be sane and happy. (Clarke, 1997: 274)

It is undoubtedly clear that Clarke does not intend readers to interpret him as suggesting that religious belief is particularly sane, and his fiction is consistent in suggesting that, as he told Ñāṇavīra on the beach in 1959, first contact will render all theist beliefs redundant. However, he is equally consistent in finding some accommodation for non-theist forms of Buddhism in his many imagined futures. This does not make him a Buddhist by any means, but this accommodation and interest predates his move to Sri Lanka, and then seems to have been sustained by his exposure to Sri Lankan Buddhist culture, most notably evidenced in *The Fountains of Paradise*.

Jerome Agel quotes Clarke discussing the purpose of sf in relation to *2001*: 'One of the biggest roles of *science fiction* is to prepare people to accept the *future* without *pain* and to encourage a flexibility of *mind*. Politicians should read science fiction, not westerns and detective stories. Two-thirds of *2001* is realistic — hardware and technology — to establish background for the *metaphysical, philosophical,* and *religious meanings* later' (Agel, 1970: 300). Clarke's affinity with Buddhism may not even cryptically make him a Buddhist. However, the fictional accommodations he lent to the religion, especially in an austere, non-theist, scientifically friendly form which perhaps derives in part from Ñāṇavīra and in part from Sri Lanka itself, suggests that this, and not the Christianity of his childhood nor any of the other religious faiths he regularly pathologized, may inform the *metaphysical, philosophical,* and *religious* meaning' he had in mind.

Acknowledgement

The author would like to thank Edward James and the editors of *Urthona* magazine for their assistance in the writing of this chapter.

Works Cited

Agel, J. (1970) *The Making of Kubrick's 2001*. New York: New American Library.

Bordwell, D. (2002) *Catechism of the Catholic Church*. London: Bloomsbury Academic.

Brandreth, G. (2000) 'Life Beyond 2001', *Sunday Telegraph*, 17 December.

Cherry, M. (1999) 'God, Science, and Delusion: A Chat With Arthur C. Clarke', *Free Inquiry* 19(2): 36–7.

Clarke, A. C. (1953/1990) *Childhood's End*. New York: Del Rey.

Clarke, A. C. (1957/1991) *The Deep Range*. New York: Bantam Books.

Clarke, A. C. (1979/1980) *The Fountains of Paradise*. London: Pan.

Clarke, A. C. (1986) *The Songs of Distant Earth*. New York: Del Rey.

Clarke, A. C. (1997) *3001: The Final Odyssey*. New York: Ballantine.

Clarke, A. C. (1999) *Greetings, Carbon-Based Bipeds!: Collected Essays 1934–1998*. New York: St Martin's Press.

Clarke, A. C. (2000) *The Collected Stories of Arthur C. Clarke*. New York: Tor.

Clarke, J. (2019) *Science Fiction and Catholicism: The Rise and Fall of the Robot Papacy*. Canterbury: Gylphi.

The Dhammapadda: The Buddha's Path of Wisdom (1985), trans. Acharya Buddharakkhita. Kandy: Buddhist Publication Society.

Feeley, G. (1990) 'Partners in Plunder Or, Rendezvous with Manna', *Foundation* 49: 58–63.

Fleetham, M. (2006) *Multiple Intelligences in Practice: Enhancing Self-esteem and Learning in the Classroom*. Stafford: Network Continuum.

Harris, E. J. (2006) *Theravada Buddhism and the British Encounter: Religious, Missionary and Colonial Experience in Nineteenth-Century Sri Lanka*. Abingdon: Routledge.

James, E. (2005) 'Arthur C. Clarke', in D. Seed (ed.) *A Companion to Science Fiction*, pp. 431–40. Oxford: Blackwell.
Kaplan, Rabbi A. (1983) *The Aryeh Kaplan Reader*. New York: Mesorah Publications.
McAleer, N. (1992) *Odyssey: The Authorised Biography of Arthur C. Clarke*. London: Gollancz.
Mintowt-Czyz, L. (2008) 'Science fiction author Arthur C. Clarke dies aged 90', *The Times*, March 19.
Ñāṇavīra (2014) *Seeking the Path*, eds. Gerolf G. P. T'Hooft, Bhikkhu Hiriko Ñanasuci and Samanera Bodhesako. IJssel, Netherlands: Path Press.
Perakos, P. S. (1979) 'Arthur C. Clarke's *Fountains of Paradise*', *Cinefantastique* 8(4): 35.
Purves, P. (Dh. Vijaya) (2018) 'Arthur C. Clarke, *2001* & Deep Time', *Urthona: Journal of Buddhism and the Arts* 34: 46–52.
Reid, R. (1997) *Arthur C. Clarke: A Critical Companion*. Westport, CT: Greenwood.
Robinson, A. (1997) 'The Cosmic Godfather', *Times Higher Education Supplement*, 10 October, URL (accessed 13 April 2020): https://www.timeshighereducation.com/features/the-cosmic-godfather/103989.article
Samuelson, D. (1982) 'Arthur C. Clarke', in E. Bleiler (ed.) *Science Fiction Writers: Critical Studies of the Major Authors from the Early Nineteenth Century to the Present Day*, pp. 313–20. New York: Charles Scribner's Sons.
Walker, M. (1978) 'Arthur C. Clarke in Sri Lanka', *Guardian*, September 14.
Westfahl, G. (2018) *Arthur C. Clarke*. Urbana: University of Illinois Press.

5

No Future?
Queering Deep Time in *The City and the Stars*

Paul March-Russell

Although *Childhood's End* (1953) and *2001: A Space Odyssey* (1968) have dominated the critical scholarship on Arthur C. Clarke's fiction, many readers regard *The City and the Stars* (1956) as his exemplary work. Edward James writes that in this novel 'Clarke was able to express the ideology and poetic vision of science fiction better than anyone else' (James, 2005a: 439). Unlike *Childhood's End*, where humanity is prohibited from deep space exploration, *The City and the Stars* reaffirms it as 'the most fitting aim for the human race' (James, 2005a: 438). For Brian Stableford and David Langford, this reaffirmation confirms the novel as 'the classic pulp sf story about the far future', in which humanity's historical role is re-established on a cosmic scale (Stableford and Langford, 2015). And yet, despite Russell Blackford's contention that it is not 'mystical to ponder the far future' or 'to wonder what forms of life or consciousness will one day supersede humanity' (Blackford, 2001: 41), there is a critical tendency either to dismiss the novel's far-future scenario as mystification or to schematize it as an allegory of the Cold War (Blackford, 2001: 37–44). In other words, a discrepancy occurs. On the one hand, *The*

City and the Stars is the epitome of sf's ideological values (humanity's manifest destiny within the cosmos); on the other hand, its very setting seems to undermine these values, to render them mystical or merely an allegory of the present.

To some extent, the problem lies with the far-future narrative itself. H. G. Wells's *The Time Machine* (1895), the speculative essays of J. D. Bernal and J. B. S. Haldane and, perhaps most of all, Olaf Stapledon's *Last and First Men* (1930) established a methodology for speculating about the deep future based upon theories of entropy and evolution. A tension persists in these narratives: on the one hand, by asserting that whatever the future contains it will always be different from now, there is an optimistic embrace of change and difference; on the other hand, by acknowledging that all structures – even the universe itself – ultimately decay, their optimism is shrouded by an underlying pessimism. Whether we call these narratives optimistic or pessimistic is ultimately down to the reader's own position, their own sense of the *telos* of history. In the final analysis, we may all be dead, but there is much to be enjoyed as we live, an appreciation heightened and made meaningful by its eventual end. For Weird fiction authors, such as William Hope Hodgson in *The Night Land* (1912), entropy is itself generative: it is the abcanny creatures that have evolved since the sun died, rather than the laboured pastiche of the narration, which give the story much of its energy.

Consequently, although far-future narratives may originate in scientific speculation, whether they be classics of the sub-genre such as Stapledon or more recent additions such as Stephen Baxter's Xeelee quartet (1991–4) or N. K. Jemisin's Broken Earth trilogy (2015–17), the sense of an ending is what gives them their dramatic appeal. The reversion to magic may be a sign of decadence in Jack Vance's *The Dying Earth* (1950) but it is also what propels the novel. Similarly, Gene Wolfe's use of a fantastical far-future setting in *The Book of the New Sun* (1980–3) throws into relief the harsh instrumentality of reason while Brian Aldiss, in *Hothouse* (1962), is intrigued more by the symbolism rather than the science of entropy. The far-future narrative, then, can be both an experiment in the depths of speculation and a critical intervention into scientific rationality. Aldiss, in his revised ending to another far-future narrative *Galaxies Like Grains of Sand* (1960), even cheekily absorbs the title of Clarke's key work: 'They shall be told,' the Highest said, his face a shadow as night fell upon the old city and the stars' (Aldiss, 1979: 188).[1]

Clarke's novel, then, is perched somewhere between these various modes. If it is indeed the epitome of far-future speculation, it can do nothing but reproduce the dialectical tensions between science and mysticism, optimism and pessimism, progress and decadence. These tensions, rather than their resolution, are precisely what lend the novel its enigmatic vitality. For, despite its apparent affirmation of the values of genre sf, *The City and the Stars* – like many other far-future narratives – also plays with those values and dramatizes their antithesis. To some extent, this is because the novel also presents one of Clarke's most extensive explorations of utopia. For James, the novel offers an 'archetypal science-fictional critique of utopia' (James, 2005b: 26), in that the technological perfection of Diaspar supplies 'a completely satisfying existence' which, without competition or struggle, is also 'wholly futile' (Clarke, 1956/2001: 33). For Tom Moylan, in an over-deterministic reading of the novel, this utopian future is simply the fulfilment of a 'capitalist-imperialist political economy' (Moylan, 1977: 154). More promisingly, Martin McGrath draws upon Michel Foucault's notion of heterotopias to find sites of temporal, spatial and social dissidence within Clarke's otherwise progressive vision of human development (McGrath, 2011: 10–13). Diaspar is such a site since it encompasses both a multitude of spaces, 'the totality of the world' (Foucault, 1986: 26) via the city's Memory Banks 'in one space [...] outside of time, and inaccessible to its ravages' (Foucault, 1986: 26), and an almost magical sense of order which, for dissidents like Alvin and the jester figure Khedron, borders upon the carceral. In other words, whilst the planned regime of Diaspar appears to be materially satisfying but spiritually void, it also embeds within itself 'counter-sites' in which all the 'sites within the culture, are simultaneously represented, contested, and inverted' (Foucault, 1986: 24). Yet, this is true not only of Diaspar itself but also of how Clarke's novel negotiates the various paradoxes within the far-future narrative.

In short, *The City and the Stars* not only dramatizes ambiguity, it is in itself ambiguous – at once, the affirmation of genre sf and its antithesis. This generic instability partially arises from its more than twenty-year long gestation, and the divergent influences that were acting upon Clarke as he wrote and re-wrote the story. But it also emerges from Clarke's unease with the very idea of futurity and, in particular, its investment in imperial and material progress. In reading Clarke's novel alongside Lee Edelman's critique of what he terms 'reproductive futurism', I also want to suggest that Clarke queers the far-future narrative even as he offers one of its most vivid depictions.

En-Weirding the Engineer Paradigm

Perhaps as a sign of the novel's intractability, critics tend to fall back upon familiar strategies for reading Clarke's fiction, most especially upon the 'engineer paradigm' which Roger Luckhurst sees as underlying the development of genre sf 'in the pre-1945 era' (Luckhurst, 2005: 52). Clarke, of course, bolstered this view through his pioneering work in telecommunications, his early non-fiction and his subsequent career as a science communicator. It is therefore no surprise to see Clarke's *A Fall of Moondust* (1961) as one of the case studies in Gary Westfahl's account of hard sf, *Cosmic Engineers* (1996). More recently, Westfahl has built upon this notion of engineered design in Clarke's fiction by emphasizing the greater structural unity of *The City and the Stars* in comparison with its original published form as *Against the Fall of Night* (1948) (Westfahl, 2018: 83–6).

Although Westfahl is ultimately more pessimistic in his reading of the novel than John Hollow's similar account (Hollow, 1983: 117–25), both critics foreground the constituent role of scientific plausibility to interpreting Clarke's fiction. The centrality of this criterion is typical of the earlier criticism on the novel by, amongst others, John Huntington, Eric Rabkin, George Slusser and Patricia Warwick. Their approach defines science fiction in terms of its handling of the scientific method, a perspective which is well-suited to consolidating the predominance of Clarke, Isaac Asimov and Robert Heinlein, all of whom had scientific backgrounds, as well as the claims to scientific knowledge by John W. Campbell, editor of *Astounding Science Fiction*. As Clarke acknowledged, the premise of *The City and the Stars* was not only indebted to the vast time-scales in Stapledon's *Last and First Men* but also to Campbell's vision of a soulless, technological far-future in his short story 'Twilight' (1934) (Clarke, 1972: 9–10). The increased importance of the Central Computer to the city of Diaspar in Clarke's revised version is also a clear response to Norbert Weiner's *Cybernetics* (1948) as well as the first workplace appearances of IBM computers in 1953.

These preferred readings for design and scientific validity not only reinforce Clarke's public image of the science communicator, but they also present a more coherent trajectory to the writing of *The City and the Stars*. Instead, the earliest drafts of the novel date back to 1935 when Clarke was still an adolescent fan of *Astounding Stories*, then edited by F. O. Tremaine. It was Tremaine who innovated pulp sf by publishing 'thought-variants', stories that were either premised on an original idea or glossed a familiar scenario in an original way, and what Tremaine called 'super-science': 'actual facts which, because they astound and confuse science, *are super-science*' (Tremaine, 1934: 9). These 'actual facts' included the paranormal writings of Charles Fort, whose book *Lo!* (1931) was serialized in *Astounding* in 1934. Clarke recollected that he found Fort's 'eccentric – even explosive – style stimulating and mind-expanding' (Clarke, 1989: 107). H. P. Lovecraft, who referenced Fort in his story 'The Whisperer in Darkness' (1931), was also published by Tremaine; his story, 'At the Mountains of Madness' (1936), was subsequently parodied by Clarke in the fanzine *Satellite* (March 1940). Clarke's parody also refers to the magazine *Unknown*, which was launched by Campbell in 1939 to explore his own pseudo- (or super-) scientific beliefs, and debuted with Eric Frank Russell's long Fortean story, 'Sinister Barrier'. In addition, both *Against the Fall of Night* and its revised version were published during Clarke's twelve-year correspondence with Lord Dunsany, whose influential fantasy novels drew upon late Victorian tropes of decadence and Celtic mysticism. As John Clute and David Langford (2019) note, Dunsany also wrote a far-future novel in 1955,

The Pleasures of a Futuroscope (albeit far more pastoral than Clarke's), while Dunsany's Jorkens tales of the 1930s may have influenced the story-telling frame of Clarke's *Tales from the White Hart* (1957).

This melting-pot of influences suggests not only affinities between *The City and the Stars* and its apparent antithesis, *Childhood's End*, written when Clarke was still 'a semi-believer' in the paranormal (Clarke, 1989: 185), it also implies that the final version was still imbricated with traces of the Weird. Indeed, the city of Diaspar echoes the Great Redoubt in Hodgson's *The Night Land*. However, whereas Hodgson's nightmare vision of a dying Earth is at least redeemed by the promise of heterosexual romantic love, 'for that which doth be *truly* LOVE doth mother Honour and Faithfulness' (Hodgson, 1912/1979: 419), Clarke's vision, equally inspired by writers such as Campbell, Stapledon and Wells, shares with Lovecraft's depiction of contemporary society as a 'cancerous machine-culture [...] a treadmill, squirrel-trap culture – drugged and frenzied with the hasheesh of industrial servitude and material luxury' (cited in Joshi, 2003: 218). Over and above the echoes of the Eloi in Wells' *The Time Machine*, the sybarite culture of Aldous Huxley's *Brave New World* (1932) and the languid 'Lotus Eaters' in Clarke's own novella, 'The Lion of Comarre' (1949), Lovecraft's dystopian vision turns upon the very pointlessness of reproduction. If Hodgson still holds out the prospect of a humane hope, premised in the true meeting of the sexes, for Lovecraft such hope is a delusion, incarcerating both sexes within the futility of capitalist consumption. As Clarke's narrator writes: 'Diaspar was all that existed, all that they needed, all that they could imagine. It mattered nothing to them that Man had once possessed the stars' (Clarke, 1956/2001: 9).

From Post-Imperial Melancholy to Reproductive Futurism

For all of its technological perfection, Diaspar is compared with the surrounding ruination of the landscape: 'it sheltered against the slow attrition of the ages, the ravages of decay, and the corruption of rust' (Clarke, 1956/2001: 9). The juxtaposition suggests that Diaspar is itself a ruin, a fragment of the technical achievement that had underwritten the Empire and from which the inhabitants have turned away: 'They did not wish to bring back the old days, for they were content in their eternal autumn' (Clarke, 1956/2001: 10). Again, for all of its accomplishment, a sense of melancholy pervades Diaspar, borne from a fear of the outside, which the inhabitants seek to lose in their playing of virtual reality 'Sagas' and the instant gratification of their material desires. Clarke's protagonist, Alvin, embodies though the unrest that these quick-fix solutions fail to satisfy: 'He was always wanting to go outside, both in reality and in dream. Yet to everyone in Diaspar, "outside" was a nightmare that they could not face' (Clarke, 1956/2001: 13).

This unease in the novel is preconditioned by two cultural contexts, both of which I want to argue are interrelated. The first stems from the decline of the British Empire during the period in which Clarke rewrote the published versions of his novel. Luckhurst, following the work of critics such as Ian Baucom, Paul Gilroy and Tom Nairn, has argued that a 'post-imperial melancholy' pervades the work of 1970s science fiction by such writers as M. John Harrison, Christopher Priest and Keith Roberts (Luckhurst, 2005: 172–4). However, the cultural introspection and clinging to seemingly safe and familiar locales that Luckhurst describes can be equally applied to the behaviour of the Diasparans: 'the Sagas had been infected by the same strange phobia that ruled all the citizens of Diaspar. Even their vicarious adventures must take place cosily indoors, in subterranean caverns, or in neat little valleys surrounded by mountains which shut out all the rest of the world' (Clarke, 1956/2001: 16).

In this regard, Clarke's novel is often compared with the contemporaneous writings of Asimov and, in particular, the Foundation Trilogy (1951–3). *The Caves of Steel* (1954), though, is a more apposite comparison since there humanity has retreated underground, has renounced its claim to space exploration, and is effectively forced to regain its place amongst the stars. This brief summary suggests strong similarities with Alvin and his attempt to reclaim humanity's cosmic destiny in *The City and the Stars*, but unlike the more Frontier-driven vision of Asimov, Clarke's narrative is imbricated with his own mixed feelings about imperial decline. Instead, more promising comparisons could be made with his British near-contemporaries such as John Christopher and John Wyndham.

In 1947, India and Pakistan had been partitioned, Burma and Ceylon (which Clarke would make his home) had gained independence in 1948, uprisings continued throughout the 1950s in Kenya and Malaysia, and in 1956 Sudan had become independent, prefiguring the Suez Crisis of 1957. Clarke's own feelings towards the break-up of Empire were ambivalent. During the Second World War, he had served as a radar specialist with the RAF, while his early novels, most notably *Prelude to Space* (1951), imagined a specifically British expansion into space exploration. On the other hand, he migrated to the newly independent Ceylon in 1956 (the year of *The City and the Stars*), ostensibly to pursue his love of scuba diving, but more likely to escape the social and sexual repression of British society (see Mike Stack's later chapter). A similar ambivalence about the glories of an imperial past is to be found in Clarke's novel.

In Clarke's fictional world, a mythology has emerged that humanity had 'for millions of years [...] expanded across the Galaxy, gathering system after system under his sway' (Clarke, 1956/2001: 236) until overwhelming defeat at the hands of the so-called Invaders had driven humanity back to Earth, traumatized, and divided between the two communities of Diaspar and Lys. This imperial myth is countered by the discovery that humanity had been unable to escape the solar system; that it was only through the agency of alien technology that it did so, and when it did 'found cultures he could understand but could not match' (Clarke, 1956/2001: 237). It was only when humanity bioengineered itself, so as to be an equal of these other civilizations, that it returned to the stars and formed 'an Empire of many races' (Clarke, 1956/2001: 238), which was doomed only by its decision to create a disembodied, 'pure mentality' known as 'The Mad Mind' (Clarke, 1956/2001: 240). Clarke's narrative becomes increasingly eschatological: although imprisoned in an artificial star, the Mad Mind will one day 'be free again' so that humanity created further mentalities, such as Vanamonde encountered by Alvin, to defeat it in a final reckoning (Clarke, 1956/2001: 240-1). In the meantime, humanity slipped through 'the great empty rents which the Mad Mind had torn' (Clarke, 1956/2001: 242) into a higher dimensional universe, leaving behind its backwoods descendants on Earth. Whereas in Asimov's cosmogony, Earth retains a semi-legendary, foundational role for the galactic empire, in Clarke's vision, the future history of Earth is no more than 'a tiny thread in an enormous tapestry' (Clarke, 1956/2001: 241), 'a belated and trivial epilogue, though one so complex that we have not been able to unravel its details' (Clarke, 1956/2001: 242).

This side-lining of the Earth as the Empire's imaginary homeland, and the enclosure of its remaining inhabitants within the technological utopia of Diaspar and the pastoral idyll of Lys, suggests not only Clarke's ambivalent relationship with colonialism but also his vicarious feelings toward human progress. Although Diaspar is vast, it is nevertheless finite so that its social order requires an environment that is homeostatic. This equilibrium is achieved by the fact that there are no new generations in Diaspar. As Alvin's tutor, Jeserac, explains, 'our ancestors learned how to analyse and store the information which would define any specific human being – and to use that information to recreate the original' (Clarke, 1956/2001: 21). Francis Crick and James Watson's description of the DNA double helix had been published in *Nature* in April 1953; crucially, they showed how the reproducibility of the intertwined structure could be understood in terms of informational code. The realization that the basis of human life was no more than a reproducible code intersected with the mathematical and cybernetic theories of figures such as John von Neumann, Alan Turing and Norbert Weiner. As Jeserac himself comments, 'the way in which information is stored is of no importance; all that matters is the information itself' (Clarke, 1956/2001: 21). In preparing for his death and rebirth in a new body, Jeserac likens his consciousness to computer storage: 'I shall go back through my memories, editing them and cancelling those I do not wish to keep [...] Nothing will be left of Jeserac but a galaxy of electrons frozen in the heart of a crystal' (Clarke, 1956/2001: 21). Instead, the Diasparans have achieved a kind of virtual immortality: 'We have all been here many, many times before' although 'only a hundredth of the citizens of Diaspar live and walk in its streets.' Meanwhile 'the vast majority slumber in the memory banks, waiting for the signal that will call them forth [...] So we have continuity, yet change – immortality, but not stagnation' (Clarke, 1956/2001: 22). By these means, in effectively short-circuiting the need for sexual reproduction, the Diasparans achieve homoeostasis but only at the expense of an expansionist vision of human progress.

The managed decline of Diaspar's imperial past and its eternal, asexual present can be compared alongside Lee Edelman's critique of what he terms 'reproductive futurism'. In his polemic, *No Future* (2004), Edelman (2004: 2-3) argues that 'however radical' the idea of 'a more desirable social order, remains, at its core, conservative insofar as it works to *affirm* a structure, to *authenticate* social order'. Political change remains bound, Edelman (2004: 2) suggests, by 'the absolute privilege of heteronormativity by rendering unthinkable [...] the possibility of a queer resistance to this organising principle of communal relations', that is to say, reproductive futurism: the sanctity of children and of the future generations to come. In contrast, Edelman (2004: 3) argues that '*queerness* names the side of those *not* "fighting for the children", the side outside the consensus by which all politics confirms the absolute value of reproductive futurism'. Edelman's (2004: 3) object is to claim that 'queerness attains its ethical value precisely [...] as resistance to the viability of the social while insisting on the inextricability of such resistance from every social structure'. Instead, bound by his own immersion in the vocabulary of Jacques Lacan, Edelman (2004: 4) refuses 'the insistence of hope as an affirmation' of the Symbolic Order, whose illusory power is grounded both in the procreative ability of the phallus and its expulsion of all social and sexual identities which are deemed to be non-procreative. Edelman (2004: 5), by contrast, delights in 'the death drive' that 'the queer, in the order of the social, is called forth to figure: the negativity opposed to every form of social viability', and the resulting *jouissance* (bliss) that follows, 'a movement beyond the pleasure principle, beyond the distinctions of pleasure and pain, a violent passage beyond the bounds of identity, meaning, and law' (Edelman, 2004: 25).

In summoning Edelman's critique, I deliberately play upon the anachronism – let alone the disparity – between his position and that of Clarke. Edelman's provocative assertion of non-heteronormative identities is indebted to the public expression of the Gay Liberation Movement of the 1970s as well as the theorization of sexuality by poststructuralists such as Lacan, Foucault and Judith Butler. Clarke, writing in Britain in the 1950s when homosexuality remained a criminal offence, is noticeably more reticent (more coded, one might say) while he would have baulked at the heavily theorized language Edelman's argument is couched within. Nevertheless, I want to suggest that there is a productive reading to be found within the very tensions between their respective positions. In particular, the hesitancy towards reproductive futurism in *The City and the Stars* is symptomatic of the post-imperial melancholy that elsewhere pervades the text.

Alvin: Queering the Weird

Unlike other dying Earth narratives then, in which the decadence and sterility of the surviving population arises from the entropy of the planet, in *The City and the Stars* it emerges from the Diasparans' decision to have no further children but to reincarnate themselves. This choice must be contrasted with the fear of an aging, childless population in both Aldiss's *Greybeard* (1964) and P. D. James's *The Children of Men* (1992), the latter one of Edelman's chosen examples. Unlike both Aldiss and James, whose narratives remain invested in the hope of reproductive futurism, Clarke's Diasparans do not face extinction but an ultimately sterile recirculation, signified by the gradual return of memories from each previous incarnation. There are no new experiences to be had, only an enforced nostalgia due to the bioengineering of the Diasparans' genetic code. In that sense, although the Diasparans negate the logic of reproductive futurism as described by Edelman, they do not cancel the repetition of 'industrial servitude and material luxury' as critiqued by Lovecraft; instead, they actively embody it. We could then argue that Clarke en-Weirds the very notion of human progress by dramatizing how it is closely aligned with the vacuity, the abysmal emptiness and horrific non-signification, of endless capitalist (re)production. This fear also underlines the post-imperial melancholy of the Diasparans that, arguably, they compensate for by creating the myth of the Invaders and the military defeat of the Empire.

The Central Computer, though, understands this horror. As Jeserac informs Alvin, he 'alone of the human race' has 'never lived before' but emerged from the Memory Banks fully intact without origin or prior experience: 'the first child to be born on Earth for at least ten million years' (Clarke, 1956/2001: 22). Alvin's quest to uncover the truth of Diaspar is also a search for self-discovery. What he learns is that he is not exceptional but that there have been thirteen other 'Uniques' before him – their purpose is, like Khedron the Jester, to 'introduce calculated amounts of disorder into the city' (Clarke, 1956/2001: 45) so that Diaspar does not stagnate. In other words, progress – even within the circumscribed limits of the city – can only be sustained by deviating from the norm. Instead of regarding Alvin as a kind of double negative, in that he negates Diaspar's negation of reproductive futurism, it is more accurate to see him and his precursors as sustaining the negativity of Diaspar. His deviation, though, from the already queer norm of Diaspar cannot be fully regulated by the Central Computer. Significantly, all the previous Uniques have 'disappeared' (Clarke, 1956/2001: 53); it is unclear whether they have died or gone missing (it is subsequently revealed that they defected and adjusted to life in Lys). Either way, although their creation is dependent upon the Central Computer and is constituent to how Diaspar regulates itself, both Alvin and his predecessors ultimately represent a excess, in Edelman's terms a *jouissance*, which is both painfully conditioned by its social context and pleasurably defies it. In other words, Alvin queers the very queerness of Diaspar, not to reintroduce a heteronormative order but to play within its libidinal economy.

Such a description, however, seems a far cry from Clarke's novel insofar as the only 'erotic games' (Clarke, 1956/2001: 29) are framed in terms of heterosexual behaviour. Clarke himself was famously reticent about the description of sexuality in his fiction, at least until *Imperial*

Earth (1975), partially because of obscenity laws, partially because of the wider age demographic for science fiction, but mostly because of Clarke's own temperament and homosexuality. Nonetheless, what I am describing here as 'queer' about Clarke's fiction is not his representation of gay or lesbian subjects, which in sf of the 1950s could only be implied, for example in Theodore Sturgeon's short story 'The World Well Lost' (1953), but a series of textual effects that disturb the 'almost completely naturalized heterosexual binary' that Veronica Hollinger sees as underwriting 'science fiction as a narrative field' (Hollinger, 1999: 2). These effects arise from the Weird elements that imbricate Clarke's novel, rhetorical devices that Luckhurst summarises as 'the slipperiness of form, a refusal to fit narrative or generic expectations' (Luckhurst, 2017: 1050), which he also equates with 'a twisting away from heteronormative destinations' (Luckhurst, 2017: 1051). Thus, within the textual lacunae of Clarke's narrative, we can read both traces of queerness and utopian negativity: glimpses of a social order other than what is defined by reproductive futurism.

Perhaps one of the clearest contradictions in the narrative is that, although Alvin is portrayed as heterosexual, he lacks any stable heterosexual attachment. The brevity of his affairs are 'famous' with his peers, their intensity in marked contrast with the 'long spells' where he shows no interest in sex as well as the level of disconsolation felt by 'his discarded lovers' (Clarke, 1956/2001: 29). The figure of Alystra embodies this long sequence of forsaken girlfriends; although she is instrumental in Alvin escaping Diaspar, he treats her with disdain: 'Ungallantly, Alvin shook his head. He knew where *that* would lead, and at the moment he wanted to be alone.' Instead, Alvin values cerebral contact over the physical: 'In a city of ten million human beings [...] there was no one to whom he could really talk' (Clarke, 1956/2001: 14).

To some extent, however, Alvin's exceptionalism links him to other superhuman beings in pulp sf, most notably Jommy Cross in A. E. van Vogt's *Slan* (1940), so that he remains reassuringly masculine for young male readers, anxious of their own entry into heterosexual conduct. Nonetheless, Alvin's physical appearance, like that of all

Diasparans, is coded feminine from a twentieth-century perspective: 'at first sight he would also have been baffled by the problem of distinguishing male from female' (Clarke, 1956/2001: 26). Nails and hair have all but disappeared; the Diasparans' bodies are smooth whilst the genitalia of both sexes are now stored internally. The necessity for sexual reproduction has vanished although heterosexual desire remains: 'in the appropriate circumstances' masculinity reasserts itself (Clarke, 1956/2001: 26). In this description of the Diasparans' sexual being, there are a number of swerves. Clarke is intent upon emphasizing the morphology of sexual evolution – that, despite outward physical differences, heterosexual desire remains continuous with the reader's time – but, like Alvin's decline of heterosexual attachment, Clarke also plays with the possibility of non-binary identities.

This strategy is important for when it comes to exploring the relationship between Diaspar and its forgotten counterpart, Lys. Whereas critics tend to describe the two communities in binary terms – one technological and impersonal, the other bucolic and intimate – Clarke's playing with non-binary identities suggests that readers should be careful of over-determining the binary opposition. For instance, Lys is both coded more masculine and more feminine than Diaspar. It is the former because sexual reproduction and reproductive futurism persist, with concomitant effects in terms of biological difference, the presence of children and inevitable mortality (although delayed for two centuries). But, it is also the latter, because reproductive futurism is tempered by the self-sufficient need to be in harmony with nature, a matriarchal power structure and the role of telepathy that binds the community together. In other words, despite its pastoral setting, Lys is shown to be just as ambiguous and double-edged as Diaspar. If in one sense, Lys is the feminine corollary to Alvin's hyper-masculinity (and it may be significant that 'lys' forms part of Alystra's name whom Alvin disavows), in another sense, Lys' function in the narrative is to draw out Alvin's queer identity. Although the experience of children, and in particular childhood play, teaches Alvin both 'tenderness' (Clarke, 1956/2001: 106) and 'the price of immortality' (Clarke, 1956/2001: 93), Alvin refuses to join his predecessors in becoming part of Lys. Equally, the Diasparans' memories of Alvin are not erased even though Lys' telepathic powers have previously done that – with help from Khedron's calculated disordering of Diaspar. Again, there are swerves here motivated by Alvin's non-affiliation with both communities, his denial both of the reproductive futurism embodied (in limited form) by Lys and its negation embodied by Diaspar. Instead of seeing the novel's ending as one in which the reproductive sterility of Diaspar is supplanted by the return to Lys' natural life-cycle, it can be read instead as one in which a new social order is gestured towards at the expense of both societies: 'Looking down upon the belt of twilight, Jeserac and Hilvar could see at one instant both sunrise and sunset on opposite sides of the world. The symbolism was so perfect and so striking, that they were to remember this moment all their lives' (Clarke, 1956/2001: 254).

In this utopian gesture, Alvin's relationships with his other mentor figure, Hilvar, and the novel's non-human characters are crucial. Although Clarke pointedly emphasizes Hilvar's heterosexuality (his attraction to Nyara), Hilvar's role ranges from physically testing Alvin to emotionally supporting him. Whereas Jeserac performs the more conventionally Oedipal function of a father-figure – a patrician-like educator – who ultimately learns from and is superseded by his pupil, Hilvar's part is that of a motherly companion. Hilvar's relative ugliness in comparison with Alvin's physical perfection echoes other pairings in ancient and classical literature, most notably that of the wild man, Enkidu, and the demi-god, Gilgamesh, in the Babylonian epic. Like Enkidu's capacity for prophecy, Hilvar's telepathic ability not only goes beyond Alvin's over-determined speech and reason but also softens and feminizes his character in comparison with Alvin. Whereas the latter is aloof and distant, Hilvar is 'good-natured', his physical and emotional strength complemented by his 'friendliness' and 'gentleness' (Clarke, 1956/2001: 113). Although there is little sign of the homoeroticism that is apparent to contemporary readers of *The Epic of Gilgamesh*, the relationship between Alvin and Hilvar is nonetheless homosocial in that Alvin bonds closer with Hilvar than any other human character, certainly more so than his ostensible love-interest, Alystra. It is further significant that Alvin's parents barely feature in the narrative and are substituted by the surrogate parental figures of Hilvar and Jeserac, since their mentorship breaks the genealogical chain of reproductive futurism.

Crucially, it is Hilvar who acts as the conduit between the giant polyp and Alvin, so that he learns about the story of the Master and the Great Ones. Ironically, unlike the Great Ones in Lovecraft's Cthulu Mythos, these seemingly omnipotent beings are the humans who departed from the universe after the incarceration of the Mad Mind. Clarke performs a sleight of hand here: on one side, he rejects the horror of Lovecraft's malign cosmos, so as to foreground an all-too-human history of vain glory, but on the other side, he leaves Alvin with the prospect of an even further future where 'Vanamonde and the Mad Mind must meet each other among the corpses of the stars' (Clarke, 1956/2001: 254). Like the Master who travelled the solar systems to teach the cosmology of humankind (and here Clarke suggests that religion tells a version, if not *the* version, of the truth), Alvin is a vatic figure who journeys the cosmos but ultimately remains on Earth. Although pivotal in humanity rediscovering its true place within the universe, Alvin is also overtaken by the narratives that he reclaims, first from the Master's servants, the polyp and the robot, and then from Vanamonde. In this regard, Alvin is a microcosm of both Diaspar and Lys, in that both communities rediscover their historical purpose only to be subordinated both by the laws of universal entropy and the cosmic struggle between the entities created by their human ancestors. By both repositioning and at the same time decentring humanity's role, typified by the heroic figure of Alvin, Clarke queers the far-future narrative through an en-Weirding of the ontology of the human race. Central yet also peripheral to the cosmic design, both humanity and Alvin in particular are bound up with the ontologies of non-humans. These include, for example, the robot of whom Alvin is only 'its probationary master' (Clarke, 1956/2001: 139) and who 'might desert him at any moment' (Clarke, 1956/2001: 153). However, whereas Lovecraft would regard this encounter as malign, Clarke sees it as benign embodied, for instance, in the careful observance of Diaspar by the Central Computer. In coming to terms with his own restless self, Alvin (and the peoples of Diaspar and Lys) come to realize their entanglement with and reliance upon Others.

In offering then what many readers see as the definitive pulp narrative of the far future, Clarke presents a vision that constantly swerves in and around the idea of futurity. To say that it is either pessimistic or optimistic is to gloss over the peculiar ambiguities of its textual effects. These effects, which are in part indebted to the legacy of Weird fiction, serve to queer the narrative in ways that encode Clarke's own homosexuality but are not expressive of it. Edelman's critique of reproductive futurism, read alongside Clarke's novel, helps us to recognize some of the ways in which Clarke contests historical and material progress, but does not categorically define them. Clarke's very reticence keeps in play the different ways in which we could read him as a gay writer without ever identifying him one way or the other. From his origins within the cultural ghetto of British science fiction, Clarke sought to communicate his wonder of the universe to as wide an audience as possible. To openly identify as 'a gay writer' at this time was neither desirable nor feasible for Clarke's wider ambitions. Yet, the fictional methods in *how* he communicated also unsettled *what* he communicated – that estrangement, so sought-after in science fiction, also served to queer the narratives that Clarke composed.

Acknowledgement

The author would like to thank Russell Blackford for his assistance in researching this chapter.

Note

1 *Galaxies Like Grains of Sand* (1960) was the first US version of *The Canopy of Time* (UK, 1959), but with a different arrangement of stories and slightly more of the interlinking narrative that Aldiss had composed. It was subsequently republished in the US in 1977, with an introduction by Norman Spinrad, and then again in the UK in 1979 with both the framing narrative and one of the stories, 'Blighted Profile', restored in a new version. 'Visiting Amoeba', which closed both the UK and US editions, was originally published as 'What Triumphs' in *Authentic* in 1957. It is unclear as to whether the revised ending was omitted from *The Canopy of Time*

out of deference to Clarke, or whether there is also an ironic allusion to Asimov's 'Nightfall' (1941).

Works Cited

Aldiss, B. (1979) *Galaxies Like Grains of Sand*. London: Panther Granada.

Blackford, R. (2001) 'Future Problematic: Reflections on *The City and the Stars*', in D. Broderick (ed.) *Earth is But a Star: Excursions through Science Fiction to the Far Future*, pp. 35–46. Perth: UWA Press.

Clarke, A. C. (1956/2001) *The City and the Stars*. London: Gollancz.

Clarke, A. C. (1972) *The Lion of Comarre and Against the Fall of Night*. London: Corgi.

Clarke, A. C. (1989) *Astounding Days*. London: Gollancz.

Clute, J. and D. Langford (2019) 'Dunsany, Lord', in J. Clute and D. Langford (eds) *The Encyclopedia of Science Fiction*, URL (accessed 19 July 2020): http://www.sf-encyclopedia.com/entry/dunsany_lord

Edelman, L. (2004) *No Future: Queer Theory and the Death Drive*. Durham, NC: Duke University Press.

Foucault, M. (1986) 'Of Other Spaces', trans. Jay Miskowiec. *Diacritics* 16(1): 22–7.

Hodgson, W. H. (1979) *The Night Land*. London: Sphere.

Hollinger, V. (1999) '(Re)reading Queerly: Science Fiction, Feminism, and the Defamiliarization of Gender', *Science Fiction Studies* 26(1): 1–14.

Hollow, J. (1983) *Against the Night, the Stars: The Science Fiction of Arthur C. Clarke*. San Diego, CA: Harcourt Brace Jovanovich.

James, E. (2005a) 'Arthur C. Clarke', in D. Seed (ed.) *A Companion to Science Fiction*, pp. 431–40. Oxford: Blackwell.

James, E. (2005b) 'Clarke's Utopian Vision', *Foundation* 93: 26–33.

Joshi, S. T. (2003) *The Weird Tale*. Holicong: Wildside Press.

Luckhurst, R. (2005) *Science Fiction*. Cambridge: Polity Press.

Luckhurst, R. (2017) 'The Weird: A Dis/Orientation.' *Textual Practice* 31(6): 1041–61.

McGrath, M. (2011) 'Against Utopia: Arthur C. Clarke and the Heterotopian Impulse', *Vector* 267: 8–14.

Moylan, T. (1977) 'Ideological Contradiction in Clarke's *The City and the Stars*', *Science Fiction Studies* 4(2): 150–7.

Stableford, B. and Langford, D. (2015) 'Far Future', in J. Clute and D. Langford (eds) *The Encyclopedia of Science Fiction*, URL (accessed 24 July 2020): http://www.sf-encyclopedia.com/entry/far_future

Tremaine, F. O. (1934) 'Super-Science.' *Astounding Stories* 13(2): 9.
Westfahl, G. (1996) *Cosmic Engineers: A Study of Hard Science Fiction.* Westport, CT: Greenwood Press.
Westfahl, G. (2018) *Arthur C. Clarke.* Urbana: University of Illinois Press.

6

ARTHUR C. CLARKE AND THE LIMITATIONS OF
THE OCEAN AS A FRONTIER

Helen M. Rozwadowski

In 1960, the bathyscaphe *Trieste* reached the bottom of the Marianas Trench at the Challenger Deep, the deepest point of the ocean. The first human to orbit the earth did not do so until two years later. Yet for three decades after the *Trieste*'s epic achievement, no further efforts were launched to revisit the deepest seafloor. Meanwhile, the Gemini and Apollo programs built on the foundation of *Mercury*'s accomplishment of orbital travel, realizing the goal of putting people on the Moon by 1969. During the 1960s, in parallel with space exploration, the oceans, particularly their third dimension, likewise attracted attention from politicians, scientists, engineers, entrepreneurs, boosters, and ordinary people. Ocean exploration, already well established by the late 1950s, paled somewhat by the late 1960s in comparison with the prospect of space travel. Any effort to understand the fascination of the 1960s with the undersea realm must grapple with the shadow of space. The momentous dive of the *Trieste* did not, as boosters confidently predicted, open up the depths to commercial development, new industries, or human occupation. Instead, the achievement of putting humans at the ocean's deepest point was interpreted by some, including Arthur C. Clarke, as signalling the end of the ocean's status as a frontier.

Although the ocean and its resources loomed large in the development of the American colonies and the young United States, awareness of the ocean had attenuated by the early twentieth century. Before the Second World War, most Americans thought about the ocean, if they did at all, as the source for seafood and a surface for steamship travel, shipping, or warfare. Submarine warfare particularly attracted attention seaward and ensured massive federal investment in marine science and technology to improve understanding of the ocean, especially the depths. After the war, the metaphor of the frontier became attached to the ocean. At about the same time, the frontier appeared as a powerful metaphor for outer space as well. To varying degrees, the metaphor resonated with perceptions of these realms as sources of material resources and as sites for cultural development. By the late 1960s, outer space had overtaken the sea as the most culturally resonant frontier. This chapter investigates why the ocean shifted from being the most promising frontier, certain to satisfy material as well as spiritual needs, to a distant second-place frontier relative to space.

Following wartime advances in oceanography, many scientists and writers, starting with Rachel Carson in *The Sea Around Us* (1951), published popular accounts about the relatively unknown realm of the ocean. These accounts identified many new uses for the sea. No longer was the ocean limited to serving as a fishing ground, a transportation surface, or a battlefield. Pursuit of wild fish would give way to cultivation of fish, plankton, and seaweed, just as farming had replaced hunting and gathering. Ranching of whales numbered among the more imaginative proposals. Extractive industries would expand to non-living resources such as minerals, chemicals, and even fresh water. No longer would people visit the ocean temporarily to engage in such activities. Instead, the seafloor would become a construction site, followed thereafter by an industrial zone where workers would participate in undersea oil drilling, submarine cargo shipping, mining, and other lucrative endeavours. Human habitation of the ocean floor would follow naturally. Technology was integral to these visions. For example, technical experts anticipated the installation of seafloor nuclear reactors to create artificial upwelling zones as well as the use of nuclear submarines for undersea cargo transport free of danger from storms on the surface. The term 'frontier' had resonance in this context because of the associations linked to it by the US historian Frederick Jackson Turner, whose western frontier was first entered by trappers and hunters, then by cattlemen and miners, then by farmers, and finally by industrialists whose work was made possible by the growth of cities. Ocean boosters likewise envisioned a shift from inefficient extraction of a small number of marine resources to modern industry and agriculture that would enable comprehensive and maximal use of the sea's bounty.

The idea for ranching whales, just as cattle had been ranched on the frontier of the Great Plains, may have been the brainchild of Arthur C. Clarke, who explored the analogy of the sea to the western plains of the United States in his 1957 novel *The Deep Range*.[1] Clarke, better known for his stories set in space, numbered among the earliest recreational scuba divers. Before his famous work *2001: A Space Odyssey* (1968), he wrote both fiction and nonfiction celebrating the promise of the ocean as a source of food and other resources, livelihood, inspiration, and insight into human nature. In both his ocean and space writing, Clarke integrated state-of-the-art science and engineering; indeed, he famously predicted the advent of communications satellites. In this chapter, Clarke's personal life and his writing serve as tools to analyse changing cultural conceptions of the ocean and to provide insight into the relative status of the oceans compared with outer space.

Clarke presented a vision of a new human relationship with the ocean, one that integrated science, recreation, industry, government, and spirituality (cf. Rozwadowski, 2004: 325–52). Promoters of the fast-growing field of oceanography likewise planned facilities and technologies based on a similar vision applied to research that linked oceanography to engineering, medicine, aquaculture, archaeology, and recreation. Rather than being limited to the study of oceanic phenomenon, this new blueprint for ocean science addressed every possible aspect of how people might work and live on and under the sea.

Shortly before the 1960s, scientists, explorers, and writers had begun to characterize the ocean, particularly the undersea world, as a frontier. Many who were involved in ocean exploration associated the sea with outer space, sometimes pointing to similarities and sometimes to contrasts between these two forbidding, yet promising, environments. As an example, consider how the engineer and popular author Seabrook Hull characterized the sea in 1964:

> Of the two great frontiers, space and the ocean, being opened up in the 20th Century, only the ocean is close, tangible, and of direct personal significance to every man, woman, and child on the face of the globe. Another war might be won or lost in its depths, rather than in outer space. It is a cornucopia of raw materials for man's industries, food for his stomach, health for his body, challenges to his mind, and inspiration to his soul. (Hull, 1964: 221)

Hull labelled both the sea and space as frontiers, and then he enumerated some of the reasons why champions of ocean exploration believed it might prove more pressing, and also more rewarding, to concentrate on the ocean. Reference to the provision of food and the potential for creating wealth echoed cultural assumptions about what the American West had offered as a frontier. In addition, the suggestion that the sea promised strength and spiritual sustenance likewise evoked associations between the western frontier and American individualism and democracy (Rozwadowski, 2018: 161–87). As Hull's quote makes clear, promoters of underwater exploration felt it held more immediate potential compared with space exploration. This was especially the case during the 1950s before Sputnik and the race for the Moon. A single invention, the Aqualung, was most responsible for opening the undersea world, not only to experts but to ordinary people as well. In 1949 Jacques Cousteau and a colleague invented the Aqualung, the first free-swimming underwater breathing set (Matsen, 2009: 51–72, 82–93). Previous underwater breathing gear included helmeted diving suits and wartime innovations such as re-breathers that used carbon dioxide scrubbers to avoid the escape of air bubbles that might reveal the diver below. Such equipment required significant expertise and was dangerous to use even for professional divers.

The Aqualung or, as subsequent generations of the technology were called, Self-Contained Underwater Breathing Apparatus, or 'scuba', was eagerly embraced by skin divers and spear fishers, and also by newcomers to the sport, including recreationalists, scientists, filmmakers, and others.

Among the early users of the Aqualung was Arthur C. Clarke. Relative to his fame for science fiction and space prognostication, Clarke is less well known for his early and enthusiastic pursuit of diving, spear fishing, underwater photography and treasure hunting; for his promotion of undersea exploration; and for his predictions of futuristic ocean industries, technologies, and uses of the sea. He dove and wrote about the oceans in the late 1950s and early 1960s, and the ideas and preoccupations found in his ocean writings appear and reappear in popular and scientific works throughout the 1960s (cf. Cowen, 1960; Carlisle, 1967; McKee, 1969). Although many of Clarke's expectations and predictions regarding the ocean were not fulfilled, they fell firmly within the range of what ocean scientists and engineers also anticipated.

In Clarke's words and deeds, and also in the minds of a generation of scientists, diver/explorers, engineers, and entrepreneurs, the ocean promised to become the premier outlet for their economic, intellectual, cultural, and social ambitions. Their embrace of the frontier analogy signalled their belief that the ocean might provide not only resources but also necessary challenges. Clarke and some of his contemporaries believed that an emerging relationship with the ocean formed part of what they considered an evolutionary trajectory for humanity. In a very concrete sense, the ocean's resources would in the near future prove essential for the survival of the growing population. But the relationship with the ocean had another dimension as well, because Clarke believed that humanity required new challenges in order to survive. People had evolved from the sea, and now the ocean's depths were expected to serve as the testing ground for both the technology and the spirit that would be required for humans to break free of the earth to explore space. Clarke's writings and biography, then, offer a window into how the ocean was perceived, how experts expected to be able to use it and its resources, and even how the ocean might figure in world history.

Despite the tremendous enthusiasm for the ocean and its potential, the sea could not quite match the appeal of space – either in Clarke's writings or in reality. In *The Deep Range*, Clarke tells the story of a failed astronaut who finds fulfilment working undersea. In the end, however, the astronaut's son chooses outer space over the ocean. Similarly, despite all the promise and enthusiasm, experiments in undersea habitats did not lead to underwater colonies, and ocean engineering did not spawn a marine equivalent of the giant aerospace industry. Oceanography remained the science of the oceans rather than an integrated sciences and engineering approach devoted to establishing a fundamentally new relationship between people and the sea.

Clarke's life and writings, both his fiction and nonfiction, provide an excellent tool for exploring the expectations that a generation of scientists and dreamers projected onto the ocean, providing new insight into a history of the ocean. Maritime history has tended to privilege human events and actions that take place on the sea, rather than the ocean itself. Environmental history offers the imperative to consider the mutual influence of nature on human history and vice versa, but, until recently, environmental historians have largely ignored the ocean (Hughes, 2006: 111–12). Those few scholars who have begun to write excellent histories of marine environments are strongly influenced by the science of ecology and by environmental, and especially fisheries, management concerns (Bolster, 2006; Taylor, 2001). But the ocean is not only a source of natural resources or a stage for the events of human history: it is a complex and changing natural environment that is inextricably connected to, and influenced by, people. Because human lungs cannot breathe unassisted in the ocean, our knowledge of it is necessarily mediated through technologies, knowledge systems, or cultural conceptions of this space – or some combination of these. Imagination may, in fact, play a larger role in our perception of the ocean, especially its third dimension, than modern science. Rather than thinking of our task as including the ocean in our histories, we might more profitably put the ocean in the centre of our stories and aim to write histories of the ocean to include human actions, habits, cultural assumptions, and expectations (cf. Rozwadowski, 2018).

Clarke and the Ocean

Clarke's interest in the ocean is often presented in the context of his dedication to space; his interest in skin diving, for instance, is supposed to have derived from his desire to experience something akin to the weightlessness of space. In addition, the period of his interest in the sea is usually bounded by identifiable start and end dates. Yet the sea, and skin and scuba diving in particular, preoccupied him throughout his adult life. In 1956 Clarke moved permanently to Sri Lanka (then Ceylon), whose beaches seemed to him akin to the platonic ideal of the beach compared to the English beach of his childhood (McAleer, 1992: 139). At age seventy-five he was still an active diver and operated diving-related businesses, including the Arthur C. Clarke Diving School, which was still in operation until its building was destroyed by the 2004 tsunami (*The Times*, 2008).

Eric S. Rabkin has argued that understanding Clarke's fiction and its sources requires knowledge of 'Clarke's exceptionally active life' (Rabkin, 1979: 9). This point is as true for his ocean-related work as for his writings about space. Between his childhood summers on the coast and 1950, when he was aged thirty-three, Clarke does not appear to have had any serious preoccupation with the ocean. In 1950, Clarke began a long-standing friendship with Mike Wilson, a young science fiction fan living and working in London as a wine steward. Wilson, who had served in the British merchant navy, army, and also marines, including service as a military frogman, told Clarke about his diving experiences in the Pacific. Intrigued, Clarke took skin diving lessons in a local pool and later rented an Aqualung to try diving in the English Channel. Clarke's friendship with Wilson, oriented around underwater activities, coincided with the years of his active writing about the ocean.

After his 1953 trip to the United States, Clarke regularly combined business travel with jaunts to dive in new and exotic locations. A trip to Tampa, Florida, provided him with an opportunity to dive with Dr George Grisinger, who introduced him to underwater photography and to the fish known as groupers (also called sea bass, these large fish were popular targets for spear fishers). In May 1953, Clarke and his group moved on to Key Largo, where he dove and also met the diver Marilyn Mayfield, whom he briefly married.

In the mid-1950s to early 1960s, Clarke embarked on a series of expeditions with Mike Wilson to dive in areas where few Western divers had previously visited. In 1954 and 1955, for example, he spent months in Australia diving on the Great Barrier Reef. One place he visited on that trip, Heron Island, became the setting for scenes in *The Deep Range* and *Dolphin Island* (1963). These expeditions were not just personal adventures; they were entrepreneurial enterprises. He and Wilson experimented with underwater diving and photography equipment and amassed experiences to write and lecture about. Their joint ventures broadened to include filmmaking, treasure hunting, underwater businesses (involving consulting, salvage, underwater surveying, and tourism), and co-authoring a juvenile picture book, *Boy Beneath the Sea* (1958), as well as *The First Five Fathoms* (1960) with an introduction by Cousteau, whom Clarke had met at a skin divers' convention in 1958.

In pursuit of novel diving experiences and new undersea places to photograph and write about, Clarke headed to Ceylon in 1956. At the time the Indian Ocean was the least familiar ocean to Western scientists. Acknowledging this, oceanographers began organizing the International Indian Ocean Expedition, a multiyear, multi-ship effort to study this sea biologically, chemically, physically, and geologically (Knauss, 1961: 1674–6). Typically for the time, organizers confidently predicted that the expedition would not only result in new knowledge but would also lead to more intensive use of the sea and its resources, including as a sink for radioactive and other wastes and as a source for much-needed protein from the sea (Hamblin, 2005, 2008; Wolff, 2010). While Clarke, in many of his writings, waxed enthusiastic about the prospect of food, energy, and other material resources from the ocean, he and Wilson had a new entrepreneurial idea in mind as they headed to Ceylon in 1956; they hoped to find historic treasure. Wreck diving was becoming a popular activity in scuba circles, and examples abounded in popular magazines such as *Life* of divers finding ancient silver and gold-laden shipwrecks using modern diving equipment (cf. Bass, 1966; Brindze, 1960: 80–94). Indeed, Wilson did discover treasure in 1961, at a wreck at Great Basses Reef where he was filming a movie. That discovery and their other expeditions became grist for a series of books, *Indian Ocean Adventure* (1961) and *Indian Ocean Treasure* (1964), about this little known part of the world.

In 1962, Clarke was diagnosed with polio. Recuperation was slow, although within a year he had managed to scuba dive, an achievement that helped motivate him to continue exercising and writing. Biographical accounts of Clarke's life often mention this period as the time when he gave up the sea; indeed, *Dolphin Island* has been called his 'farewell to the sea' (McAleer, 1992: 165). The reality is more complex.[2] The conclusion that he had left the ocean behind seems to have derived both from his physical weakness and also from the fact that his publications after this point focused again on space after years of preoccupation with the ocean. For example, 1964 was the start of his vibrant, productive partnership with Stanley Kubrick. Yet as he sought out scientists and government experts to discuss space flight and weather satellites, Clarke remained actively engaged with the sea. He continued to dive until the end of his life; he continued to live in Sri Lanka, enjoying its beaches and reefs, and he also maintained an active interest in businesses related to diving. In Clarke's writings after 1964, his conceptions of the ocean and space continued to be closely intertwined.

The Ocean in Clarke's Writings

Any attempt to create a strict separation of Clarke's interests and work related to the ocean and space is destined to fail. In 1958, in the midst of his obsession with the ocean, he wrote essays that were later published in *Profiles of the Future* (1962), a book of predictions that included much on space but also forecast the advent of submarine and hovercraft cargo transport and other futuristic uses of the sea. In the same work he relied on the analogy of sail power to argue for the equal likelihood of, first, cheap nuclear energy and, subsequently, very high-speed transport drawing natural energy from the upper atmosphere. He explained, 'After all, there is nothing fundamentally absurd about the idea. We sailed the seas for thousands of years in fuel-less ships, powered by the free energy of the winds' (Clarke, 1962/1967: 63). In 1962, he published the collection titled *From the Ocean, From the Stars*, making clear the parallels he drew between the two realms. In the fall of 1960, the same year he published *The Challenge of the Sea* and struggled financially with supporting his and Wilson's diving and other endeavours, he wrote the novel *A Fall of Moondust* (1961), a story set on the Moon inside a tourism vehicle that sinks into a 'sea' of dust. Stories such as 'The Road to the Sea', written in the 1950s but included in the 1962 collection *Tales of Ten Worlds*, likewise demonstrate the similarities Clarke saw between space and the ocean.

Clarke's unwillingness to differentiate strongly between oceans and space may have derived from his conviction that human exploration of space was a natural extension of an evolutionary journey that began with movement of sea creatures onto land. In *The Deep Range*, as one of his characters gazes over great plankton farms and whale herds, he reflects that, 'Man had come back to the sea, his ancient home, after aeons of exile; until the oceans froze, he would never be hungry again' (Clarke, 2001: 259). Other writers shared this perception. The German rocket scientist Wernher von Braun, in his introduction to Clarke's *Challenge of the Sea*, mused that humans might be compelled to explore the sea because 'the sight of it evokes subconscious and vestigial memories of his primal beginning.' Then von Braun continued, 'From a poetical, but not too farfetched, viewpoint, we on earth can consider the bottom of the sea as man's point of departure on his extremely long trip to outer space.' He elaborated that life, which began in the depths, then moved onto land, and, 'after a brief pause', would continue upward into space (von Braun, 1960: 7–8). Jacques Cousteau likewise framed the human relationship in evolutionary terms, although looking forward rather than backward. At the World Congress on Underwater Activities in London in 1962, Cousteau declared, 'A new species of human being is evolving, Homo aquaticus' (cited in Matsen, 2009: 160).

The evolutionary trajectory from the ocean to space that Clarke imagined fundamentally involved technological innovation. For example, he surmised that the invention of a one-man gravitator might 'do for mountains what the aqualung has done for the sea [...] It is only a matter of time before tourists are floating all over the Himalayas, and the summit of Everest is as crowded as the seabed round the Florida Keys or off Cannes' (Clarke, 1962/1967: 58-9). Similarly, after discussing the achievement of the bathyscaphe *Trieste*, Clarke turned to consider space: 'In our own time, men have peered through the portholes of a bathyscaphe into a region, only inches away, where they would be crushed in a fraction of a second by the pressure of a thousand tons on every square foot of their bodies [...] Centuries in the future, and light-years from Earth, there may be men peering out of portholes into the still more ferocious environment of a dwarf star' (Clarke, 1960a: 99, 111). Even in the arena of cultural understanding and expression, sea and space were connected in Clarke's mind. Reflecting on the literature accompanying America's frontier settlement he decided, 'Space flight has, therefore, very little in common with aviation; it is much closer in spirit to ocean voyaging, which has inspired so many of our greatest works of literature' (Clarke, 1960a: 88-9).

The frontier analogy was particularly important for Clarke, who was among the first writers to elaborate on it to make sense of human interaction with both oceans and space. Clarke's vision of the frontier derived from that made popular by Frederick Jackson Turner who theorized that the western frontier had forged a distinct, democratic American culture and provided an outlet for the restless energy of its people. Turner first articulated his argument about the influence of the frontier in American history in 1893, at the very moment that the US Census Bureau declared the western frontier to be closed. To politicians and others, the obvious problem emerged of finding new outlets for expansion; solutions included overseas territories, Alaska, polar regions, and even the frontier of new knowledge, especially discoveries in the natural sciences.

By the mid-1950s, the ocean, too, had acquired the status of frontier, as observers including Clarke expected the sea soon to provide food to feed a growing population as well as mineral and other critical resources including fresh water. In November 1953, the American Association for the Advancement of Science included at its annual meeting a special session on 'The Sea Frontier', which included topics ranging from the geology of ocean basins to the productivity and biological resources of the sea, to the potential for extracting resources such as fresh water or minerals (Taylor, 1953: 275–78). A 1954 advertisement in *Life* magazine placed by the American Petroleum Institute declared, 'In the open waters of the Gulf of Mexico, against every hazard of wind, wave, and sudden storm, sea-going oilmen are opening up a new American frontier' (American Petroleum Institute, 1954: 152). Even when the word 'frontier' was not invoked, its associations were: 'This wet world, as many are belatedly beginning to realize, may hold the key to [human] survival on this planet – not only in terms of attack and defense but in terms of minerals, chemicals and food ... Beneath the sea, man is still a tentative intruder, just learning how to farm and mine its depths.' This characterization of the ocean appeared in a 1962 *Life* article, describing a novel 300-foot instrument-vehicle for ocean exploration, the *Floating Instrument Platform* (or *FLIP*), designed by and built for researchers at Scripps Institution of Oceanography ('We Race for the Ocean's Secret', 1962: 40–3). While *FLIP* was mainly intended as a stable platform for performing delicate acoustic measurements, work with explicit military applications, the enthusiasm surrounding such new technological means for probing the sea frequently used the frontier analogy.

Futurists believed that, like the western frontier, the sea would be the site of dramatic innovation in transportation, communication, and other technologies. As with all his work, Clarke's ocean-focused writing rested on his knowledge of contemporary science and technology. As he did for space (famously predicting earth-orbiting satellites for telecommunication), he envisaged uses that people would soon make of the sea and its resources. Stories from *Tales from the White Hart*

(1957), dating from the days when Clarke first met Wilson, included two works that evoked anticipated new uses of the ocean. 'The Man Who Ploughed the Sea' revolved around a plan to extract minerals from seawater, and 'Cold War' revealed a scheme by California to destroy Florida's appeal to tourists by landing icebergs on Miami Beach. Both proposals, although presented by Clarke in the context of Harry Purvis's tall tales, were believed by experts to be firmly within reach or nearly so by the late 1950s and early 1960s (Carlisle, 1967: 83–94; Cowen, 1960: 265–9; McKee, 1969: 165–79). The communication with dolphins depicted in *Dolphin Island* reflected the work of physician and neurophysiologist John C. Lilly in such books as *Man and Dolphin* (1961) and *The Mind of the Dolphin* (1967). Farming the sea, as outlined in *The Deep Range*, likewise seemed an obvious and achievable goal to scientists and engineers (Cowen, 1960: 245–74).

Not the Last, Nor the Best, Frontier

Clarke's novel *The Deep Range* provides a window into the nature and extent of the frontier analogy in his conception of the ocean. Starting with its title, *The Deep Range* leans on the image of the cowboy and cattle-driving frontier. In the opening scene, Whale Bureau warden Don Burley sits in his one-man scout sub preparing to battle the killer whales that are destroying the whales he tends. He feels a kinship with ancient shepherds guarding flocks but more so with ranchers of the American West: 'Yet far nearer in time, and far closer in spirit, were the men who had marshalled the great herds of cattle on the American plains [...] They would have understood his work, though his implements would have been magic to them' (Clarke, 2001: 254–5). The analogy is not perfect; Clarke compares the whales being protected and herded to bison, which were exterminated in favour of introduced cattle, whereas Burley's charges are 'native' whales. In other parts of the ocean of this future earth, vast plankton farms stand in for endless wheat fields.

The goal is for humanity to move from exploitation of the sea using a hunting model to a farming model, which Clarke articulated in his nonfiction work (Clarke, 1960a: 92-111). This trajectory bears the imprint of Turner's frontier thesis, which described an inexorable progression on the frontier whereby cattlemen and miners replaced the trappers and traders who were the first European settlers to expand into the American West. After the cattle ranchers and miners came the farmers, the first of whom had small subsistence farms. Farming grew more intensive and settlements larger until cities and industries formed. The inevitable outcome, as described by Turner and predicted for the ocean by Clarke, included access to food resources, wealth from extractive and productive industries, undersea living, and the continued development of individuals and political and social institutions.

As Clarke himself pointed out, there were limits to the applicability of the frontier analogy: 'The parallel with the old-time cowboy is obvious, but it cannot be taken too far' (Clarke, 1960a: 101). Rather than the fixed borders of western cattle ranches, the ranches of the sea would move from the polar regions where whales fed to the warmer waters where they gave birth and raised their young. Such migration would make it impossible for individual countries to operate such an enterprise, so Clarke's vision for the future included a radical internationalization of all aspects of life and politics. Likewise, while 'the great gold rushes of a century ago may be repeated on the sea bed [...] prospectors will not be grizzled old-timers working alone. They will be multi-million dollar corporations employing armies of scientists and technicians' (Clarke, 1960a: 121).

The Deep Range uses the characteristic trope from maritime literature of describing the training of a neophyte to introduce the reader to the ranching business and the vessels and technologies it employs (Foulke, 1997: 1-26). In the novel, Burley, after killing a great white shark to protect a mother whale and her two calves, reports to the main office in Brisbane to induct Walter Franklin into the ranks of whale wardens. Although Burley does not pry into Franklin's personal situation, it does not escape his notice that the newcomer is on 'the wrong side of thirty' and obviously a spaceman; 'you could tell them a mile away' (Clarke, 2001: 265). Under Burley's tutelage, Franklin not only learns the job but also gains an appreciation for the ocean, coming to recognize it as resembling space in some ways and yet distinct in others. Just before the training ends, Burley takes Franklin into the middle of a herd of whales, an experience that provides 'one of the great moments of his life', akin to his first glimpse of earth from space: 'Amid the gigantic creatures, Franklin felt the same awe and the same awareness of cosmic forces as he had in space' (Clarke, 2001: 342–4). At peace with the new direction for his life, Franklin 'had lost the freedom of space, but he had gained the freedom of the seas. It was enough for any man' (Clarke, 2001: 346).

Indeed, Clarke signalled in both this novel and elsewhere in his writings that the ocean offered greater challenge and more profound mystery than space. He believed that the deep ocean 'may still remain utterly savage – the last wilderness of the world' (Clarke, 1960a: 93), even when continents have been tamed from poles through deserts (Clarke, 1960a: 176). In the novel, Franklin marvels at technical accomplishments such as the globe-circling fences of high-pitched sound created by nuclear-powered generators on the deep seafloor, wondering what earlier people might have thought. 'In some ways,' he reflects, 'it seemed the greatest and most daring of all man's presumptions. The sea, which has worked its will with man ever since the beginning of time, had been humbled at last. Not even the conquest of space had been a greater victory than this' (Clarke, 2001: 300). Such an admission that the ocean poses greater challenges than space is striking, coming as it does from the mouth of a character who had experienced outer space. Franklin's continued thoughts make the point even more strongly – that the oceans will ultimately present a greater challenge than space: 'And yet – it was a victory that could never be final. Slowly, Franklin was coming to terms with the sea, as must all men who have dealings with it' (Clarke, 2001: 301).

Franklin's pursuit of the great sea serpent provides a concrete manifestation of the lingering mystery of the sea. In *The Challenge of the Sea* Clarke gave serious consideration to the possibility that the ocean still hid yet undiscovered monsters as big and strange as the sperm whale and the giant squid. Franklin discusses with his colleagues a faint echo on the sonar screen that he chased with his mini-sub but lost. His fellow wardens warn him not to discuss the episode with reporters, but among themselves, they appear convinced that it had been 'nothing less than the Great Sea Serpent.' Franklin initially tries to tell himself to let go of this particular mystery, musing, 'the oceans still held many secrets and would retain them for ages yet to come.' He finds himself, however, unable to let go of his fascination with this puzzling challenge (Clarke, 2001: 359–62). Working deftly within the layers of bureaucracy of his government office, he manages to acquire and deploy remote sensing equipment to begin a study of unexplained phenomena of the deep. After analysing several months of echoes, he moves all the recorders to one location and collects data that reveal a very large, thin animal that lives at 20,000 feet and comes halfway to the surface twice a day, presumably to feed. An official search launched to find the sea serpent ends with the tragic loss of Burley's sub and the painful lesson to Franklin of the ocean's dangers.

People seem more firmly in control of the ocean and its resources closer to the surface. Franklin rises to the directorship of the Bureau of Whales and faces a set of challenges to its whole operation. The long running conflict with the Plankton Bureau over ocean space, in which the plankton farm administrators argue that their bureau produce far more food more efficiently, starts to heat up. More importantly for the plot, Franklin learns of experiments with training killer whales to help herd whales, as sheepdogs herd sheep, and also efforts to build and use an automatic milking device for whales. He mentions the idea of milk from whales in an interview and suddenly finds himself and his bureau under determined attack by the Buddhist leader, the Maha Thero. Franklin is forced to take seriously calls to end the killing of whales. Secretly, Franklin and the other wardens had always felt that whales were different from other animals, perhaps closer to humans in intelligence. Most of them disliked the necessity of killing the whales and even the necessity of destroying the killer whales that preyed on them. Facing political and moral pressures from many directions, Franklin decides to speak out publicly in support of the Maha Thero's proposal, even at the likely cost of his own professional advancement.

As tied to the ocean as Franklin has become, his decision to take a stand against killing whales derives, oddly, from his former – and apparently continuing – allegiance to space exploration. Of the various arguments presented by the Maha Thero, one he presents privately to Franklin posits the inevitable future meeting between man and extraterrestial life, who would likely judge humanity on the basis of how humans treated other creatures. Clarke's ultimate ranking of space as a more important frontier than the ocean becomes clear at the novel's end when Franklin watches his son leave earth to begin a career as a spaceman: 'To his son, he willingly bequeathed the shoreless seas of space. For himself, the oceans of this world were sufficient.' As he faces the stars after his son's rocket disappears, Franklin whispers to himself, 'Give us another hundred years [...] and we'll face you with clean hands and hearts – whatever shape you be' (Clarke, 2001: 488). The end of *The Deep Range*, then, offers a hint to the limitations of the ocean as a frontier relative to outer space.

Conclusion

The Deep Range provides a window into the relationship between the ocean and outer space in the minds of boosters for the exploration of both places. Like other works by Clarke, this novel reflects popular conceptions of the ocean in the 1950s and 1960s as a frontier offering material resources as well as the possibility for human expansion and progress. While Clarke derived his view of the frontier from Turner, his vision differed from Turner's in important elements. Turner identified the close of the American frontier as the US Census Bureau did, with the announcement that the 1890 census could no longer identify a 'frontier line' behind which empty land beckoned settlers (Turner, 1996). In contrast, in *Profiles of the Future*, Clarke claimed as an end date for the frontier 1869, the year in which the first transcontinental railroad was completed. Clarke's starting date, 1492, alludes to Christopher Columbus's discovery of the New World. Turner, however, did not glorify explorers; to the contrary, his heroes were the farmers and ranchers who went west and stayed there, not explorers who went ahead then returned to report back. Indeed, he hardly mentioned explorers or exploration at all. To Turner, the frontier was fundamentally an economic entity, albeit one with powerful political and cultural resonances. To Clarke, and to his contemporaries in the 1950s and 1960s, frontier was tied to discovery, to newness. Clarke contended that 'the ocean will keep us busy for centuries to come' (Clarke, 1962/1967: 82). This claim was presented, however, with a significant caveat. To Clarke, after the achievement of the *Trieste* just two years before – just as with the successful spanning of the continental United States in 1869 – the task of dealing with the remaining parts of the ocean, although admittedly vast, 'will only be a mopping-up operation' (Clarke, 1962/1967: 83).

Clarke shared with Turner the assumption that finding alternative frontiers as outlets would be essential for the continued existence and development of society. While some frontiers would serve as sources for humanity's physical needs, such as food and mineral resources, Clarke explained, 'The spiritual need is less apparent, but in the long run it is more important.' Other planets would not, he predicted, offer a solution to the problem of overpopulation because space colonies would require too much support from Earth, at least at the outset. 'If we are looking for living space for our surplus population, it would be far cheaper to find it in the Antarctic – or even on the bottom of the Atlantic Ocean,' he warned. Space settlements would, however, provide a significant intellectual and emotional contribution to the 'stay-at-homes', those people who did not leave Earth to colonize new planets. Using strikingly Turnerian language, Clarke continued, 'They will know, as they watch their TV screens, that History with a capital H is starting again' (Clarke, 1962/1967: 84–5).

This formulation leans on Turner's argument that the close of the frontier in 1890 ended what he identified as the first period of American history. Yet Turner's cyclical nature of how the frontier shaped people and the nation implied that a turn to a new frontier provided a chance to start over. Unexplored areas of ocean might still function in some ways as frontier, particularly because of the almost unimaginably vast scale of new resources that Clarke's generation expected from the depths. The ocean, however, had a crippling limitation compared to space, namely that ocean exploration – although at an early stage and still promising to keep people 'busy for centuries to come' – would one day end. The ocean, in short, ultimately lacked the starting-over element. What made space a better frontier, to Clarke, was its infinity. The space frontier, he argued, was 'beyond all possibility of exhaustion' (Clarke, 1962/1967: 83). As an uncloseable frontier, space would remain immune to the restrictions of earthly frontiers.

Notwithstanding the limitations he assigned to the ocean relative to outer space, Clarke had bold and ambitious expectations for human use of the sea and its resources. His writings reveal attitudes toward the ocean that influenced how its resources were perceived and used. His language and the content of his writings depicted an ocean that strongly resembled the western frontier as described by Turner and others since, complete with seemingly unlimited economic potential and great social and cultural power. Clarke conveyed breath-taking optimism about the expected scale and extent of new uses for the ocean and, predictably for his time, exhibited blindness about what groups of people would and would not be involved in or benefit from a deepening human relationship with the ocean (Limerick, 1992: 249–61). Embedded in his view of the ocean as a frontier was the bedrock assumption that the sea should be systematically and maximally exploited, just as the resources of the American West had been.

Science and technology would, to Clarke and contemporary ocean enthusiasts, enable new and intensified uses of the sea and marine resources. Oceanography existed not simply to increase understanding of the ocean and its contents and processes, but to facilitate exploitation. In 1969, the US committees on oceanography and ocean engineering, which planned for the proposed International Decade of Ocean Exploration, reflected this view. The overall goal articulated for the Decade was '*To achieve more comprehensive knowledge of ocean characteristics and their changes and more profound understanding of oceanic processes for the purpose of more effective utilization of the ocean and its resources*' [italics in original]. The sentence immediately following this goal in the Steering Committee report pressed the point:

'The emphasis on utilization was considered of primary importance' (Committee on Oceanography, 1969: 2).

Clarke and his contemporaries had plans for using the ocean that reflected more accurately their desires than anything inherent about the ocean environment itself. The sea, like other elements of the natural world, did not simply bend to the will of the engineers and entrepreneurs of the 1950s and 1960s, however much they expected it to do so. The technologies, industries, and capabilities that Clarke and others predicted – such as atomic submarine engines transporting cargo underwater in giant rubber bags, massive-scale farming of plankton or ranching of whales, profitable mining of a host of minerals and metals from seawater, or the possibility of communication with whales and dolphins – did not come to fruition. While the offshore oil and gas industry did emerge, other undersea industries involving workers operating, even living, deep under water did not. In 1969 the experimental saturation diving program, SEALAB III, was terminated after the death of diver Barry Cannon during emplacement of the habitat. Two years earlier, the Apollo program continued after the fiery death of three astronauts on the launch pad. There are many reasons for the failure of the dreams for using the ocean harboured by the likes of Clarke and his contemporaries – and for the continuation of space exploration when it seemed, to ocean enthusiasts, that the promise represented by *Trieste* and SEALAB went regrettably unfulfilled.

Because the space frontier overshadowed the ocean frontier in the decades after the Second World War, it is essential to examine these frontiers relative to one another. The ocean possessed characteristics recognized as associated with Turner's frontier: resources to fuel economic development and increase standard of living as well as the setting for the outlet of human energy and the progressive development of human culture. At times the space and ocean frontiers seemed similar, but analysis of the writings and life of Clarke, who immersed himself in both of these realms, reveal a crucial difference. The value of the ocean frontier rested in the vastness of its potential economic resources. Space, however, was ultimately judged a better frontier because of its potential to serve human spiritual and cultural needs endlessly into the future.

Articulation of this difference offers insight into current ocean issues. It illuminates the frustration expressed by ocean boosters from the post-war period to the present that ocean exploration is wrongly neglected relative to exploration of outer space. Boosters of ocean exploration apparently have a hard time arguing that earth-bound exploration is not simply a 'mopping-up operation'. The cultural promise offered by the infinite extent of space came to resonate more strongly, by the end of the 1960s, than the fading dreams of the fabulous wealth to be derived from the ocean's depths. The stubborn persistence in viewing the ocean in terms of its economic resources has contributed to massive global overfishing, depletion of other marine resources, and cascades of unintended ecosystem effects. While concepts of conservation and preservation were applied to land at the turn of the twentieth century, and Aldo Leopold articulated the need for a 'land ethic' in 1949, recognition of the ocean as an environment in need of protection and ethical treatment has emerged slowly (Safina, 2002–3: 2–5). The enthusiastic identification of the ocean as frontier created a legacy for human use and understanding of the sea and its resources that remains with us to the present.

Acknowledgement

This is a shorter, slightly updated version of the article as it originally appeared in *Environmental History* 17(3) (2012). The author remains grateful to the University of Connecticut Humanities Institute for support during 2008–9, while researching the chapter, and support from the Connecticut Space Grant College Consortium while writing it. The paper was enriched by comments from participants in the Maritime Conference in the Humanities, held at the Massachusetts Maritime Academy, October 23–5, 2009, from colleagues at the Humanities Institute, and also from anonymous reviewers. Special thanks go to Nancy Shoemaker, Walter Woodward and Michael Robinson.

Notes

1 Clarke published his whale ranching scheme in *Popular Science* (November 1960). Other commentators and popular writers likewise wrote about the whale ranching idea, sometimes crediting Clarke; see, for example, Pehoda (1967) and Pinchot (1966). There were references to dolphin milk before Clarke, most notably, biochemists studied the properties of dolphin milk; see Lillian Eichelberger et al. (1940). The 'Kuroshio Ranch' in Tosa Bay, Japan, is currently marketed for eco-tourist activities, such as whale and dolphin watching. *The Deep Range* was based on a short story of the same name published in *Argosy* in April 1954.

2 Clarke's so-called turn away from the sea also coincided with the departure of Wilson from his household; Wilson, and later his wife and first child, had lived with Clarke, whose household often included close friends who were not relatives. As was the case with Wilson, these friendships were often both personal and business ones. All of Clarke's joint ventures and activities with Wilson were oriented around the ocean, mostly involving diving. After Wilson and his family moved out, they continued their many business partnerships until a falling out in the late 1960s ended communication between them entirely. Clarke's active engagement with the ocean in his writings declined in step with the increasing distance between him and his former diving partner, and it seems likely that the two trends were related.

Works Cited

American Petroleum Institute (1954) 'US Oilmen Challenge the Sea', *Life* (7 June): 152.

Bass, G. F. (1966) *Archaeology Under Water*. New York: Praeger.

Bolster, W. J. (2006) 'Opportunities in Marine Environmental History.' *Environmental History* 11(3): 567–97.

Brindze, R. (1960) *All About Undersea Exploration*. New York: Random House.

Carlisle, N. (1967) *Riches of the Sea: The New Science of Oceanology*. New York: Sterling.

Clarke, A. C. (1960a) *The Challenge of the Sea*. New York: Holt, Rinehart and Watson.

Clarke A. C. (1960b) 'Will a Hungry World Raise Whales for Food?', *Popular Science* (November): 74–6, 216.

Clarke, A. C. (1962/1967) *Profiles of the Future*. New York: Bantam.

Clarke, A. C. (2001) *The Ghost of the Grand Banks and The Deep Range*. New York: Aspect/Warner Books.
Committee on Oceanography, National Research Council and National Academy of Sciences and Committee on Ocean Engineering, National Academy of Engineering (1969) *An Oceanic Quest: The International Decade of Ocean Exploration*. Washington, DC: National Academy of Sciences.
Cowen, R. C. (1960) *Frontiers of the Sea*. New York: Bantam.
Eichelberger, L, E. S. Fetcher, Jr., E. M. K. Geiling, and B. J. Vos (1940) 'The Composition of Dolphin Milk', *Journal of Biological Chemistry* 133: 171–6.
Foulke, R. (1997) *The Sea Voyage Narrative*. Boston: Twayne.
Hamblin, J. D. (2005) *Oceanographers and the Cold War: Disciples of Marine Science*. Seattle: University of Washington Press.
Hamblin, J. D. (2008) *Poison in the Well: Radioactive Waste in the Oceans at the Dawn of the Nuclear Age*. New Brunswick: Rutgers University Press.
Hughes, D. J. (2006) *What is Environmental History?* Cambridge: Polity.
Hull, S. (1964) *The Bountiful Sea*. Englewood Cliffs: Prentice-Hall.
Knauss, J. A. (1961) 'The International Indian Ocean Expedition', *Science* 134 (3491): 1674–6.
Leopold, A. (1949) *A Sand County Almanac*. New York: Oxford University Press.
Limerick, P. N. (1992) 'Imagined Frontiers: Westward Expansion and the Future of the Space Program', in R. Byerly, Jr. (ed.) *Space Policy Alternatives*, pp. 249–61. Boulder: Westview Press.
McAleer, N. (1992) *Arthur C. Clarke: The Authorized Biography*. Chicago: Contemporary Books.
McKee, A. (1969) *Farming the Sea*. New York: Thomas Y. Crowell.
Matsen, B. (2009) *Jacques Cousteau: The Sea King*. New York: Pantheon Books.
Pehoda, R. W. (1967) *Designing the Future: The Role of Technological Forecasting*. Philadelphia: Chilton Book Co.
Pinchot, G. B. (1966) 'Whale Culture: A Proposal', *Perspectives in Biology and Medicine* 10(1): 33–43
Rabkin, E. S. (1979) *Arthur C. Clarke*. Mercer Island: Starmont House.
Rozwadowski, H. M. (2004) 'Engineering, Imagination, and Industry: Scripps Island and Dreams for Ocean Science in the 1960s', in H. M. Rozwadowski and D. K. van Keuren (eds) *The Machine in Neptune's Garden*, pp. 325–52. Canton: Science History Publications.

Rozwadowski, H. M. (2018) *Vast Expanses: A History of the Oceans*. London: Reaktion Books.

Safina, C. (2002/3) 'Launching a Sea Ethic.' *Wild Earth* (Winter): 2–5.

Times, The (2008) 'Sir Arthur C. Clarke', 19 March, URL (accessed 17 February 2021): https://www.thetimes.co.uk/article/sir-arthur-c-clarke-the-times-obituary-38csw6qlkks

Taylor, J. E. (2001) *Making Salmon: An Environmental History of the Northwest Fisheries Crisis*. Seattle: University of Washington Press.

Taylor, R. L. (1953) 'Association Affairs', *The Scientific Monthly* 77(5): 275–8.

Turner, F. J. (1996) *The Frontier in American History*. New York: Dover.

von Braun, W. (1960) 'Introduction to A. C. Clarke', *The Challenge of the Sea*. New York: Holt, Rinehart and Watson.

'We Race for the Ocean's Secret: Ship Flips for Science – and a Lagging US' (1962) *Life* (21 December): 40–3.

Wolff, T. (2010) *The Birth and First Years of the Scientific Committee on Oceanic Research*. SCOR History Report 1.

7

The Extensions and Obsolescence of Man in *2001* and *2010*

Andrew M. Butler

There is a moment in 'The Obsolescence of Man' (1960) when Arthur C. Clarke rejects the idea that humanity invented tools: 'it would be more accurate to say that *tools invented Man*' (Clarke, 1962/1973: 228). He has just described how prehuman anthropoids discovered that sticks and stones could be used as tools to dig, to kill animals and to kill other anthropoids. The best tool-users became *Homo sapiens*. Eight years later, Stanley Kubrick's film of *2001: A Space Odyssey* (1968), from a script by Kubrick and Clarke, dramatized a similar breakthrough, as a hominid starts using animal bones as tools, including as weapons. Striking one bone down upon another, the hominid catapults the second into the air – and the film leaps ahead two million years, matching the prehistoric object with a near-future space vehicle, probably a nuclear weapons satellite. Marcio Caraccio notes that this cut elides 'the long series of technological advances that brought humanity from using bones as weapons to building artificial satellites' and 'combines temporal discontinuity with spatial continuity' (Caraccio, 2015: 78), focusing us upon the way in which human evolution involves technology 'augmenting the human body'

(Caraccio, 2015: 78). The agency for this giant leap in abilities must be called into question, as the hominid seems to have been provoked into his discovery by an enigmatic black monolith, a form which is rediscovered on the Moon and in outer space. But certainly the benefits and dangers of tools are central to the film of *2001: A Space Odyssey* and its companion novel, as well as Clarke's sequel, *2010: Odyssey Two*, and its adaptation, *2010: The Year We Made Contact* (dir. Peter Hyams, 1984). In this chapter I will discuss these ambiguities in relation to the ideas of Sigmund Freud, Martin Heidegger and Jacques Derrida, among others, as all of them have discussed the relationships between humanity and tools.

Books and Films

Stanley Kubrick began his voyage towards the making of *2001: A Space Odyssey* two months after the release of *Dr Strangelove, Or How I Learned to Stop Worrying and Love the Bomb* (1964), suggesting to Clarke that they collaborate on 'the proverbial good science fiction movie' (cited Krämer, 2010: 18). He wished to explore the impact of first contact with aliens on humans and to produce a more optimistic film than *Dr Strangelove*. Clarke responded positively and sent some initial ideas, drawing on his short story 'The Sentinel' (first published as 'Sentinel of Eternity' in *10 Story Fantasy* [1951]), and noted that he was developing the alien uplift of humans theme in *Childhood's End* (1953). They agreed to meet in New York in April to discuss their ideas. Clarke's novel, originally titled *Journey Beyond the Stars*, was then drafted in lieu of a film script to submit to MGM in December 1964. The studio gave Kubrick the go ahead in February 1965.

Kubrick relocated to England to start filming and continued to work on the outline. For example, Jupiter was substituted for the novel's Saturn, with the former being used for a slingshot acceleration and course adjustment in the novel – even though Douglas Trumbull had already shot test footage of the ringed planet. Clarke notes he 'often had the strange experience of revising the manuscript *after* viewing rushes based upon an earlier version of the story – a stimulating, but rather expensive, way of writing a novel' (Clarke, 1982: xi). While the novel often *tells* the readers what is going on, the film *shows* it, Kubrick abandoning voiceover and paring down speech. Alex North's soundtrack was rejected in favour of an orchestral score – including works by Richard Strauss, Richard Wagner, and György Ligeti – to which Geoffrey Unsworth's long takes and fluid moving camera and Ray Lovejoy's edits seem to be choreographed. *2001: A Space Odyssey* is not therefore a standard novelization nor adaptation, but was still used as a promotional tool, both to bring in Clarke's existing readership and to reveal one interpretation of an enigmatic film.

In time, Clarke became a household name, gaining larger advances for novels such as *Rendezvous with Rama* (1973), *Imperial Earth* (1976) and *The Fountains of Paradise* (1979), and fronting the first of several television series on the supernatural and pseudoscience, *Arthur C. Clarke's Mysterious World* (1980). *Rendezvous* won the major sf novel awards (the Hugo, the Nebula, the Locus and the John W. Campbell), *Fountains* gleaned a Hugo, and *Imperial* and *Fountains* got Nebulas. But the puzzles left by the endings of the film and book of *2001* meant that there was pressure upon Clarke to write a follow-up, *2010: Odyssey Two* (1982).[1] Clarke explains that it 'is something much more complex than a straightforward sequel to the earlier novel – or the movie. Where these differ, I have followed the screen version; however, I have been more concerned with making this book self-consistent, and as accurate as possible in the light of public knowledge' (Clarke, 1982: xiv). This latter aim matches a tendency in his novels since the mid-1970s to interleave chapters that are as much popularization of scientific papers and science journalism as to add to the narrative. Explaining a satisfying enigma with an unsatisfactory solution can be an anticlimax; as reviewer Peter Stockill notes, 'By answering questions raised by *2001*, *2010* reduces the profundity of the former' (Stockill, 1983: 35).

MGM/UA acquired the film rights and approached director Peter Hyams, Kubrick having passed on the project. At first, Hyams was reluctant, since *2001* had been an influence on his own films, including *Capricorn One* (1977) and *Outland* (1981), but he was convinced that it felt different enough from *2001* that there would be no comparison:

it would be a 'big, exciting thriller that's very accessible and emotional, and is, ultimately, overwhelmingly touching' (Lipari, 1984: 61). Hyams obtained Kubrick's blessing and persuaded Clarke that they could collaborate on the screenplay via email and modems. In the final release, however, only Hyams is credited as writer, in addition to directing, producing and acting as cinematographer.

Hyams's script follows the general outline of the source novel, but changes the identity of many of the secondary characters – Walter Curnow and Max Brailowsky are just buddies rather than lovers on the *Alexei Leonov* mission to salvage *Discovery One* and Dr Katherina Rudenko becomes male.[2] As Robert Shelton argues, Hyams's 'expedient goal seems to be to simplify Clarke's novel [...] He avoids narrative complications and literary allusions' (Shelton, 1987: 259). For example, the Chinese mission to explore Jupiter's moon Europa is omitted, with a probe and a pod from the *Leonov* surveying Europa and the monolith they find in orbit around the gas giant. Hyams inserts several letters home from Floyd (Roy Scheider), suggesting that he was worried that the audience would not be able to follow the plot, something that Kubrick seems to have taken on trust. Additionally, Hyams expands the Cold War context and the possibility of nuclear war, which adds tension to the Soviet-American mission to retrieve *Discovery One*.

2001: Humans Using Tools

It is an overstatement that tool usage distinguishes humans from animals – see other primates, dolphins, corvids, octopus, for example – but it is the human species that has most frequently found ways of expanding their capabilities with objects. In *Civilisation and its Discontents* (1930), Sigmund Freud argues:

> With every tool man is perfecting his own organs, whether motor or sensory, or is removing the limits to their functioning. Motor power places gigantic forces at his disposal, which, like his muscles, he can employ in any direction; thanks to ships and aircraft neither water nor air can hinder his movements. (Freud, 1985: 279)

Humanity could first move only at walking speed, but riding animals and using boats could improve upon this and increase the range they could travel. Steam, internal combustion, and jet technology could be applied to trains, cars, and aeroplanes; rockets meant that the atmosphere was no longer a limit to distance. Clarke notes that in space exploration 'most of our energies will be devoted to protecting our frail and sensitive bodies against the extremes of temperature, pressure or gravity' (Clarke, 1962/1973: 239). Meanwhile, technology such as glasses, telescopes, microscopes, contact lenses, telephones, radio, email programs, and so on would extend the range of the senses of sight and hearing. Inventions such as cameras, films, records, audio cassettes, MP3s, and writing act as artificial memories and preserve experiences. Freud suggests that

> Long ago he [humanity] formed an ideal conception of omnipotence and omniscience which he embodied in his gods. [...] To-day he has come very close to the attainment of this ideal, he has almost become a god himself. [...] Man has, as it were, become a kind of prosthetic God. (Freud, 1985: 280)

Bows and arrows, guns, cannons, and nuclear weapons allow such godlike humans to defend themselves from a distance.

In the philosophy of Martin Heidegger, tools have a more psychological role in our relation to the universe. For Heidegger, we are thrown into Being (*Dasein*) and spend much of our time trying to distract ourselves from the thought that we might be thrown out again – so even relationships with others are tools. Tools such as the 'axe and gun and canoe and wagon' (Clarke, 1968/1998: 77) are examples of technology, for Heidegger both a human activity and a means to an end: 'The manufacture and utilization of equipment, tools, and machines, the manufactured and used things themselves, and the needs and ends that they serve, all belong to what technology is' (Heidegger, 1993: 312). Technology is a form of bringing-forth, 'a mode of revealing. Technology comes to presence in the realm where revealing and unconcealment takes place' (Heidegger, 1993: 319). Garry Leonard (2011: 53) applies these ideas about technology to various sequences in *2001: A Space Odyssey*, describing the process in which the hominid unconceals the tool in the bone: 'The discovery of how to use the club as a bone is really an "unconcealment" that fosters a mode of thinking that it is fair to call "technological"'. Natural artefacts are unconcealed as human resources. The hominid becomes central to the cinema screen and to history: there is a before and after to this unconcealment.

In Clarke's novel, the prehistoric hominid Moon-Watcher uses a stone and then a bone club, knife and awl. Such basic tools allow a subsisting group to progress to being a thriving clan, because the unconcealment makes it easier to kill and butcher animals. They become better at attacking rival tribes. As Sherryl Vint (2009: 230) notes, 'The hominids achieve technology and its benefits (freedom from fear of the night, freedom from hunger) at the same time that they invent weapons and become territorial (claiming the watering hole permanently instead of occupying it)'. Tools here distinguish the human from the non-human and alter the existing social order, although at this point in (pre)history, 'The human/animal boundary – which marks one killing [of a human] as murder and the other [of an animal] as noncriminal – has yet to be articulated' (Vint, 2009: 231). Some tools have a right and a wrong end to be on and not all tool use is always appropriate.

But technology and its connection to unconcealment may also undercut humanity's position in the universe. In his *Introductory Lectures to Psychoanalysis* (1917), Freud (1991: 326) suggests that 'the naïve self-love of men has had to submit to two major blows at the hands of science', namely Copernicus's astronomy and Darwin's theory of evolution. Freud felt that psychoanalysis and his identification of the unconscious mind offered a third blow with his conception of the unconscious. However, Donna Haraway (2007: 12) describes a fourth blow, the 'cyborgian', as we merge with our technology. Hybridity, supplementation and prosthetic enhancement have been a dominant experience of the last fifty or more years.

In 'The Obsolescence of Man', Clarke (1962/1973: 243) discusses the developing power of computers and points to the just coined term 'cyborg', where machines are connected to or made part of the human body, to modify or run its functions. He envisaged that a human could become 'a spaceship or a submarine or a TV network' (Clarke, 1962/1973: 243). Marshall McLuhan, in *Understanding Media: The Extensions of Man* (1964) and later works, imagined (with some ambivalence) a networked global village which would draw upon the communications satellites Clarke had imagined, and discussed how the electronic media – such as it was in the early 1960s – extends the central nervous system. The body, in particular the mind, may well close down some of the senses in response: 'Such amplification is bearable by the nervous system only through numbness or blocking of perception' (McLuhan, 1964: 43).

Clarke (1962/1973: 240) was aware of the roles of machines to act as bodily prosthetics and cheerfully suggests that '"extension [of the human intellect]" may be replaced by "extinction"'. Tools as prostheses may supplement human capabilities, but 'supplement' has the double meaning of extension (as in dietary or newspaper supplements) and substitute. In Jacques Derrida's (1998: 144) terms, the supplement 'adds itself, it is a surplus' but 'It adds only to replace. It intervenes or insinuates itself *in-the-place-of* (Derrida, 1998: 145). The tool, the prosthetic, is an extension *to* and a replacement *for* the human, with consequent implications for humanism. New tools make old ones obsolete. The abilities of HAL, the ultimate tool, make the *Discovery One* crew supplementary to requirements and thus dispensable, even disposable.

Moon-Watcher and his kin have unconcealed much technology and developed social networks, but the truth they have found does not include the monolith. While Clarke might not have thought of them this way when he wrote the novel and film script – although this has become evident in *Odyssey Two* – the monoliths are tools. In the book, Floyd reflects upon the epochal change between the implements of the European settlers of new colonies and those of the 'Spaceborn', those who have grown up off-planet: 'their tools would not be axe and gun and canoe and wagon; they would be nuclear power plant and plasma drive and hydroponic farm' (Clarke, 1968/1998: 77). It appears that humanity has developed under its own steam after the initial stimulus of the monolith, but it is unclear whether this is a matter of free will rather than extra-terrestrial intervention.

Once the film has moved to the year 2001, we only see humans off Earth, where survival of fragile bodies requires tools such as spacesuits, rockets, space stations, space pods and *Discovery One*. The characters search for the meaning behind the monolith found on the Moon, another discovery on the brink of unconcealing. The computer HAL monitors and controls the life support systems of *Discovery One*, opens and closes hatches and doors remotely, facilitates communications within the ship and with Earth, and does all of this without the need for sleep. Additionally, HAL has gained or been programmed with a personality — arguably, he is the most developed character in the film. HAL can think for the crew. The novel explains that HAL would pass the Turing Test (as described in Clarke, 1962/1973: 231) and by any reasonable judgement *is* thinking, and his ability to demonstrate emotion helps enables humans to believe he is sentient. The film suggests that emotions smooth relations with humans — in other words they are tools used by a tool.

But the crew are on the wrong side of this tool. It is not certain in the book or film why HAL fails – this is clarified in both versions of *2010* – but the first symptom of this is when the ship's radio dish is about to fail. Bowman and Poole find nothing wrong with it and HAL blames human error, part of his emotional makeup being supreme confidence. We are repeatedly told that no HAL unit has ever failed or miscalculated, although the engineers have foreseen the need for a COMPUTER MALFUNCTION warning sign.

HAL's major aim is to protect the mission – and knows that it is not just an exploration of Jupiter (film) or Saturn (book) – but a rendezvous with the destination of the signal sent by the monolith on the Moon. Bowman only learns this after he has dismantled HAL's memory. HAL's actions may be a programming glitch, akin to trying to resolve conflicting Asimovian Laws of Robotics which demand protection of humans and itself whilst obeying orders. Reaching the destination of the signal may outweigh the need to protect the crew. This does not necessarily explain the apparently mistaken diagnosis of instrument failure.

Bowman and Poole discuss whether HAL is competent to run the mission and decide to switch the computer off — not using a tool might be safer than using a broken one. But despite their precaution of talking away from HAL's microphones, they do not realize that they are being lip-read. HAL decides that their decision jeopardizes the mission and must remove them. It might be that Clarke had read D. F. Jones's *Colossus* (1960), in which a supercomputer decides that people are getting in the way of keeping the peace after it contacts its Soviet twin. Still, the *Discovery One*'s mission to find out what it is near Saturn/Jupiter surely cannot succeed without humans to observe — unless HAL's monitors supplement or replace them. It is at this point that Poole is cut adrift in space and dies. HAL switches off life support for the three astronauts who are in deep sleep and Bowman is nearly stranded outside the ship.

Bowman uses various tools to outwit HAL's refusal to obey his orders, triggering explosive bolts to break back into the ship and holding his breath to survive the vacuum. He then must use Allen keys to dismantle HAL. As Bowman removes each memory board, HAL regresses to a more childlike state and returns to basic functionality. Bowman can then use other tools — a spacesuit and a pod — to extend his life support as he has his close encounter with the monolith.

This encounter is the most baffling sequence of *2001*. We get a series of colours and shapes, psychedelic landscapes, with Trumbull using his slitscreen technique to produce striking visuals. Kubrick maintains continuity editing by cutting between this and Bowman, his eyes echoing HAL's panoptic red eye, his helmet reflecting each strange new vision. He sees what feels like an infinite series of sublime images.

Thanks to the novel's description of the space monolith as a Star Gate, we can take the string of experiences to be a voyage into the interior of the object, which breaks with normal four-dimensional time and space. It could also be a voyage into Bowman's perceptions, as he evolves to the next stage of humanity. We see him as an older man in a highly decorated, Regency-style, bedroom, looking at an even older version of himself, before he is seen lying in the bed, gesturing towards another monolith. Finally, we see a foetus, first above the bed and then — after the camera moves towards the monolith, filling the screen with black — orbiting around Earth. The musical leitmotif of

Richard Wagner's 'Also sprach Zarathustra' (1896) returns from earlier in the film, and the end credits roll.

In the book, one of Bowman's/the Star Child's first actions is to destroy nuclear weapons in orbit around the Earth, removing one of humanity's deadlier tools: 'the circling megatons flowered in a silent detonation' (Clarke, 1968/1998: 236). Here concludes one trajectory in tool development in parallel with the great span of history between hominid and space farer: 'The spear, the bow, the gun and finally the guided missiles had given him weapons of infinite range' (Clarke, 1968/1998: 48). This detail reveals a difference between the pacifist Clarke and the war-obsessed Kubrick: whereas the former was broadly optimistic about the future, the latter, although he wanted this follow-up to *Dr Strangelove* to be positive, was anticipating Armageddon. The Moon-Watcher and Star Child (an Earth watcher) both wonder what to do next with their newfound abilities: 'But he would think of something' (Clarke, 1968/1998: 46; cf. 236). These lines echo the chief of the Science Bureau, Pierre Duval, in *Childhood's End*: 'We will think of something' (Clarke, 1953/1956: 44).

What neither the book nor film of *2001* reveal or unconceal is the nature of the aliens that have supplemented human evolution and how they benefit from this intervention. In various places, Clarke posits his Third Law: 'Any sufficiently advanced technology is indistinguishable from magic' (Clarke, 1962/1973: 39). To Moon-Watcher, the monolith might as well be magical, for all his understanding of what is going on and despite Heidegger's claims. For film viewers, the enigmas of the monoliths and the journey through the Star Gate, not to mention Bowman's eventual destination and transformation as Star Child, might as well be magic too. All limits to the Star Child's functioning have been removed. If *2001* were not located as science fiction, then we might read it as fantasy. The unseen aliens are beyond our comprehension. Clarke's Third Law has inspired several variants, including Michael Shermer's: 'Any sufficiently advanced extra-terrestrial intelligence is indistinguishable from God' (Shermer, 2002: 33). Indeed, Clarke (1973: 253) had suggested during the production of *2001* that 'M-G-M doesn't know it yet, but they're paying for the first

$10,000,000 religious movie'. This seems an odd – presumably ironic – thing to say for a professed atheist.

The monoliths are presented as if they are teaching machines, in the book displaying images on their surface. When rotated ninety degrees, the monoliths' proportions mimic the cinema screen. Leonard suggests 'Kubrick has positioned the film-viewing audience as so many apes gathered before a monolith (the movie screen)' (Leonard, 2011: 58). The film teaches, even as we project onto and — through identification — into the screen: 'Kubrick has "used" the movie screen to create an equivalent experience for the viewer of being an "ape"' (Leonard, 2011: 59). We are to the (unseen) aliens as the apes are to us. *2001* across various media is another tool, extending the visions of Clarke and Kubrick around the world and beyond their deaths: a teaching machine, even if the lesson itself is ambiguous. I. Q. Hunter (2013: 48), more a devotee of Kubrick than of Clarke, sees the novel as 'a handy primer and a crib to a wholly unconventional film'.

2010: Humans as Tools

As HAL demonstrates, the greater the tool becomes, the more it controls the person who uses it, who becomes an extension of the tool. As Clarke notes of computers, 'even machines *less* intelligent than men might escape from our control by sheer speed of operation. And in fact, there is every reason to suppose that machines will become much more intelligent than their builders' (Clarke, 1962/1973: 232). The bigger the tool, the more people it impacts upon. Tools and users are inseparable. The lesson of *2010* is that civilization is a tool – both controlling the people who dwell within it and those who rule or run it. On board the *Leonov*, reflecting on what has gone wrong with HAL and his role in the disaster of *Discovery One*, Floyd is of little specialist use to the team, instead working on maintenance and being a night watch. Just before a rebooted HAL informs him that they must evacuate the Jovian system, he realizes that he is a tool.

The crew of the *Leonov* come to the same conclusion about the monoliths:

'We're talking about these things as if they're persons – intelligent entities. They're not – they're *tools*. But general-purpose tools – able to do anything they have to. The one on the Moon was a signalling device – or a spy, if you like. The one that Bowman met – our original *Zagadka* [puzzle] – was some kind of transportation system. Now it's doing something else, though God knows what. And there may be others all over the Universe.

'I had just such a gadget when I was a kid. Do you know what *Zagadka* really is? Just the cosmic equivalent of the good old Swiss Army knife!' (Clarke, 1982: 191–2)

It seems a large leap from a device that has a knife, a corkscrew, cap remover, awl, and so forth, to a block with golden ratio dimensions and an apparently infinite interior, but we are prepared for this by the supplement of bone by spacecraft. The crew remains in partial ignorance as to how the tool is being deployed and certainly by whom.

Dave Bowman — the surname is surely no accident — is also a tool, having reached the next stage in human evolution through his encounter with the Jovian monolith and is now being used to explore time and space. At first, he does not quite use the word, realizing 'he was being used as a probe' (Clarke, 1982: 123). But after a few more explorations, he glimpses the nature of what he has become: 'He was being used as a tool, and a good tool had to be sharpened, modified – adapted. And the very best tools were those who understood what they were doing' (Clarke, 1982: 144). Quite why the superior beings are using him rather than observing reality directly is unclear, but the monolith has been used as an educational tool, to upgrade him to a superior tool. He is a human supplement and a supplement to/for the aliens.

Before Jupiter is transformed into a star by an exponentially increasing number of monoliths, a final message is shared by HAL:

ALL THESE WORLDS ARE YOURS – EXCEPT EUROPA.
ATTEMPT NO LANDINGS THERE. (Clarke, 1982: 206)

This is a moment equivalent to God speaking to Adam and Eve and giving them dominion over the Garden of Eden and the animals and plants within it, with the exception of two trees; humanity has been given freehold of the clear majority of the solar system. This new star, Lucifer, produces enough light to mean that there is little night for much of the year, bringing the species to a new utopia: 'the end of night had vastly extended the scope of human activity, especially in the less-developed countries' (Clarke, 1982: 210). Energy costs reduce, outside activities increase, crime is less prevalent and so on. The new environment is something to be exploited, albeit for the common good, although it might be objected that this seems naively utopian. Jupiter's orbit would certainly mean that it is obscured by the Sun for parts of the year and the diurnal cycle may well disrupt the ecosystem more than Clarke acknowledges.

The same optimism is seen in *2010: The Year We Made Contact*, and this is emphasized by the way Lucifer ends the Cold War. Peter Krämer notes the change Kubrick had made from Clarke's novel by removing the nuclear space weapon, and that Hyams restores this theme in his overall story arc: 'Hyams's sequel returns us to the very beginnings of Kubrick and Clarke's joint science-fiction project in 1964' (Krämer, 2010: 101). Kubrick had already explored the insanity of mutually assured destruction in *Dr Strangelove* and presumably did not wish to repeat himself. The space race, especially with John F. Kennedy's wish to put a man on the Moon by the end of the 1960s, was a soft power extension of Cold War propaganda, but seems absent from the 1968 film.[3] There may be an awkwardness to the encounter between Dr Heywood Floyd (William Sylvester) and Dr Andrei Smyslov (Leonard Rossiter) on Space Station 5, but that is more due to procedure than aggression. In *Odyssey Two*, Floyd seems quite comfortable with Russians and pragmatic about etiquette.

In the late 1960s, American involvement in Vietnam and the civil politics of Black, women's and gay rights were beginning to call American values into question – the uncomplicated hero no longer seems appropriate. Dominic Janes observes that Keir Dullea playing Bowman is 'anything but a conventional possessor of phallic potency in his close encounter with the monolith at the climax of the film' (Janes, 2011: 64). The collapse of traditional certainties was further emphasized by the resignation of Richard Nixon over the Watergate break-in and subsequent cover-up and the withdrawal from Vietnam.

Whilst on television *Star Trek* had expressed heroism within a multicultural crew (cf. Worland, 1988), in *2001*'s wake science fiction cinema was to become more ambiguous (Butler, 2012).

By the end of the 1970s, a new right-wing politics had emerged, catalysing an attempt to recuperate the straight white male American hero. Inspired by the success of *Star Wars* (George Lucas, 1977), Hollywood cinema became dominated by what Andrew Britton calls 'Reaganite entertainments' (Britton, 2009: 47), whose neoliberalism 'anticipates a gorgeous re-flowering of capitalism in which the good things will be born again under the aegis of the microchip once a flabby politic has been slimmed down and its cancerous growths excised' (Britton, 2009: 109). These films reassure us with and about fathers or father figures, infantilize their viewers, side-line women characters, dazzle with special effects, and warn about the dangers of nuclear weapons in the wrong (Russian) hands. According to Peter Bamford, *The Year We Made Contact* 'is dragged down by its pessimistic Cold War machinations, evacuating the lyrical and mesmerizing flow of *2001* to make way for a recognizable starscape of angular, bulky spacecraft and feuding, territorial governments on the brink of war' (Bamford, 2002: 228). When Floyd is woken on board the *Leonov*, to be briefed about the US-Soviet skirmish in Central America, he is reminded by the Soviet crew that 'they are patriotic military officers and he is the enemy' (Shelton, 1987: 263). The Russian crew supplement their state in a conflict with Floyd on behalf of America. Eventually, they do cooperate, for survival.

Another change in the film is a coda to the final message from HAL:

USE THEM [the worlds] TOGETHER
USE THEM IN PEACE

Here the solar system is seen as resources. In Heidegger's words, 'the work of modern technology reveals the real as standing-reserve' (Heidegger 1993: 21). As Leonard suggests in his Heideggerian reading, we are encouraged to view 'our surroundings as a totally available "standing reserve," or ready-to-hand, awaiting our discovery of its function preparatory to submitting it to our use' (Leonard, 2011: 60). The right of the aliens to gift humanity the solar system is not disputed, nor is humanity's right to accept it; it is at the heart of the imperialist ideology that territory is there to benefit the occupiers.

Conclusion

The extra-terrestrial gifts echo the start of *2001*; as John Rieder (2009: 91) observes, 'The intervention of the monolith has the effect [...] of making the ape-man's discovery of tools into a gift'. Intelligence and society have not developed entirely through human agency, but rather through alien intervention and control. Humanity may have as little free will as their tools. The optimism of Clarke's imagined evolution of human from hominid to space-farer is transformed into an historical inevitability in which the ingenuity of the species seems downplayed. The aliens are helicopter parents – albeit ones who seem to have lost interest in their charges in favour of the Europans. Stockill's reading is that 'the experiment with man on Earth has been a failure' (Stockill, 1983: 36), but perhaps their previous interference with humanity and ongoing interference in the development and protection of the Europans is still a result.

The point of the films is to emphasize our decentred identities – for all the visible creativity in technology, we are as much the product of our tools as producers of them; 'tools invented man' (Clarke, 1962/1973: 229). The parallels drawn between hominids and humans and the psychedelic Star Gate sequence and its aftermath are unconcealings of the truth, although the nature of this truth is unclear – in practice it reminds us that we have both made conceptual breakthroughs and experienced major blows to our 'naive self-love' (Freud, 1991: 326). We have also been under the microscope. Clarke (1962/1973: 244) might note that 'most people will feel it is a rather bleak prospect for humanity if it ends up as a pampered specimen in some biological museum', but that is effectively what we are in these books. Kubrick's reinsertion of a monolith into the mise en scène at the end of *2001* should remind us that we too are tools and a standing-resource, even Heidegger argues that 'because man is challenged more originally than are the energies of nature, i.e., into the process of ordering, he never is transformed into mere standing-reserve. Since man drives technology forward, he takes part in ordering as a way of revealing' (Heidegger, 1993: 323). But people *are* a resource, in the ideology of neoliberalism, the philosophy of Heidegger and the universe of 2001/2010. Other people both distract us from being thrown out of Being and can assist us in being. Resources are finite and although humanity may be extended, this cannot be infinitely done. One day, humanity will also become extinct.

Notes

1 Two further sequels followed, *2061: Odyssey Three* (1987) and *3001: The Final Odyssey* (1997), but are outside the scope of this chapter and have yet to be filmed. Three books, collectively labelled *A Time Odyssey* and co-written with Stephen Baxter, are 'orthogonal' to the tetralogy: *Time's Eye* (2003), *Sunstorm* (2005) and *Firstborn* (2007). The open ending of *Rendezvous* led to *Rama II* (1989), *The Garden of Rama* (1991) and *Rama Revealed* (1993), largely written by Gentry Lee.

2 Shelton (1987: 264) notes that Brailowsky and Zenia Marchenko (a late addition to the *Leonov* crew) and Curnow and Rudenko are engaged to be married by the end of *Odyssey Two*: 'His bisexuals are, as it were, redeemed [...] by entering into "happy-ever-after" heterosexual unions'. But this is to erase bisexual identity – a bisexual man married to a woman can still be bisexual.

3 Leonard suggests it is in the film in an oblique form: 'But if Kubrick cannot depict the moment before and after our own cleared world, he can defamiliarize it and open it up as a site of establishing a mode of thinking establishing an experience of being, thereby imparting a political and cultural message that the cold war's arms race, is not the inevitable doomsday scenario it appears to be' (Leonard, 2011: 59). The jump-cut from bone to spaceship represents the unrepresentable.

Works Cited

Bamford, P. (2002) 'Peter HYAMS', in Y. Allon (ed.) *Contemporary North American Film Directors: A Wallflower Critical Guide*, pp. 227–9. London: Wallflower Press.

Britton, A. (2008) 'Blissing Out: The Politics of Reaganite Entertainment', in B. K. Grant (ed.) *Britton on Film: The Complete Film Criticism of Andrew Britton*, pp. 97–154. Detroit, MI: Wayne State University Press.
Butler, A. M. (2012) *Solar Flares: Science Fiction in the 1970s*. Liverpool: Liverpool University Press.
Caracciolo, M. (2015) 'Bones in Outer Space: Narrative and the Cosmos in *2001: A Space Odyssey* and Its Remediations', *Image [&] Narrative* 16(3): 73–89.
Clarke, A. C. (1953/1956) *Childhood's End*. New York: Ballantine.
Clarke, A. C. (1962/1973) *Profiles of the Future*. London: Pan.
Clarke, A. C. (1968/1998) *2001: A Space Odyssey*. London: Orbit.
Clarke, A. C. (1973) *Report on Planet Three and Other Speculations*. London: Corgi.
Clarke, A. C. (1982) *2010: Odyssey Two*. London: Granada.
Derrida, J. (1998) *Of Grammatology*. Trans. Gayatri Chakravorty Spivak. Baltimore: Johns Hopkins University Press.
Freud, S. (1985) *Civilisation and its Discontents* (1930), in *Civilisation, Society, and Religion*, pp. 251–340. London: Pelican.
Freud, S. (1991) *Introductory Lectures on Psychoanalysis*. Harmondsworth: Penguin.
Haraway, D. (2007) *When Species Meet*. Minneapolis: University of Minnesota Press.
Heidegger, M. (1993) 'The Question Concerning Technology' (1954), in D. F. Krell (ed.) *Basic Writings: from 'Being and Time' (1927) to 'The Task of Thinking' (1964)*, pp. 311–41. London: Routledge.
Hunter, I. Q. (2013) 'From Adaptation to Cinephilia: An Intertextual Odyssey', in T. Van Parys and I. Q. Hunter (eds) *Science Fiction Across Media: Adaptation/Novelisation*, pp. 43–63. Canterbury: Gylphi.
Janes, D. (2011) 'Clarke and Kubrick's *2001*: A Queer Odyssey.' *Science Fiction Film and Television* 4(1): 57–78.
Krämer, P. (2010) *2001: A Space Odyssey*. London: Palgrave Macmillan.
Leonard, G. (2011) 'Technically Human: Kubrick's Monolith and Heidegger's Propriative Event', *Film Criticism* 36(1): 44–67.
Lipari, J. (1984) '2010 Men', *Film Comment* 20(6): 60–3.
McLuhan, M. (1964) *Understanding Media: The Extensions of Man*. New York: McGraw-Hill.
Rieder, J. (2009) 'Spectacle, Technology and Colonialism in Wim Wenders' *Until the End of the World*', in M. Bould and C. Miéville (eds) *Red Planets: Marxism and Science Fiction*, pp. 83–99. London: Pluto.

Shelton, R. (1987) 'Rendezvous with Hal: *2001/2010*', *Extrapolation* 28(3): 255–68.
Shermer, R. (2002) 'Shermer's Last Law', *Scientific American* 286(1): 33.
Stockill, P. (1983) 'The Culmination of the Mythology', *Vector* 117: 34–7.
Vint, S. (2009) 'Simians, Subjectivity and Sociality: *2001: A Space Odyssey* and Two Versions of *Planet of the Apes*', *Science Fiction Film and Television* 2(2): 225–50.
Worland, R. (1988) 'Captain Kirk: Cold Warrior.' *Journal of Popular Film and Television* 16(3): 109–17.

8

'ALL THESE WORLDS ARE YOURS EXCEPT EUROPA'
TRANSHUMANISM AND THE ETHICS OF TERRAFORMING

Alexey Dodsworth-Magnavita

Transhumanism is a political and cultural movement that sustains, among various ideas, the importance of broadening our ethical perspective in order to encompass non-human beings. In a wide range of aspects, transhumanist's ethical proposals share affinities with the moral lessons to be found in Arthur C. Clarke's fictional works. For example, whereas the Russian rocket scientist Konstantin Tsiolkovsky saw outer space as subservient to human expansion, famously arguing that 'Earth is the cradle of humanity but one cannot live in the cradle forever' (cited in Redd, 2013), Clarke wrote in *Childhood's End* (1953) that 'The planets you may one day possess. But the stars are not for man' (Clarke, 2010: 137). There are at least two reasons for this human limitation. The first is biological: humanity cannot survive within deep space contexts, so it would be necessary not only to terraform other planets, but also to enhance our bodies and longevity, which would make us post-human. The second is ethical, that is, the experience of overcoming our limitation to planet Earth demands we surpass our tendency to be guided by an anthropocentric mindset.

This critique of anthropocentrism underlines the philosophy of transhumanism and its attitude towards the terraforming of other worlds.

Transhumanism and the Space Endeavour

The 'Transhumanist Declaration' (first drafted in 1998 and revised multiple times) begins by advocating 'the possibility of broadening human potential by overcoming aging, cognitive shortcomings, involuntary suffering, and our confinement to planet Earth' (Aegis et al., 2013: 54). At first sight, this statement seems to align itself with the sentiments of Tsiolkovsky rather than Clarke. However, their similarities are restricted to the merely common purpose of expansion into space. When it comes to achieving their goal, there are important ethical disagreements between Tsiolkovsky and transhumanism that cannot be underestimated as, for example, the role played by humanity in this cosmically expanded future.

On the one hand, Tsiolkovsky seems to defend a strong anthropocentrism, a kind of manifest destiny beyond the boundaries of our planet, when he says:

> Men are weak now, and yet they transform the Earth's surface. In millions of years their might will increase to the extent that they will change the surface of the Earth, its oceans, the atmosphere and themselves. They will control the climate and the solar system just as they control the Earth. (cited in Brody, 2005)

Conversely, transhumanists tend to remove the human being from any claim to universal privilege. The seventh proposal of the Transhumanist Declaration advocates for 'the well being of all sentience, including humans, non-human animals, and any future artificial intellects, modified life forms, or other intelligences to which technological and scientific advance may give rise' (Aegis et al., 2013: 54). That is, according to a transhumanist perspective, ethics cannot be anthropocentrically sustained due to the fact the notion of value derives from *sentience* instead of *intelligence*. This shift in perspective complements the cultural impact of the Moon landings and of seeing the Earth from outer space (Poole, 2008). Astronauts report a sensitivity, euphoria or spiritual connection to the planet known as 'the overview effect'. In 1969, Rusty Schweikart described his feelings during a spacewalk: 'When you go around the Earth in a hour and a half, you begin to recognize that your identity is with the whole thing' (cited in O'Neill, 2008).

Most people, though, have not had the opportunity of experiencing such a sensation. Whilst on the one hand, transhumanism rejects the arrogance of anthropocentrism, on the other hand, it resists being restricted to planet Earth. Although solutions to ageing, cognitive impairment and pain may be welcomed by many, the colonization of other worlds tends to be rejected by public opinion (Randolph, 2004: 35–9). Critics of space exploration tend to emphasize that our own planet has serious problems to be solved, therefore money spent on outer space should be spent here on Earth, on more pressing matters such as health-care research. Arguably, though, these criticisms are a false dilemma, given that space research offers strong benefits to our everyday applied technology (Bennington-Castro, 2015).

Above all the benefits, space exploration could help us protect and conserve our own planet, for example through asteroid mining. As pointed out by several researchers (Blair, 2000; Lewis, 1996; Sonter, 1998), asteroid mining is not only economically feasible but it is also environmentally ethical, given that we can minimize the exploitation of our world. Planet Earth is so rare in so many ways that it could be protected as a sanctuary while almost all mining could be made by space settlements. (The database Asterank offers the costs and benefits of off-world mining as opposed to current terrestrial industries [Webster, n.d.].) Additionally, by mining these barren bodies, we could monitor and divert potential planetary threats.

In short, to explore alien sites is a way to spare the Earth, which is in accordance with the transhuman statement that the long-term survival of sentient beings should be taken as a priority. If we intend to make it real, one of the practical solutions is investment in space programmes. Otherwise, we are likely to perish possibly as a result of man-made climate change, the exploitation of finite fossil fuels or the slippage of diseases between species. Space research should not be seen as an *expense* but as an *investment* whose rewards are not only for humans but also for other sentient beings. As Anna Wilks acknowledges, even though 'it is not, in principle, morally impermissible to prioritize the value of human beings given their [...] capacity for *self-legislation*', 'this does not grant free reign to human beings in their treatment of less intrinsically valuable life forms [...] since, as living beings, they still possess some *degree* of intrinsic value' (Wilks, 2016: 192).

Terraforming and Environmental Ethics

Although a space programme, whose needs are not exclusively anthropocentric, is intellectually conceivable, arguments persist such as the environmental damage that may be done to other worlds even if they are barren:

> An extension of human ethics to animals and thence to other organisms if taken to the next step would include an extension of ethics to abiotic objects (be they rocks, rivers or ringed planets) even if they do not contribute to a living ecosystem. [...] The turbulent atmosphere of Neptune, the volcanic activity on Jupiter's moon and the chemical reactions of the surface-atmosphere interface of Venus could fulfil many definitions of what it is to be 'alive'. (Marshall, 1993: 234)

This kind of argument, known as 'cosmic preservationism' or 'cosmocentrism', is also sometimes based upon aesthetics: 'by studying Mars I have come to recognize beauty of an unearthly kind in its pale colours and pure, ancient landforms. On the face of it, the destruction of this beauty would seem to be a terrible loss, and this alone provides a clear, if defeasible objection to terraforming' (McMahon, 2016: 217).

Such justifiable criticisms are derived from the unsustainable human impact upon our own terrestrial environment, which has led to the call for urgent solutions if we are to leave a viable world for future generations. Although it is unlikely that we will extinguish *all* life on Earth, we increasingly make planetary conditions unfeasible *for ourselves*, as well as for other native species. Environmental ethics, then, are not just an altruistic concern regarding nature but above all a matter of survival. As a result of this new understanding, ethical philosophy has broadened its focus and is no longer restricted to the interaction among humans. Bioethics focuses on the moral relationship between humans and all organic life-forms, whether sentient or physically alive. Whereas G. W. F. Hegel once observed, regarding our desire to describe how the world ought to be, that 'the owl of Minerva begins its flight only with the onset of the dusk' (Hegel, 1991: 23), bioethics deals with emerging problems in a world whose time is, contrary to Hegel, still not too late. Even if we consider philosophy an insufficient tool when it comes to thinking of the future, it is possible and desirable to build a bridge connecting philosophy and fiction in order to anticipate dangers and to act before they come true.

In an interview given to the entertainment website The A. V. Club, Clarke argued that 'fiction is more than non-fiction in some ways. [...] You can stretch people's minds, alerting them to the possibilities of the future, which is very important in an age where things are changing rapidly' (Robinson, 2004). In several of Clarke's fictional works, he warns us that Earth is not separate from the rest of the universe and that to deny this truth is a dangerous mistake. Our planet has suffered global extinctions caused by extraterrestrial factors, such as the Cretaceous-Paleogene Event, when an asteroid collided with the Earth's surface and extinguished more than seventy-five per cent of the species (including the dinosaurs). There is no guarantee that cosmic extinctions will not recur. Instead, the human presence on Earth is comparatively recent and we delude ourselves by thinking of our world as existing in a stable state. Throughout the Earth's formation, comets and meteors brought much of the existing water, while we remain vulnerable to the effects of supernovae and gamma ray bursts (Galante and Hovarth, 2007). Instead, by visualizing the Earth as part of a dynamic, cosmic system and in deploying anticipatory thought experiments, the literary imagination is integral to the practical application of environmental ethics.

Clarke's *Rendezvous with Rama* (1973), for example, begins with a moral criticism of our tendency to act only when it is *too late*. Clarke starts by describing some real cosmic events that happened in our recent past. By remembering the Tunguska event on 30 June 1908, he emphasizes how vulnerable we are, given that 'Moscow escaped destruction by three hours and four thousand kilometres – a margin invisibly small by the standards of the universe'. He also remembers the Sikhote-Alin meteorite falling close to Vladivostok in 1947 'with an explosion rivalling that of the newly invented uranium bomb' (Clarke, 1973/2006: 1). Yet, we do not take serious safeguarding measures because we have still not been hit in a way that really hurts us. Thus, in order to demonstrate how random and indifferent the universe is, Clarke offers us a drastic fictional scene in which northern Italy is totally destroyed by thousands of tons of rock and metal falling from the sky:

> The cities of Padua and Verona were wiped from the face of the Earth; and the last glories of Venice sank forever beneath the sea as the waters of the Adriatic came thundering landward after the hammer blow from space.
>
> Six hundred thousand people died, and the total damage was more than a trillion dollars. But the loss to art, to history, to science – to the whole human race, for the rest of time – was beyond all computation. (Clarke, 1973/2006: 2)

Clarke's (2011: 8) warning, though, is clear from the very beginning of the book: 'Sooner or later, it was bound to happen'. Therefore, why should ethics spread its wings when it is *too late*? It is not ethical to keep ignoring our responsibilities as the intelligent species we are. Clarke and the transhumanists are in total accordance in this point: our intelligence gives us not more rights but more *responsibility*.

Another example of how science fiction may be of assistance to ethical philosophy is demonstrated by an actual ethical dilemma involving Europa, one of the moons of Jupiter. When *2001* and *2010: Odyssey Two* were written, respectively in 1968 and 1982, the concept of circumstellar habitable zone (CHZ) was quite restricted. In that time, CHZ was defined as a specific distance between a planet and its star where liquid water may be found. However geocentric this perspective seems, it makes sense to look for life signatures outside planet Earth by taking into account parameters that are similar to ours. The search for environments that sustain liquid solvents is the most rational thing to do. Thus, the first astrobiological rule is: we must follow the water. In our particular solar system, CHZ is limited to the region occupied by the Earth, almost reaching Mars. As for Jupiter, Saturn and their moons, those are very far from this border. Therefore, the moon Europa should harbour, at best, only frozen water.

However, in *2010*, Clarke describes Europa as possessing a massive liquid ocean: 'It was an ocean world, its hidden waters protected from the vacuum of space by a crust of ice. In most places the ice was kilometers thick, but there were lines of weakness where it had cracked open and torn apart' (Clarke, 1982: 178). In fact, Clarke anticipated not only the alien ocean, but also described the natural forces that could allow liquid water on Europa:

> Because it's so far from the sun, Europa's surface temperature is extremely low – about a hundred and fifty degrees below freezing. So one might expect its single ocean to be a solid block of ice. Surprisingly, that isn't the case because there's a lot of heat generated inside Europa by tidal forces – the same forces that drive the great volcanoes on neighboring Io. So the ice is continually melting, breaking up, and freezing, forming cracks and lanes like those in the floating ice sheets in our own polar regions. (Clarke, 1982: 55)

In principle, it does not seem reasonable to demand that science fiction ought to always be 'scientifically correct'. Fiction has obligations of coherence in relation to the universe which it depicts, which is not necessarily our own. Nevertheless, the curious thing is that in this specific case, by imagining vast oceans on moons where no liquid should exist, Clarke was right.

In September 2003, while the probe Galileo was analysing Europa, scientists realized that that moon had been harbouring a liquid ocean three times deeper than the terrestrial ones. That was the first time in which humanity faced an ethical dilemma regarding a possible alien ecosystem: should NASA keep exploring that site, and in doing so risk a possible Galilean contamination with terrestrial bacteria, or would it be wiser to destroy the probe, colliding it with Jupiter? The second alternative was chosen as not only the most ethical thing to do, but also the one that would provide interesting scientific data. As a scientist, in imagining Europa's then undetected liquid ocean,

Clarke was aware of other factors that could be present and prevent water from freezing. But as a writer, Clarke posed the question: How must we eventually deal with the primitive alien life to be found there? In 1982, this question might have been dismissed as 'fictional', 'speculative' at best, but it now describes a real-life ethical dilemma: the transition from the anthropocentric model of outward human expansion to a transhuman/Clarkean model that might be termed 'zoo-' or 'biocentric'.

Bioethical Models

Environmental ethical models are based on a fundamental question: Among all existing things, which one possesses 'intrinsic value' and which one possesses 'instrumental value'? The latter is the easier of the two to define, being the set of things or entities that are more or less useful for other creatures. The degree of utility, though, is contingent and depends upon the context. The former is more controversial, since the adjective 'intrinsic' evokes the idea of a being that possesses value on its own and for its own sake, even if there is no external observer who recognizes such value. Such beings may eventually be useful to each other, but due to the fact they are intrinsically valuable, they deserve rights and a special consideration, regardless of whether they are useful or useless in contingent contexts. However, without an external observer, who is necessarily a sentient being, all things in the universe are nothing but matter. So how could we affirm something is intrinsically valuable for its own sake? According to some philosophers, it would be more appropriate to nominate this category as 'truncated intrinsic value' (Callicott, 1985: 257–75): since the concept of 'value' is rationally created, intrinsic value is in no way antecedent to reason. For religious people, in contrast, there is an *a priori* value emanated by God that does not depend on any external observer. In spite of these disagreements, an external observer able to recognize this value is demanded.

Thus, the problem arises whereby, in admitting the concept of intrinsic value, what criterion establishes the boundary that separates what is merely instrumental from what is intrinsically precious? There is no simple answer to such a question. It is possible to demonstrate at least four models, though, that are based on different conceptions of intrinsic and instrumental value. After describing these models, we can then ask which of them better suits both transhumanists and Clarke's fiction.

Table 1 shows the four models in addition to their central moral principles and consequently their basal justification (Fogg, 2000).

Table 1. Four bioethical models

Ethical Theory	Central Moral Principle	Basis of Intrinsic Value
Anthropocentrism	Categorical Imperative	Reason
Zoocentrism	Principle of Utility	Sentience
Biocentrism	Respect for Life	Life
Cosmocentrism	Sanctity of Existence	Uniqueness

Cosmocentrism is the only one of the models to be incompatible with projects of terraforming or asteroid exploration because, even if the alien world is barren, it retains intrinsic value and must remain untouched. The stronger cosmocentric argument claims that our limited consciousness has no right to interfere in alien contexts, for they are valuable in their *uniqueness*. The value of life derives from our own interests since we are living beings whereas inanimate beings – like rocks – may well exist in a blissful state only afforded to non-living beings, and therefore we have no right to intervene in such contexts (Marshall, 1993: 227–36). However, one could also argue that worlds do not exist in isolation – as we know from the history of Earth's formation, matter and energy are exchanged between them. Since humanity is not indivisible from nature, we potentially have as much right to interact with another world as an asteroid full of bacteria is naturally free to infect a barren world with life. Although the counter-argument would be to point out the sanctity of the local eco-system, as barren as that may be, to say that inorganic beings are blissful in themselves is arguably a kind of sophistry. Since we have no way of knowing what they feel – if at all – they could equally exist in a state of despair, silently crying for an external agent that grants them life (Fogg, 2000: 205–11).

Conversely, an anthropocentric perspective asserts that the only intrinsically valuable beings are the rational ones, given that they are able to make moral decisions. Under the perspective of great monotheistic religions, humanity has a special ontological status because we are the favoured ones within the whole of the divine creation, the very image and likeness of God, therefore endowed with an *antecedent intrinsic value*. The secular perspective, as in the form of Kantian ethics, demands no gods but also defends a special ontological status for our species by claiming that since intrinsic value is our own creation it applies only to us.

It may be tempting to define anthropocentrism as environmentally destructive, since everything that is not a human being is viewed as merely instrumental. Ignorance, however, is rather a contingent element of anthropocentrism, not its essence at all. There is the possibility of an environmental anthropocentrism characterized by its enlightened self-interest in establishing a non-predatory relationship with the ecosystem (Fogg, 2000: 205–11). Given that humanity depends on a huge set of instrumentally valuable beings (plants, animals, inanimate objects), it is possible to conceive a kind of anthropocentrism that takes future generations into account. Besides, even if nature is seen as an instrument, it can still be taken care of. There is a proverb whose origin is unknown, sometimes attributed to Native Americans, sometimes to Asians, which says: 'we have not inherited the land from our ancestors, but borrowed it from our grandchildren'. Therefore, anthropocentrism is not incompatible with our survival neither with our expansion toward other worlds. On the contrary, since humanity is allegedly so special, we must care for instrumentally valuable things since we depend upon them.

However, under a zoocentrist point of view, even when a secular anthropocentrist argues that only rational entities can be intrinsically valuable, a complicated moral trap is built. If a secular anthropocentrist were to take his/her grounds seriously, we might say that people in a coma or mentally incapacitated are only instrumentally valuable.

If reason is the real core of intrinsic value, why are some individuals with very low intelligence not considered mere instruments? Besides, if reason claims to be the ontological basis for ethics, we should take into account a wide range of non-human primates who are able to use tools and to differ between right and wrong in many ways. The zoocentric ethical model enlarges the intrinsic value range by attributing it to any sentient creature. It therefore complements transhumanism, in which every sentient creature is intrinsically valuable and should not, under any circumstances, be seen as merely instrumental. Lawsuits, for example, have already been filed in several countries in order to recognize the intrinsic value and rights of apes and other mammals (Coelho, 2013; Gavin, 2014; Giménez, 2015; Ynterian, 2017). Veganism also surfaces in some transhuman manifestos (Pearce, 2007), whilst the cloning of various foods straight from the cells of living animals (Schaefer, 2018) means that farm animals could hypothetically be freed from their instrumental condition. Considering that 25% of Brazilian land is currently nothing more than pasture for cows (Dias-Filho, 2014), this territory could also be freed to become green-planned, ecologically clean cities with an enhanced quality of life for both humans and animals.

From a zoocentric perspective, when it comes to space exploration and terraforming, a dilemma occurs if – and only if – the world we intend to colonize is already inhabited by sentient creatures. But for biocentrism, a sentience-centred ethics is absolutely unsatisfying, since intrinsic value is conferred upon every living being. From a biocentric perspective, the act of terraforming a planet would be permissible only if there is no life in that world whatsoever. However, to reach such a certainty about the absence of life is a rather difficult task. A planet like Mars, for example, may be almost entirely barren, but it may harbour life in some still not explored niche.

Science fiction often describes the conflict between these competing models. Clarke, though, constantly highlights the trauma that arises in the transition from an anthropocentric to a zoocentric, sometimes biocentric model. Zoocentrism can be found in *Childhood's End*, when the aliens known as the Overlords impose an ultimatum: no animal should be exposed to unnecessary suffering or to degrading entertainment. Determined to keep their tradition untouched, Spanish people perform a bullfight. At first, there seems to be no reaction from the Overlords. However, in the very moment the bullfighter's sword strikes the bull, all humans who attend the event feel the exact same pain as the animal. The Overlords, though, only forbid animal suffering in terms of human entertainment. They continue to permit humanity to kill animals for food. Nevertheless, although the novel's zoocentric element is limited, the overall narrative makes it very clear that anthropocentricism is a stage to be overcome. In that respect, the transition from human to post-human foreshadows *2001*, in which the Starchild protects Europa's alien eco-system. In *2010*, Europa has become a biotic world under the tutelage of the Starchild.

Therefore, which answer can we offer to the ethical problems surrounding the terraforming of Mars or any other planet? It depends upon the presence of life already there – and the criteria by which we determine its status as 'life'. From the point of view of a mature anthropocentric ethics, the answer would be 'yes, we should do it', and an eventual native life would be protected as scientifically interesting (or, in other words, instrumentally valuable). In terms of a cosmocentric ethics, we should be restricted to our own planet. From a zoocentric or biocentric point of view, a planet in which we find life deserves to be preserved the way it is, and also to be protected. However, if the planet is barren, biocentrism would argue we have *the moral obligation of spreading life in there*, given that life is better than non-life.

Conclusion: Terraforming and Transhumanizing

If we consider 'humanity' to be a condition connected to our current shape and mind, we will never inhabit other worlds as 'humans'. At most, we could inhabit extraterrestrial simulations of planet Earth in which we can preserve our human condition. The act of terraforming an alien world implies transforming our own existence not only genetically but also morally. The possibility of enhancing ourselves through ethical biotechnological interventions is a typical transhuman proposal. This possible transformation from human into 'something else' is established in the eighth point of the Transhumanist Declaration: 'we favour morphological freedom – the right to modify and enhance one's body, cognition, and emotions' (Aegis et al., 2013: 55).

With regard to terraforming and space exploration, it might be that concepts such as intrinsic or instrumental value are less important, since discussion of them tends to focus upon rights rather than responsibilities. Maybe the points to consider are:

1 If all things in the universe possess equal value, then nothing is special. It is perfectly possible to think that all things in the universe possess intrinsic value, so planets have the right to be preserved the way they are, as cosmocentrism claims, but our practical actions constantly demand decisions about what is most valuable. While cosmocentrism privileges the sanctity of individual worlds, this claim also entails a balancing-act with another key aspect of cosmocentrism: that life is better than non-life. At some point, according to transhumanism, humanity will need to leave the Earth and make changes not only to other worlds but also to ourselves if we want to survive. It is unlikely in this scenario that future generations will choose collective suicide because of an exclusive cosmic-preservationist imperative.

2 It is also possible to think that all life is equally valuable, as biocentrism advocates, but that our own choices contradict such a theory. In curing a disease in humans or non-human animals, we make a judgement call that this life is better than the lives of millions of bacteria. It is theoretically possible, though, to pursue the compromise of preserving the native biota of extraterrestrial sites as far as possible. Perhaps, as Clarke suggests, a post-human entity endowed with cosmic consciousness, such as the Starchild, is able to endorse biocentrism, given that it would be like an angel or a god.

3 For the moment, it is indeed very hard to devise an ethical model beyond the one that currently guides us: an enlightened form of anthropocentrism. In realizing that reason does not endow us with more rights but more responsibility, we then have the moral obligation of minimizing suffering and taking care of beings we consider to be valuable instruments. And by taking into account that 'valuable' is a contingent adjective, we should never underestimate something that does not seem currently useful. A mature anthropocentrism must take into consideration the needs of future generations. A responsible action demands we make choices when facing dilemmas, and even if all things in the universe are seen as only

instrumentally valuable, that does not mean that they should be treated with no consideration. Our rational skills make us able to understand ourselves not as holders of special rights but as endowed with responsibility. It may be that an enlightened anthropocentrism will evolve into a fully-fledged zoocentrism: such seems to be the trajectory in Clarke's novels including *Childhood's End* and the *2001* sequence.

4 Whereas inanimate entities are universally commonplace, and no effort is needed to guarantee their existence, sentient life is a rare and fragile element subject to the vagaries of chance. Only rational beings are able to defend such rarity from the possibility of extinction. Only rational beings are able to act responsibly and to commit to preserve emerging life in other worlds. As rational beings, we are able to sow the seeds of life throughout the cosmos, restoring to that word its Ancient Greek meanings of 'beauty' and 'order'. Amidst the apparent randomness of existence, we can find an underlying harmony but only by embracing the indeterminate nature of things.

We are, so to speak, potential Starchildren, able to establish ethical plans that enable life to keep its existence or flourish on other worlds. Humans have remarkable powers and incredible technology. We can destroy everything, we can keep pretending our world is everlasting, or we can assume the protection of our world as a moral duty. As the fifth point of The Transhumanist Declaration says, 'reduction of risks of human extinction and development of means for the preservation of life [...] must be pursued as urgent priorities' (Aegis et al., 2013: 54).

Our potential is still mostly unrealized and, as pressure groups such as Extinction Rebellion argue, we are at a dangerous crossroads. Like the Starchild at the end of *2001*, we are looking at our own planet with fascination, and the power of life and death lies in our hands. In *2001*, Bowman's experience of passing through the Star Gate is akin to the condition of nirvana: he is transformed not only into the Starchild but into a kind of bodhisattva, a protector of worlds.

An ethical evolution follows the cosmic enhancement from human to Starchild and so, in *2010*, even the primitive biota inhabiting Europa becomes valuable to the point that an ultimatum is communicated to the human race: 'All these worlds are yours except Europa.

Attempt no landing here' (Clarke, 1982: 277). Clarke's message is crystal clear: humanity is only a staging-post in a long process through which consciousness flows; it is not a final form in itself. Insofar as we stretch our minds by contemplating the starry sky and even moving toward new worlds, our sense of wonder and compassion becomes greater. That is the overview effect we all *may* experience some day. In the meantime, the stars maintain their glorious indifference towards us. Still, we can continue to imagine.

Works Cited

Aegis, K. et al. (2013) 'The Transhumanist Declaration', in M. More and N. Vita-More (eds) *The Transhumanist Reader*, pp. 54–5. Chichester: Wiley-Blackwell.

Bennington-Castro, J. (2015) '10 Ways Space Technology Benefits our Earthly Existence', *USA Today*, URL (accessed December 2019): https://www.usatoday.com/story/tech/personal/technologylive/2015/10/09/10-ways-space-technology-benefits-our-earthly-existence/73657820/

Blair, B. R. (2000) 'The Role of Near-Earth Asteroids in Long-Term Platinum Supply', unpublished conference paper, Space Resources Roundtable II, Golden.

Brody, D. S. (2019) 'Terraforming: Human Destiny or Hubris?', *Space*, URL (accessed December 2019): https://www.space.com/1208-terraforming-human-destiny-hubris.html

Callicott, J. B. (1985) 'Intrinsic Value, Quantum Theory, and Environmental Ethics', *Environmental Ethics* 7(3): 257–75.

Clarke, A. C. (1953/1982) *Childhood's End*. New York: Ballantine/Del Rey..

Clarke, A. C. (1973/2006) *Rendezvous with Rama*. London: Gollancz.

Clarke, A. C. (1982) *2010: Odyssey II*. Maryland: Ballantine Books.

Coelho, S. (2013) 'Dolphins Gain Unprecedented Protection in India', *Deutsche Welle*, URL (accessed December 2019): https://www.dw.com/en/dolphins-gain-unprecedented-protection-in-india/a-16834519

Dias-Filho, M. B. (2014) *Diagnóstico das Pastagens no Brasil*. Belém: Embrapa Amazônia Oriental.

Fogg, M. J. (2000) 'The Ethical Dimensions of Space Settlement', *Space Policy* 16(3): 205–11.

Galante, D. and Hovarth, J. E. (2007) 'Biological Effects of Gamma-Ray Bursts: Distance for Severe Damage on the Biota', *International Journal of Astrobiology* 6: 19–26.

Gavin, R. (2014) 'Appeals Panel to Weigh Personhood for Chimpanzee'. *Times Union*, URL (accessed December 2019): https://www.timesunion.com/local/article/Appeals-panel-to-weigh-personhood-for-chimpanzee-5797943.php

Giménez, E. (2015) 'Argentine Orangutan Granted Unprecedented Legal Rights', *CNN*, URL (accessed December 2019): https://edition.cnn.com/2014/12/23/world/americas/feat-orangutan-rights-ruling/

Hegel, G. W. F. (1991) *Elements of The Philosophy of Right*, trans. H. B. Nisbet. Cambridge: Cambridge University Press.

Lewis, J. S. (1996) *Mining the Sky*. New York: Perseus Books.

McMahon, S. (2016) 'The Aesthetic Objection to Terraforming Mars', in T. Milligan and J. S. J. Schwartz (eds) *The Ethics of Space Exploration*, pp. 209–20. Geneva: Springer.

Marshall, A. (1993) 'Ethics and the Extraterrestrial Environment'. *Journal of Applied Philosophy* 10: 227–36.

O'Neill, I. (2008) 'The Human Brain in Space: Euphoria and the "Overview Effect" Experienced by Astronauts', *Universe Today*, URL (accessed December 2019): https://www.universetoday.com/14455/the-human-brain-in-space-euphoria-and-the-overview-effect-experienced-by-astronauts/

Pearce, D. (2007) 'The Abolitionist Project', *The Hedonistic Imperative*, URL (accessed December 2019): https://www.hedweb.com/abolitionist-project/index.html

Poole, R. (2008) *Earthrise: How Man First Saw the Earth*. New Haven, CT: Yale University Press.

Randolph, C. (2004) *American Perception of Space Exploration*. Philadelphia, PA: Center for Cultural Studies & Analysis.

Redd, N. T. (2013) 'Konstantin Tsiolkovsy: Russian Father of Rocketry', *Space*, URL (accessed December 2019): https://www.space.com/19994-konstantin-tsiolkovsky.html

Robinson, T. (2004) 'Interview: Arthur C. Clarke', *The A. V. Club*, URL (accessed December 2019): https://www.avclub.com/arthur-c-clarke-1798208319

Schaefer, G. O. (2018) 'Lab-Grown Meat', *Scientific American*, URL (accessed December 2019): https://www.scientificamerican.com/article/lab-grown-meat/

Sonter, M. J. (1998) 'The Technical and Economic Feasibility of Mining the Near-Earth Asteroids', unpublished conference paper, 49th International Astronautical Federation Congress, Melbourne.

Webster, I. (n.d.) *Asterank*, URL (accessed December 2019): https://www.asterank.com/

Wilks, A. F. (2016) 'Kantian Foundation for a Cosmocentric Ethic', in T. Milligan and J. S. J. Schwartz (eds) *The Ethics of Space Exploration*, pp. 181–94. Geneva: Springer.

Ynterian, P. A. (2017) 'Cecilia, First Chimpanzee Released by Habeas Corpus', *The Great Ape Project*, URL (accessed December 2019): https://www.projetogap.org.br/en/noticia/cecilia-first-chimpanzee-released-by-habeas-corpus/

9

Dark Forest or Grand Central
Self and Other in Liu Cixin and Arthur C. Clarke

Lyu Guangzhao

'Everything that I write', says Liu Cixin, winner of the 2015 Hugo Award for Best Novel, 'is a clumsy imitation of Arthur C. Clarke' (Qin, 2014). Despite his humbleness and reverence to his mentor 'who brought [him] along onto the path of science fiction' (Liu, 2013: 28), Liu has managed to be identified as both a 'neo-classicist' (Wu and Fang, 2006: 36–9), inheriting the elements and concerns of Anglo-American Golden Age science fiction, and probably the most influential figure in the New Wave of Chinese science fiction (Song, 2013: 86–102).

The comparison between the stories of Liu Cixin and Arthur C. Clarke reveals a number of similarities especially related to the sublime, the shaping of ethnic and world images, the control of narrative time and space, and the detailed description of science fictional technologies (Liu and Li, 2016: 134–41), indicating their shared obsession in scientism and technological optimism. Therefore, given Clarke's impact, Liu has not only subverted the 'utilitarian paradigm' (Wu, 1989: xxxvi) of the Chinese science fiction that came before him but has also become 'China's answer to Arthur C. Clarke' (Rothman, 2015).

Despite these similarities, though, there is a marked difference between Clarke and Liu when it comes to the question of whether alien civilizations will be harmful or beneficial to humanity. Clarke's fictional universes tend to be benevolent and harmonious, where 'the survival [of humans] is not everything' (Clarke, 1985: 727), since the transcendence brought about by the contact with advanced but well-meaning aliens is far more important. On the contrary, Liu in *The Three Body Problem* trilogy (2006–10), also known as the Santi trilogy, believes that civilizations will have to 'hide [themselves] well; cleanse [others] well' (Liu, 2017: 561), because everyone is confined in a cage-like universe called the 'Dark Forest'. Yet, is there a not-so-obvious logic shared by both of them? Would it be safe to just embrace Clarke's alien benevolence without second thought in order to avoid Liu's Dark Forest? What in the real world can be inferred in the two cosmic images? Seemingly, the Other would always be reduced to the sameness of the Self, while the uniqueness and diversity, represented by the crowded universe portrayed by both Clarke and Liu, would be replaced by homogeneity and absolutism.

Grand Central and Dark Forest

Regarded by Roger Luckhurst as 'the British writer who comes closest to the American model of SF' advocated by John W. Campbell (Luckhurst, 2005: 133), Clarke blended the 'scientific and technological know-how with his sense of optimism about the future of human development' (Mann, 2001: 106), with detailed literary presentation and imagination of 'either established or carefully extrapolated science as its backbone' (Nicholls, 2019). Clarke's 'optimism', in this case, while serving as the source of his imaginative and vivid descriptions of Good Samaritan aliens, refers not only to his vision of what science can potentially achieve but also to the positive impact of science upon the morality of human or alien civilizations.

Therefore, Clarke can be considered indispensable to the 'undercurrent of imagery that perceives aliens in neutral or even positive terms' during the decades when science fiction had 'for the most part abandoned' the stereotype of the Bug-Eyed Monster (Beatie, 1989: 59). Focusing instead upon 'the longing for an evolutionary leap that will release humanity from its current limitations' (Luckhurst, 2005:133), Clarke preferred to present a benevolent universe shepherded by an omnipotent, God-like civilization standing for rationality and morality. Human flaws, such as wars and violence, would thus be eventually purified through direct or indirect contact with highly advanced alien races who, instead of striving to eliminate other civilizations with their technologies, would rather altruistically protect human beings from 'powers and forces […] beyond anything that [humans] can ever imagine' (Clarke, 1953/2017: 157) and instead 'encourage its dawning' (Clarke, 1968/1998: 208) amidst other alien species.

Among the different versions of benevolent alien portrayed by Clarke, the Overlords in *Childhood's End* (1953) are probably one of the most representative images. Upon their arrival, the Overlords show 'an immense, tolerant understanding of mankind' (Clarke, 1953/2017: 15) and, through their technology and governance, remove 'at once the […] obstacle to the happiness of mankind' (Clarke, 1953/2017: 22). Human beings enter a Golden Age where 'ignorance, disease, poverty and fear had virtually ceased to exist', and the memory of war fades 'into the past as the nightmare vanishes with the dawn' (Clarke, 1953/2017: 78). Although the betterment of human society is 'paralleled by a decline in science' (Clarke, 1953/2017: 82), due to the insurmountable technological gap between humanity and the Overlords, this becomes the basis for 'a generation of children' to 'transcend physical reality and join the "Overmind"' (Roberts, 2006: 213): the Clarkian transcendence of humanity.

Even more surprisingly, it seems that the protection offered by the Overlords to prepare human beings for such a transcendence was all for free. Unable to evolve further and play any 'further part in the story of the universe' (Clarke, 1953/2017: 212), the Overlords came to Earth, under instruction from the Overmind, simply to 'bring something new and wonderful into the world' (Clarke, 1953/2017: 206). Although allowing humanity to evolve naturally without the Overlords' intervention might have resulted in a dangerous 'havoc' to the stars, it would 'not have been the threat to them [the Overlords]' (Clarke, 1953/2017: 213). This said, the Overlords have in fact provided life-or-death guidance to humanity, as well as other worlds that can travel 'along the road [they] can never follow' (Clarke, 1953/2017: 215), on behalf of the Overmind, which is beyond even their comprehension. Therefore, the altruistic nature of the Overlords and their compassion for humanity have essentially made them 'the saviours of man' and their 'envy' (Clarke, 1953/2017: 217) while humanity's potential to join the Overmind has made them, in turn, 'very human' (Beatie, 1989: 61).

The Overlords' counterpart in *2001: A Space Odyssey* (1968) appears far less human and more mystical, acting not as a protector but, to a large degree, the creator of human civilization. Although in possession of the technological power that makes them 'lords of the Galaxy', and even capable of existing beyond 'the reach of time' and 'the tyranny of matter' (Clarke, 1968/1998: 209), this unknown alien race retains 'the awe, and wonder, and loneliness' it had felt – feelings that had inspired them to 'set forth for the stars' (Clarke, 1968/1998: 207) and sow the seed of intelligence. While having intentionally modified and tinkered with the destiny of various species on the Earth through the Monolith, they literally granted Moon-Watcher's clan – perhaps the father of the entire human race – the abilities to make tools and think beyond basic questions of food and survival. One of Moon-Watcher's descendants, three million years later, is transformed into a transcendental being under the gaze of those 'omnipotent' creatures (Clarke, 1968/1998: 233): a second-stage evolution that resembles the climax to *Childhood's End*. Presumably in part inheriting the alien's mind, the Starchild dismantles the 'circling megatons' to make for 'a cleaner sky' (Clarke, 1968/1998: 252), showing little indication of violence or aggression in its nature. The numerous star-gates left behind for a newly born intelligence to '[escape] from its planetary cradle' constitute a 'Grand Central Station of the Galaxy' (Clarke, 1968/1998: 205) connecting every corner in the universe.

Here, interstellar communication and contact are expected, encouraged and cherished, which would only be possible if those highly developed creatures had long before got rid of their hostility towards each other, indicating the benevolence and rationality brought forward by scientific advancement.

However, in Liu's stories, this portal would be humanity's doomsday. While Clarke has conceived a Grand Central Station in perhaps the best of all possible universes, Liu endeavours to build 'the worst of all possible universes [...] in which existence is as dark and harsh as one can imagine' (Liu, 2014): a universe under the laws of the 'Dark Forest' where 'the only moral imperative is the recognition of zero morality, and all intelligent species compete to destroy other species' (Song, 2018: 116). Instead of practicing the benevolent help of Clarke's Good Samaritan aliens, Liu's denizens, once spotting their neighbours, automatically 'open fire and eliminate them' (Liu, 2016: 521) – a will to survive where 'people will become non-people' (Liu, 2016: 480). The ultimate transcendence of humanity with the aliens' help is nowhere to be seen, and any exposed location of a potential civilization, whether 'an angel or a demon, a delicate infant or a tottering old man' (Liu, 2016: 521), at once attracts merciless and annihilative attack from its enemy – that is, everyone else.

In *The Three Body Problem* trilogy, Liu's Dark Forest, in the opposite of Clarke's benign universe, is based on two ostensibly self-evident axioms: (1) 'survival is the primary need of civilisation'; and (2) 'Civilisation continuously grows and expands, but the total matter in the universe remains constant' (Liu, 2016: 6). The Dark Forest is therefore a Social Darwinist scenario. Subject to an assumption that all the entities participating in the game of survival 'are mortal and degradable and they need to consume materials and energy in order to survive or minimise degradation' under an 'omnipresent problem of local and immediate scarcity' (Hodgson and Knudsen, 2012: 33), Social Darwinism would only be valid with 'the pressure of population growth on resources [that] generated a struggle for existence among organisms' (Hawkins, 1997: 31). Therefore, in this case, the permanent struggle for existence and the resource scarcity are the core elements that have made our universe a Dark Forest:

Every civilisation is an armed hunter stalking through the trees like a ghost, gently pushing aside branches that block the path and trying to tread without sound [...] The hunter has to be careful, because everywhere in the forest are stealthy hunters like him. If he finds others [...] there's only one thing he can do: open fire and eliminate them. In this universe, hell is other people. An eternal threat that any life that exposes its own existence will be swiftly wiped out. (Liu, 2016: 521)

Since intelligent life, represented by the Trisolarans, can be found in the nearest neighbour of humanity's sun, the universe must be crowded by countless civilizations fighting for limited resources – a conflict that can never really cease because of the impossibility of identifying whether other worlds are benevolent or malicious (through 'the chain of suspicion'), and of the possibility that even the weakest civilization, if neglected and remaining at large, may one day become a serious danger due to a 'technological explosion' (Liu, 2016: 517–21). Therefore, annihilation becomes the safest, even the most economical solution.

Realizing this universal truth, humanity manages to stop the Trisolarans' military invasion by threatening to broadcast the locations of both Earth and Trisolaris, making both civilizations marked targets for other deadly hunters in the Dark Forest. Ultimately, though, this effort is in vain, since eventually everyone in the universe, including the attackers, will be the victim. This pessimistic ending underlines that 'the nature of [Liu's] universe is fundamentally amoral' (Song, 2018: 120). The Clarkian transcendence of humanity is unthinkable in the Dark Forest, where it is replaced by the 'autotomy' of hunters in the game of survival: 'If I destroy you, what business is it of yours?' (Liu, 2016: 446).

The Self, the Other and the Chain of Suspicion

Clarke, then, tends to treat the universe as a kind place benevolent to the survival and transcendental evolution of humanity, where 'any conceptual breakthrough will only strengthen our resolve and teach us to live as a unified race instead of as warring factions' (Mann, 2001: 108). Liu, after developing 'an ever-deeper attachment to the heart and soul of [science fiction]', noticed a 'sudden [yet uncomfortable] waver' of his moral beliefs, and carefully set up an experiment in *The Three Body Problem* trilogy into how humanity could adapt to 'extreme situations' (Liu, 2013: 29).[1] He challenged Clarke's benign view via the introduction of the Dark Forest applicable to every single creature in his fictional universe, advanced or primitive, where benevolence and enlightenment are replaced by holocaust and eradication. Here, the famous Monolith in *2001*, a 'passive yet almost arrogant display of geometrical perfection' (Clarke, 1968/1998: 185), has even become 'a supercilious demonstration of power' (Liu, 2016: 444–5).[2]

However, despite the ostensible contrast in their conceptions of the universe, Clarke and Liu do share one thing in common through their presentations of human-alien contact – the superiority of the Self over the Other. This dynamic, while operating under a 'prevailing trend in epistemological reflection [...] to reduce objectivity more and more to the subject' (Adorno, 1973: 176), regards the Self as the fixed starting-point from which to make sense of the Other. In science fiction, though, it should not be viewed only in terms of an interaction 'between terran self and alien other' (Malmgren, 1993: 15). The Trisolarans, the Overmind and the builders of the Star Gate could all, on their own terms, be regarded as versions of the Self looking upon the human civilization as the distant Other. Here, the central Self would 'confer meaning upon [the Others] by either helping or forcing [them] to adopt a particular world view and to define [their] positions therein' (Cavallaro, 2001: 121). Therefore, being the Self is not the privilege of humanity, given that, if put in the Nietzschean manner, when you (the Self) look long into an abyss (where you think could reside various possibilities of the Other), the abyss also looks into you.

From this perspective, Liu and Clarke are also involved in such a 'theory of knowledge known as "other minds"' and, in the process of looking into the abyss, concerned with the following issues: (1) 'whether we can know that other beings have thoughts and feelings and, if so, how we can know it'; (2) 'whether, assuming we could establish beyond doubt that other beings indeed have mental lives, we could know that they resembled our own'; and (3) 'whether we could interpret other beings' behaviour (physical, cultural, linguistic) as a reliable reflection of how they think and feel' (Cavallaro, 2001: 122). The answers to these questions, to a large degree, determine the author's attitude towards the human-alien encounter and eventually shape their overall image of the fictional universe. In this case, while facing a potential contact with aliens, things and creatures that humanity knows little about, Liu has claimed rather clearly that 'we should be ever vigilant, and be ready to attribute the worst of intentions to any Others that might exist in space' (Liu, 2015: 430): a motto that every hunter in his Dark Forest would firmly hold as the truth.

This kind of 'worst intentions' ascribed to the Other, in *The Three Body Problem* trilogy, can be most distinctly identified in the 'chain of suspicion' that appears as one of the premises of Liu's universal theory of the Dark Forest, initially illustrated in the 'Battle of Darkness'. After humanity's space-based army is annihilated by a single Trisolaran space probe (Liu, 2016: 463), the seven human warships that survive this disaster find themselves in an eerie situation – while the planet that they once called home has been turned into a 'death trap' by the Trisolarans, the ships have 'to accept the responsibility of carrying [human] civilization forward [...] to fly onward, and fly far [into the unknown]' (Liu, 2016: 470), taking the hostile universe as their final resting-place. Despite or because of their precarious situation, 'vipers [...] come out [...] climbing up people's souls' (Liu, 2016: 482), warning them of a subtle yet unspeakable relation among the remaining spaceships: since their cosmic journeys will be calculated by millennia, all their resources, including fuel, part replacement and hibernation necessities, are only enough for a single ship along with a limited number of crew members. Therefore, Liu poses a similar question to that of Tom Godwin in his story 'The Cold Equations' (1954), either 'someone must die, or everyone will die' (Liu, 2016: 486). Who, or which ship, will be the lucky one? In this 'extreme situation', Liu proposes one of his most significant thought experiments:

'We don't want to become devils [to kill others], but who knows what they're thinking.'
'Then we're already devils, or how else could we think of them as devils unprovoked?'
'Very well, then we won't think of them as devils, [...] [but] the problem remains.'
'Because they don't know what we're thinking.'
'Suppose they know that we're not devils?'
'The problem still exists.'
'They don't know what we're thinking about what they're thinking about us.'
[...]
'That carries on in an endless chain of suspicion: They don't know what we're thinking about what they're thinking about what we're thinking about.' (Liu, 2016: 488)

In face of an 'insurmountable wall' (Liu, 2016: 488), the human survivors divide into seven self-enclosed entities based upon the ships to which they belong, each seeing the other as unapproachable and incomprehensible, and their own entity as the Self whose survival is thus endangered by the existence of the Other. This is the motive for the 'Battle of Darkness', but also the 'microcosm of cosmic civilisation' (Liu, 2016: 516).

Through introducing the 'chain of suspicion', Liu constructs an unbreakable polarity between Us and Them, the Self and the Other, which is also applicable to his larger image of the entire universe. All the hunter civilizations in the Dark Forest, under Liu's manifesto that 'the universe is big, but life is bigger', suffer from the relative scarcity of resources since 'the total amount of matter in the universe remains constant' (Liu, 2016: 6). Any hypothetical attempt for friendly communication is daunted, and then stopped, by the possibility of exposing the location of their planet to apocalyptic danger, and by the impossibility of dissolving the 'chain of suspicion' due to the vast distance and biological differences between alien civilisations. Therefore, given that 'survival is the primary need of civilisation' (Liu, 2016: 6), the only safe way for the Self is to annihilate the dangerous and unreachable Others at first sight.

Meanwhile, the myopic concentration upon the Self is strengthened further in *The Three Body Problem* trilogy by neglecting the distinguishable features of the Other. Here in the 'chain of suspicion', the 'morality and social structure [of other civilizations]' is unrelated, because 'regardless of whether civilisations are internally benevolent or malicious, when they enter the web formed by chains of suspicion, they're all identical' (Liu, 2016: 519). Being identical in the eyes of the Self, the Others whose 'factors of chaos and randomness in the complex makeups of every civilised society in the universe get filtered out by the distance' (Liu, 2016: 5–6) become 'just a collection of points in space with a clear mathematical configuration' (Liu, 2016: 233). In other words, in the universe crowded by numerous civilizations, the idealized Self is the only entity who has agency in Liu's story, and the only identity in which all the races see themselves. On this account, the bodily and behavioural symbols of the Others beyond the reach of the Self, accordingly, are deprived by a means termed as 'dehumanisation' by the sociologist Zygmunt Bauman, which 'starts at the point when, thanks to the distantiation, the objects [...] can and are reduced to a set of quantitative measures' (Bauman, 1989: 102).

Through his conception of the Dark Forest, Liu has managed to conceive, in science fictional terms, a binary opposition between the Self, who has to deny any potential communication with other 'hunters', and the Other, whose unique features – social, behavioural and ideological – are all stripped away and 'viewed with indifference' (Bauman, 1989: 103). Since the Self could be any civilisation that regards their survival as the only priority, Liu establishes 'an arena for a Hobbesian war of all against all, in which the only possible relation between sentient beings [whose sentient characteristics will be deprived when viewed as the Other] is antagonism' (Malmgren, 1993: 18), a universe 'whose evolution comes down to an embodiment of the principle of "Civilisations as a wolf to Civilisation"' (Lem, 1986: 247). The polarity between the narcissistic Self and the unapproachable Other, as well as the consequent annihilative war, concurs with the real-world legacy of the political scientist Samuel Huntington's controversial argument that war 'rarely ends permanently' and is never 'marked by [...] comprehensive peace treaties that resolve central political issues' (Huntington, 2002: 291). These irresolvable political issues, while echoing with the dilemma in *The Three Body Problem* trilogy between the survival of civilizations and the relative resource scarcity in the universe, prefigures a Dark Forest where 'In our eyes, the stars appear as ghosts; in the eyes of the stars, we appear as ghosts' (Liu, 2017: 564). Even so, Liu's misanthropic imagery by no means indicates his agreement with Huntington or his advocacy for an all-against-all future, through which he manages to raise his concerns regarding the ever-increasing conflict in contemporary China between science and humanity.

The Gardener and the Weed

In contrast with the pessimistic, amoral imagery of Liu's science fictional universe, Clarke's 'particular brand of optimistic Hard SF has inspired many writers the world over' (Mann, 2001: 108). But interestingly, his conception of a benevolent and friendly universe fostering an eventual transcendence of humanity, guided by a God-like and Good Samaritan alien Messiah, also indicates the same polarity between the Self and the Other, only in a different way. This time, the dynamic between the two ends of Liu's chain of suspicion is apparently not annihilative or malicious to each other in terms of how they interact, but it is through these interactions that they also reveal 'a reduction of the other to the same [of the Self]' (Levinas, 1979: 43).

In this case, according to Bauman's usage of Claude Lévi-Strauss's terminology, two formulae can be attributed to the polarity of Self and Other demonstrated in Clarke's novels: (1) the 'anthropophagic' strategies that suggest to '"[eat] up" the strangers so that they are assimilated by the body of the eater and become identical with its other cells, having lost their own distinctiveness'; and (2) the 'anthropoemic' strategies that aim to '"[vomit]" and "[spit] out" those "unfit to be us", either isolating them by incarcerating them inside the visible walls of the ghettos or the invisible (though no less tangible for this reason) walls of cultural prohibitions', or in other words 'by round-ing them up, deporting them or forcing them to run away' (Bauman, 2000: 175–6). The seemingly transcendent and visionary ending of *Childhood's End*, where humanity is absorbed 'into something greater and totally alien' (James, 1994: 78), becomes less reassuring to the degree that the Overmind sees itself as the source of justice and peace in the universe. The Overmind, a super-egotistical version of the Self, imposes its mysterious yet centralized idea upon human beings and other intellectual civilizations – a process where humanity, while losing its unique and distinctive characteristics, is reduced to a part of the Others who need to be absorbed into the self-sameness of the Overmind.

Therefore, humanity, as observed by Jan Rodricks the stowaway, 'could never be more than an inferior species' who has been 'preserved in an out-of-the-way zoo with the Overlords as keepers' (Clarke, 1953/2017: 223), and who will eventually be 'eaten up', trained and educated by the Overmind who 'must be the sum of many races' (Clarke, 1953/2017: 215). Throughout *Childhood's End*, human beings are guided by the Overlords into an understanding of their place within the hierarchy of the universe, under the doctrines and values forced by the Overmind who views humanity, as well as any other worlds, 'in the early flower of [their] civilisation', 'the clay that is being shaped on that wheel' (Clarke, 1953/2017: 215). The ostensibly harmonious universe dominated by the Overmind who maintains the final interpretation of its spreading and incorporative ideology should instead be regarded 'as a collection of so many "problems" to be solved, as a "nature" to be "controlled", "mastered" and "improved" or "remade", as a legitimate target for "social engineering", and in general a garden to be designed and kept in the planned shape by force' (Bauman, 1989: 18).

Despite previous positive interpretations of Clarke's cosmic benevolence, his conception of the Self-Other dynamic still indicates a potential danger. Here in this garden, the vegetation (the Other) is divided into 'cultured plants' to be taken care of, the last generation of human children protected by Karellen as well as the Overmind whom they will finally become, and 'weeds' to be exterminated, namely the rest of humanity and any other Earth species who might interfere the children's transformation: 'All the trees and grass, all the living creatures that had inhabited this land, flickered out of existence and were gone' (Clarke, 1953/2017: 239). These dehumanized children are deemed to be the only significant beings in the universe according to the designs of the Overmind, while the Other remains meaningless and therefore should be sacrificed. As Karellen says, 'The stars are not for Man' (Clarke, 1953/2017: 157), because deep space is the reserved place for the 'cultured plants' – those able to either join or serve for, and thus be 'eaten up' by, the Self (the Overmind), while the Other, considered 'unfit', is 'spat out' and confined as a 'prisoner' (Clarke, 1953/2017: 105).

Similarly, the Overmind's counterparts in *2001* can also be seen as followers of Bauman's 'anthropophagic' and 'anthropoemic' strategies. Identifying Moon-Watcher's clan, among 'many species on land and in the ocean' (Clarke, 1968/1998: 208), as the chosen ones who might possess the Mind (the very symbol to distinguish the Self from the Other), the owners of the Star Gates 'became farmers in the fields of stars; they sowed, and sometimes they reaped [...] sometimes, dispassionately, they had to weed' (Clarke, 1968/1998: 208). Hence, the cultivation of the Mind, when Moon-Watcher and his companions are 'compelled to follow the lesson' (Clarke, 1968/1998: 18) and in this way 'programmed' (Clarke, 1968/1998: 20) to use simple tools, is positively viewed as a leap in human evolution; the first step in humanity's transcendence from the brutish Other to the omnipotent Self: Bowman's abandonment of name and body, and his transformation into the Starchild. However, the other creatures in the universe, who also undertook the training yet failed to uncover the Monolith, are forever trapped in their 'planetary cradle' (Clarke, 1968/1998: 207) and thus locked out of the ascent of Mind.

From this perspective, the seemingly benevolent and harmonious cosmic community described by the metaphor of the Grand Central Station, which connects numerous intellectual civilizations triggered by the enlightenment via the same creator, appears more as a representation of the dominance and controlling power of the Self over the Other – the inferior beings that cannot survive without following the universal guidance and being assimilated as an indistinguishable cell of the 'eater'. Although both images of the Self in *2001* and *Childhood's End* are well-known for their highly developed technology, morality and rationality, the way in which they are presented still forms a Clarkian world where 'one can be "master"' and a fictional universe where 'transcendence is possible and can lead to true superiority: a universe in which masters may justify their status as part of the Order of Things' (Erlich, 1987: 122). This hierarchy is particularly dangerous in the sense that 'a staunch preacher and defender of rationality', the prototype of the God-like beings in the two stories, could be easily turned into 'the most sinister, cruel, bloody-minded ruler' (Bauman, 1989: 203), who may one day usher in the Holocaust of the Other.

Conclusion

When granted the Clarke Award for Imagination in Service to Society in November 2018, Liu again paid homage to his mentor: 'As a sci-fi writer, I have been striving to continue Arthur C. Clarke's imagination [...] I have always written about the magnitude and mysteries of the universe, interstellar expeditions, and the lives and civilizations happening in distant worlds' (Liu, 2018). Inheriting from Clarke a steadfast scientism and technological optimism, Liu does not, however, reconstruct the benevolent and enlightening Clarkian cosmic environment where humanity can reach an ultimate transcendence with the altruistic help of powerful aliens. Instead, under the premises of Social Darwinism, he has conceived of 'the worst of all possible universes' where civilizations are hostile and malicious to each other, and to survive in such a dangerous universe, humans have to endeavour to become the 'fittest'.

Despite their different conceptions of the universe and the nature of alien life-forms, Liu and Clarke coincide in their understanding of the dynamic between Self and Other. In *The Three Body Problem* trilogy, Liu introduces a chain of suspicion where every civilization sees themselves as the only subject with agency, and in so doing become the absolute Self while other beings are reduced to mere points, identical to one another, unreachable and incommunicable that should be eradicated. By contrast, *Childhood's End* and *2001* envision a garden-like hierarchy, but in which the master Self, empowered by science and rationality, either consumes or rejects the Other. Although such visions have earned Liu and Clarke global reputations, the real-world legacies of genocides from the Jewish Holocaust to those in Cambodia, Rwanda and Myanmar point out the risk of the all-against-all Hobbesian war or the domination of a central power based upon the subjugation of the Other to the Self.

Notes

1 This article, published in the 2013 special issue of *Science Fiction Studies* on Chinese science fiction, was revised and abridged during the translation. In the original version published in 2009, Liu Cixin drew upon Tom Godwin's short story, 'The Cold Equations' (1954), and extended this discussion by proposing a rather utilitarian paradox – whether to save six billion people by letting one hundred million of us die. His answer, which can be implied from a later interview (Jiang and Liu, 2011: 65–6), is a definite yes.

2 In *The Dark Forest*, Liu Cixin explicitly quotes from Arthur C. Clarke concerning the monolith, which is often viewed as the homage that Liu paid to his mentor, but meanwhile he makes a change in describing the embedded meaning of the Monolith from 'the geometrical perfection' to 'the display of alien power'. In the English version, however, the translator Joel Martinsen ignores Liu's wording difference while maintaining Clarke's original narration (Liu, 2016: 444–5).

Works Cited

Adorno, T.W. (1973) *Negative Dialectics*, trans. E.B. Ashton. London: Routledge.
Bauman, Z. (1989) *Modernity and the Holocaust*. Cambridge: Polity Press.
Bauman Z. (2000) *Liquid Modernity*. Cambridge: Polity Press.
Beatie, B.A. (1989) 'Arthur C. Clarke and Alien Encounter: The Background of *Childhood's End*', *Extrapolation* 30(1): 53–69.
Cavallaro, D. (2001) *Critical and Cultural Theory: Thematic Variations*. London: The Athlone Press.
Clarke, A.C. (1968/1998) *2001: A Space Odyssey*. London: Orbit.

Clarke, A. C. (1985) *2001: A Space Odyssey; The City and the Stars; The Deep Range; A Fall of Moondust; Rendezvous with Rama*. London: Heinemann/ Octopus.

Clarke, A. C. (1953/2017) *Childhood's End*. London: Pan.

Erlich, R. D. (1987).'Ursula K. Le Guin and Arthur C. Clarke on Immanence, Transcendence and Massacres', *Extrapolation* 28(2): 105–29.

Hawkins, M. (1997) *Social Darwinism in European and American thought, 1860–1945: Nature as Model and Nature as Threat*. Cambridge: Cambridge University Press.

Hodgson, G. M. and T. Knudsen. (2012) *Darwin's Conjecture: The Search for General Principles of Social and Economic Evolution*. Chicago, IL: University of Chicago Press.

Huntington, S. P. (2002) *The Clash of Civilizations and the Remaking of World Order*. London: The Free Press.

James, E. (1994) *Science Fiction in the Twentieth Century*. Oxford: Oxford University Press.

Jiang, X. and B. Liu (2011) 'Niansui Zhongguo Kehuan Xiaoshuo de Santi Xilie' ['The Three Body Trilogy that Crushes Chinese Science Fiction'], *China Book Review* 2: 63–9.

Lem, S. (1986) *Microworlds: Writings on Science Fiction and Fantasy*. London: Harvest/HBJ.

Levinas, E. (1979) *Totality and Infinity: An Essay on Exteriority*, trans. Alphonso Lingis. London: Martinus Nijhoff Publishers.

Liu, C. (2013) 'Beyond Narcissism: What Science Fiction Can Offer Literature', trans. Holger Nahm and Gabriel Ascher, *Science Fiction Studies* 40(1): 22–32.

Liu, C. (2014) 'The Worst of All Possible Universes and the Best of All Possible Earths: *Three Body* and Chinese Science Fiction', trans. Ken Liu, URL (accessed 14 November 2018): https://www.tor.com/2014/05/07/the-worst-of-all-possible-universes-and-the-best-of-all-possible-earths-three-body-and-chinese-science-fiction/

Liu, C. (2015) *The Three Body Problem*, trans. Ken Liu. London: Head of Zeus.

Liu, C. (2016). *The Dark Forest*, trans. Joel Martinsen. London: Head of Zeus.

Liu, C. (2017) *Death's End*, trans. Ken Liu. London: Head of Zeus.

Liu, C. (2018) 'Remarks by Imagination Awardee Cixin Liu', The Clarke Foundation, URL (accessed 22 April 2020): http://www.clarkefoundation.org/wp-content/uploads/2018/11/Liu-Cixin-Speech.pdf

Liu, G. and Y. Li (2016) 'The Acceptance of Arthur Clarke in *The Three-Body Problem* by Liu Cixin', *Foreign Literature Studies* 2: 134–41.

Luckhurst, R. (2005) *Science Fiction*. Cambridge: Polity Press.

Malmgren, C. D. (1993) 'Self and Other in SF: Alien Encounters', *Science Fiction Studies* 20(1): 15–33.

Mann, G. (2001) *The Mammoth Encyclopaedia of Science Fiction*. London: Robinson.

Nicholls, P. (2019) 'Hard SF', in John Clute and David Langford (eds) *The Encyclopaedia of Science Fiction*, URL (accessed 22 April 2020): http://www.sf-encyclopedia.com/entry/hard_sf

Qin, A. (2014) 'In a Topsy-Turvy World, China Warms to Sci-Fi – Liu Cixin's "The Three-Body Problem" is Published in U. S.', *The New York Times* (10 November), URL (accessed 14 November 2018): https://www.nytimes.com/2014/11/11/books/liu-cixins-the-three-body-problem-is-published-in-us.html?_r=2

Roberts, A. (2006) *The History of Science Fiction*. Basingstoke: Palgrave Macmillan.

Rothman, J. (2015) 'China's Arthur C. Clarke', *The New Yorker* (6 March), URL (accessed 22 April 2020): https://www.newyorker.com/books/page-turner/chinas-arthur-c-clarke

Song, M. (2013) 'Variations on Utopia in Contemporary Chinese Science Fiction', *Science Fiction Studies* 40(1): 86–102.

Song, M. (2018) 'Liu Cixin's *Three-Body Trilogy*: Between the Sublime Cosmos and the Micro Era', in Dale Knickerbocker (Ed.) *Lingua Cosmica: Science Fiction from around the World*, pp. 107–28. Urbana: University of Illinois Press.

Wu, D. (1989) 'Looking Backward: An Introduction to Chinese Science Fiction', in D. Wu and P. D. Murphy (eds) *Science Fiction from China*, pp. xi-xli. London: Praeger.

Wu, Y. and X. Fang (2006) 'Liu Cixin yu Xin Gudian Zhuyi Kehuan Xiaoshuo' ['Liu Cixin and Neo-classical Science Fiction'], *Journal of Hunan University of Science and Engineering* 27(2): 36–9.

10

'Big Dumb Objects', Conceptual Breakthroughs and the *Technologiade* in Arthur C. Clarke and Iain M. Banks

Joseph S. Norman

Space opera is obsessed with cosmic anomalies, ancient relics from lost civilizations, and colossal structures somewhere between planet-sized spaceships and piloted planets. This trope is widely known as the 'Big Dumb Object' (BDO), a term coined by Roz Kaveney in 1981. While the BDO appears in sf as far back as the 1930s, it is closely associated in the popular imagination with two works by Arthur C. Clarke: *2001: A Space Odyssey* (1968) and *Rendezvous with Rama* (1973). The appearance of these texts coincided with the early sf reading of a later British star, Iain M. Banks. Banks prolifically read sf from the famous yellow-jacketed Gollancz classics range during the 1970s and 1980s (Murray, 2002), a series that included several of Clarke's works, and, many years later, Banks would identify Clarke as a major influence on his writing (Rawlison, 2009). This influence is clearest upon his ten-text series featuring the 'Culture', Banks's name for his personal vision of an interstellar, utopian meta-civilization, which he envisioned whilst drafting the novel *Use of Weapons* in 1974. It is in the fifth Culture book *Excession* (1996), however, that Banks would most prominently include a BDO (the novel's titular object), which he uses to subvert the parameters of the trope as developed and popularized by Clarke.

Clarke and Banks respectively wrote and begun developing some of the most quintessential space opera at the turn of the 1970s, a fertile period in the Search for Extraterrestrial Intelligence (SETI), including the NASA-funded study Project Cyclops in 1971 and reception of the famous 'WOW signal' at the Ohio State SETI program. Although the radical reformulation of sf during the 1960s and 1970s known as the New Wave had encouraged an anti-space opera streak, prominent examples of the sub-genre were published during these decades, most notably Samuel R. Delany's *Nova* (1968), Larry Niven's *Ringworld* (1970) and Frederik Pohl's *Gateway* (1977). It was not until the mid-1980s that editorials in *Interzone* magazine would instigate a revival with Banks's Culture series at the forefront. *Excession* forms one part of Banks's broader project of using the Culture series to explicitly overturn the conventions and politics of Golden Age space opera, which he saw as often conservative, imperialistic and right-wing (Newman, 1986: 41–2).

While the parallels between the work of Clarke and Banks have not yet been comprehensively explored, Paul Kincaid notes that Banks's Culture story 'Descendent' (1986) 'reads like a variation' on Clarke's 'Summertime on Icarus' (1960) (Kincaid, 2017: 38), with both sharing the theme of a stranded man walking on a moon to survive. Banks also pays a playful homage to Clarke in his novella 'The State of the Art' (1989) in which a character attends a dinner party dressed in a '*2001*-style spacesuit with a zig zag across the chest' (Banks, 1991: 172). This chapter continues this exploration by placing *Excession* and *Rendezvous with Rama* in the context of Istvan Csicsery-Ronay's concept of the *technologiade*, drawing upon the four-stage narrative model for sf – Nova, Cognitive Estrangement, Conceptual Breakthrough, Topia – outlined by John Clute in *Pardon This Intrusion* (2011). I briefly trace the history of the BDO, outlining the ways in which it is developed by Banks and Clarke, and explore the philosophical and linguistic effects of the BDO in terms of sf's rational sublime. I compare Banks's vision of utopia in the Culture series with the seemingly anti-utopian stance of Clarke, and argue that *Rendezvous* is a quintessential example of Csicsery-Ronay's 'techno-Robinsonade' while *Excession* is a successful subversion of space opera.

Methodology: (New) Space Opera, the *Technologiade* and Techno-Utopia

BDOs are an important part of what Csicsery-Ronay identifies as sf's 'distinctive myth or storytelling formula': 'the *technologiade*, the epic of the struggle surrounding the transformation of the cosmos into a technological regime' (Csicsery-Ronay, 2008: 217). There is no better illustration of the *technologiade* than Stanley Kubrick's famous match cut from raised femur to bone-like far-future spacecraft in the film version of *2001*, which describes the trajectory of humankind's development, from our evolutionary past into our future colonization of space, using our reliance upon the mastery and application of tools. The *technologiade* is conveyed through one of two 'dialectically related forms': 'the expansive *space opera* and the intensive techno-Robinsonade' (Csicsery-Ronay, 2008: 217). Banks's *Excession*, for example, follows many space-operatic conventions in the vast, intergalactic scale it achieves and the various world-systems it describes (empires, federations, hegemonies, civilizations, etc.). John Clute and David Langford define the Robinsonade as 'the romance of solitary survival in such inimical (though ultimately compliant) terrains as desert islands (or planets), seen as a success-story' (Clute and Langford, 2018). *Rendezvous* therefore, in which a small group of scientists explore an alien location, the deserted spacecraft Rama, modernizes such a narrative into the quintessential techno-Robinsonade.

In each case, these BDOs represent the emergence of a previously unpredicted and radically new development, which may prove to be a new stage of techno-scientific development or a kind of mystical appearance. As such, the initial appearance of this novum forms the first stage of Clute's narrative model, which charts the same pattern of radical techno-scientific change as Csicsery-Ronay's *technologiade*: the effects of the novum upon those who see it and interact with it (cognitive estrangement), the changes in thought and techno-science that it represents (conceptual breakthrough), and finally the new socio-political effects that it potentially ushers in (topia).

Nova: BDOs, Macrostructures, Alien Artefacts

The first appearance of the BDO in sf can be traced back to Olaf Stapledon's *Star Maker* (1937), which makes reference to a type of megastructure that encompasses a star in order to exploit its energy. This hypothetical phenomenon became known as a 'Dyson Sphere', following Freeman Dyson's influential 1960 paper 'Search for Artificial Stellar Sources of Infrared Radiation' (Langford, 2012). Dyson described the concept as the logical consequence of the escalating energy needs of a technological civilization and would be a necessity for its long-term survival. Banks regularly described the Orbitals (Os) he developed for the Culture series as Dyson Spheres, a variety directly inspired by the titular object of Niven's *Ringworld*: an approximately 1.6 million-km-long ring that encircles a sun-like star, producing its own artificial gravity. Banks's Os feature a hugely powerful artificial intelligence (AI) at their core, known as the Hub, which coordinates the everyday state bureaucracy of this habitat.

Langford and Peter Nicholls, however, offer a definition of the BDO as 'vast enigmatic constructions' which shifts the focus away from such human endeavour:

> As a rule these have been built by a mysterious, now-disappeared race of alien intellectual giants [...] and humans can only guess at their purpose, though the very fact of being confronted by such artefacts regularly modifies or confounds their mental programming and brings them that much closer to a conceptual breakthrough into a more transcendent state of intellectual awareness. (Langford and Nicholls, 2018)

Nicholls suggests the alternative terms 'megalotropic sf' and 'alien artefacts' (Nicholls, 1997), while the entry itself offers 'Macrostructure' as a more specific and accurate alternative. Yet this term, while useful, fails to convey the mysteriousness of artefacts like Clarke's Monolith and Rama, or Banks's Excession. The term does, however, operate as a general descriptor for huge constructions, without suggesting a purpose for their existence or the identity of their builder. I therefore use macrostructure as a neutral umbrella term for four main types:

1 the BDO, as described above, whose sense of wonder is achieved by mystery, its frequently extraterrestrial origins and its promise of conceptual breakthrough;

2 Artificial Habitats: huge human-made homes in space, such as Banks's Os and General Systems Vehicles (GSVs), Ringworlds, etc., or numerous megatextual examples of the generation starship;

3 smaller but still Big *Practical* Objects, such as the space elevators in Clarke's *Fountains of Paradise* (1979) or Banks's *Feersum Endjinn* (1994), created for a specific purpose, usually highly functional and which convey a sense of wonder through the careful build-up of rational explanation that such a feat of engineering *is not impossible* for human beings to achieve, and with the potential for other radically new projects; and

4 Big *Sentient* Objects, such as the planet-sized extra-terrestrials that Banks named 'Giant Behemauthors' in *Look to Windward* (2000), conveying a sense of wonder simply by the fact that *biological* entities can exist at such a great size.

This chapter is primarily concerned with the first of these macrostructures. Jerome Winter argues that the Golden Age 'trope of salvaging ancient, hyperadvanced alien technology' becomes an 'intertextual reference point for the movement known as New Space Opera to be found, for instance, in Iain M. Banks' (Winter, 2016: 1). Winter draws parallels between Banks and Clarke, noting that 'the trope has reached saturation point, incubated perhaps by the monolith-spawned Star Child in Stanley Kubrick's *2001: A Space Odyssey*' (Winter, 2016: 1), which had developed from Clarke's short stories 'The Sentinel' (1951) and 'Encounter in the Dawn' (1953).

The manner in which Clarke and Banks use the various BDOs they feature in their fiction may differ in certain respects, but they are all ultimately linked by a strong suggestion that they have been *constructed* artificially rather than evolved naturally. In 'The Sentinel', the monolith – that most famous of BDOs – is a 'glittering pyramidal structure, twice as high as a man, that was set in the rock like a gigantic many-faceted jewel' (Clarke, 2001b: 305) located on the Moon – a form that suggests ancient human monuments, such as the ziggurats of Mesopotamia and the pyramids of Ancient Egypt. It is even suggestive of widely discredited 'ancient astronauts' hypotheses about extraterrestrial contact with early human civilizations: the BDO narrative that underwrites the space opera franchise *Stargate* (1994–). By the time Clarke developed his earlier stories into the novelization of *2001*, the monolith had become 'a rectangular slab, three times his [Heywood Floyd's] height but narrow enough to span with his arms, and it was made of some completely transparent material', located on a moon of Saturn, which later glows with a 'milky luminescence' (Clarke, 1968/2000: 12–13), and emanates a kaleidoscopic display of light, shape and colour. Having considered a pyramidal shape for the monolith in his eponymous film, Kubrick eventually opted (for practical reasons) for a black, slab-like cuboid located on Jupiter (Agel, 2018). Similarly, the titular object from Clarke's *Rendevzous* is an object shaped and constructed in a manner that makes it clearly artificial, 'a cylinder so geometrically perfect that it might have been turned on a gigantic lathe' (Clarke, 1973/2006: 9), while the Excession that Banks describes is a colossal black-bodied sphere that suddenly appears in space. The evolving shape of the monolith across media maintains a consistent logic, with each change in shape maintaining a desire to suggest an object that seems impossible to appear as a product of nature, and which must have been fashioned by sentient, intelligent creatures, with possibly extraterrestrial-humanoid, but probably extraterrestrial-alien, origins.

Effect: BDOs, The Sublime and Cognitive Estrangement

BDO are not just distinguished from other macrostructures by shape, however, but also, as Langford and Nicholls's definition emphasizes, by their effect. It is certainly true that, for much of the texts, the characters in *Rendezvous*, *2001* and *Excession* can do little more than speculate upon the purpose of the BDOs they face. But BDOs do more than simply confound, with the effect that they have upon those who face them often achieving that of the sublime: 'a response to a shock of imaginative expansion, a complex recoil and recuperation of self-consciousness coping with phenomena suddenly perceived to be too great to be comprehended' (Csicsery-Ronay, 2008: 146).

However, as Christopher Palmer explains, the sense of sublime excess operates differently to that of Romantic narrative forms such as the Gothic, tending to be 'itself of a particular, carefully focused – or restricted – kind. The BDO is not spooky or in some palpable way haunted' (Palmer, 2006: 97). Instead, the BDO's sublime effect is achieved by focusing on the contrast between the power and scale of the Object and the relative insignificance and banality of the humans who view it, avoiding the breathless 'lofty language' that Harold Bloom argues has long been 'vital to the effect' (Palmer, 2006: 97). Palmer, for example, notes Clarke's 'deliberately flat language and refusal of sensationalism in *Rendezvous*' (Palmer, 2006: 105). While its name, taken from the supreme deity in certain denominations of Hinduism, evokes mysticism, Palmer's observation is never clearer than in Clarke's comment that, from a distance, Rama appears 'almost comically like an ordinary domestic boiler' (Clarke, 1973/2006: 17). In *2001*, Clarke's descriptions become slightly less mundane. When the ape-man Moon-Watcher observes the Monolith, 'a rectangular slab [...] made of some completely transparent material', 'there were no natural objects' to which he could compare it (Clarke, 1968/2000: 29). Yet it is ultimately the perfect simplicity of the Monolith's geometric shape, highlighting its non-organic origin, which achieves the sublime effect here, rather than an abundance of elaborate descriptive language, as is also the case with Rama: the geometrical perfection and functionality of its design convince the Space Advisory Council that it is not 'a natural object' (Clarke, 2006: 17).

Similarly, Farah Mendlesohn could be describing Clarke's style when she observes that, in Banks's novels, the sublime effect is ultimately achieved when 'the bathetic supports the baroque' and 'Prosaic observation becomes the vector for grandeur' (Mendlesohn, 2005: 565). The ancient Culture citizens who first view the Excession find it almost completely impenetrable to study. While Banks is occasionally prone to overenthusiastic verbosity, this is not the case with his description of the Excession, the external physical attributes of which are rarely conveyed beyond an initial, brief technical report, containing some of the hardest (pseudo)science in the series. Breaking down this report, we learn that the Excession is centuries old, without precedent to the seemingly omnipotent Culture and therefore top secret, largely impervious to study, completely static, and probably inactive. As Kincaid notes: 'It is, therefore, like the black monolith in Arthur C. Clarke's *2001: A Space Odyssey*, a perfect and insoluble mystery' (Kincaid, 2017: 78). Similarly, Rama also remains a mystery in many respects, for, while it is clearly of alien origin, first contact for humanity is denied: 'its builders and its crew may be long gone or dead', it is 'very old, yet seems new, or perhaps ageless' and probably 'only functioning, not, say, living or expressing itself' (Palmer, 2006: 98). Faced with objects so familiar and yet so strange in the nature of their context, scale and origin, it is difficult for the reader/viewer not to conclude that these stellar anomalies must potentially yield radical possibilities. As with the Monolith and Rama, Banks uses a mixture of carefully developed understatement, the mundane and the mysterious to achieve a sense of sublime wonder.

Both Clarke and Banks placed limits upon the possibilities that their BDOs represent, given their ultimately rationalist and materialist worldviews. Banks adopted an intentionally Suvinian approach, and would not allow elements of the spiritual or supernatural into his work, while Clarke often surprised his readers and critics by blurring the lines between the advanced technology and magic that his famous dictum placed upon a spectrum. As Clute and Nicholls explain: 'With "The Sentinel" came the first clear appearance of the Clarke paradox: that the man who of all sf writers of his generation was most closely identified with knowledgeable, technological Hard SF was at the same time strongly attracted to the metaphysical, even to the mystical' (Clute and Nicholls, 2019). John Sutherland goes further, suggesting that 'The work of Arthur C. Clarke [...] is saturated with a religiosity which probably derives from Stapledon's cosmic humanism' (Sutherland, 1979: 177). Clarke did not seem uncomfortable with such formulations, allegedly calling *2001* 'the world's first billion dollar religious movie' (Clarke, 1999: 110). Csicsery-Ronay, however, contests such notions by arguing that Clarke's stories are 'explicitly about a *materialized* transcendence,' much as is the case with Banks, while it is actually Kubrick's filmic representation of Clarke's ideas that 'could lead in precisely the opposite direction' (Csicsery-Ronay, 2008: 169). Ultimately, the BDOs described by Banks and Clarke are rationalized to varying degrees, but largely negating the irrational, supernatural sublime of the Gothic for that of the rational, mathematical sublime.

Rama and the Excession, then, achieve the shock of the radically new but they are not merely examples of famous nova in fiction, aspects of the 'SF world which differ immeasurably from our given world' (Clute, 2011: 26). They act as nova *within* the author's fictional universes: the Excession is almost as much a 'new thing' to the hyper-advanced Culture as it is to Banks's readers. Similarly, in Clarke's *Childhood's End* (1953), the intervention of the Overlords cognitively estranges the inhabitants of late twentieth century Earth, revealing their Cold War reality to be a defective paradigm that conceals a cosmic truth. The Excession also allows for the Culture to potentially experience a radical reappraisal of the universe and its place within it: even if not revealed as actually defective, it is clearly not as omniscient or omnipotent as it believes. Clarke's hard-working astronauts in *2001* may come to understand that they too follow a defective account of humankind's history, with us revealed as minor characters in one chapter of an on-going universal narrative.

Paradigm Shifts, Outside Context Problems and Conceptual Breakthroughs

BDOs, clearly mysterious and of non-human origin, force human beings to look at themselves and their societies anew, potentially to an extent radical enough to constitute a conceptual breakthrough, defined by Nicholls as overturning 'a generally held way of looking at and interpreting the world' (Nicholls, 2016). The Excession seems uniquely able to travel through the system of nested-universes, arranged like the peel of an onion, which exists in the Culture series.

Rama, becoming more enigmatic the more facts are uncovered, awes humanity by the potential suggested in the bio-robotic nature of its creators. The Monolith is also evidence of a vastly superior alien intelligence with the capacity to travel freely through time and space. Each, therefore, potentially offers humanity access to such developments.

If Banks's language relating to the Excession is restrained and scientific, then, in its first and final transmission, the Object itself breaks its silence with a striking and beautiful kind of poetry: 'call me highway call me conduit call me lightning rod'. Far from a kind of annoyance in space, this 'excessively powerful' entity is revealed to be not only capable of travelling through universes, but is itself merely a channel through which something greater runs: 'the overarch bedeckants in their great sequential migration across the universes' (Banks, 1996: 'Epilogue'). The untranslatable name of these universes suggests still further levels of inter-species incommunicability. The multiversal breakthroughs represented by the Excession and the bedeckants forms the end of a chain of conceptual breakthroughs in politics, culture and economics suggested to have occurred within Banks's utopian Culture: moving beyond capitalism, social inequality, religious belief, patriarchy and imperialism. Banks's BDO, then, not only expands humankind's understanding of outer space: it potentially allows for the Culture to continue its utopian expansion into the cosmos, achieving the *technologiade* transformation without spatial limitations. Robert Duggan, drawing upon the motif of George Orwell's essay 'Inside the Whale' (1940), argues that 'Banks's Excession persistently stimulates his readers to think about the possibilities of higher dimensions and new contexts, and opens up space Outside the Whale in which a different way of life might be possible' (Duggan, 2018: 245). In doing so, the series enables us to do what Fredric Jameson calls, in *Archaeologies of the Future* (2005), 'thinking the break', creating space for the ideological refusal of capitalism.

Nicholls's conceptual breakthrough is something like an inverted version of what Banks refers to in the Culture series as an Outside Context Problem (OCP), an instance of colonial first contact where a relatively less-developed civilization encounters another in a higher-stage of development 'rather in the same way a sentence encountered a full stop' (Banks, 1996: 71). If a conceptual breakthrough brings progress and transcendence, the OCP brings violence, domination and enslavement. As Kincaid explains: 'The Excession itself, appearing from nowhere, unmoving, silent, featureless, stands as a metaphor for how much the Culture still doesn't know' (Kincaid, 2017: 81). Until the transmission of its message, the powerful sphere could deliver either breakthrough or OCP. It achieves a level of mystery and threat commensurate with the Gothic, 'a writing of excess' (Botting, 2010: 1), and signified by its name: 'Excession; something excessive. Excessively aggressive, excessively powerful, excessively expansionist; whatever' (Banks, 1996: 93). With the ease with which it destroys the craft that originally discovered it, the Excession could prove to be the Culture's own full stop. Just as the Culture and its antagonists, the Affront, prepare for war, so too Rama is nearly destroyed by the Hermian colony who deem it too much of a potential threat.

Ultimately, however, Rama and the Excession do not reveal themselves to be either OCP or breakthrough: the Excession releases its tantalizingly obtuse final message before disappearing again, while Rama, having capitalized on solar energy, slingshots away from the Earth to continue the journey which is its real, yet still ultimately mysterious, purpose. The Excession's transmission suggests that the Culture has been denied such a breakthrough because 'the reaction to my presence indicates a fundamental unreadiness as yet for such a signal honour' (Banks, 1996: 'Epilogue'). Clearly, the conceptual breakthrough has to be earned and BDOs can be as stubborn as they are powerful. Mendlesohn suggests *Excession* to be a book on manners for the content of many peripheral sub-plots (Mendlesohn, 2005: 562), and the Culture's relations with the Excession are suggested to be one narrative of etiquette that Banks's famously polite utopia has yet to master. Similarly, the Overlords in *Childhood's End*, who establish close relations with humans, stagger the revelation of their true nature to us strategically, deeming us too immature to handle contact with such superior and extraterrestrial entities.

While *Rendezvous* and *Excession* deny its characters a breakthrough, both versions of *2001* culminate in sf's ultimate breakthrough sequence: Bowman's journey through the Star Gate and his apotheosis as the Starchild. Bowman's breakthrough can only be presented to the reader/viewer 'by analogy, inasmuch as the new state cannot be described in a terminology which itself belongs to the old paradigm' (Nicholls, 2016). Banks's series also includes the potential for a kind of post-human super-being in a process known as 'Subliming' although, as Jim Clarke notes, this process 'exists within the Culture universe, not beyond it as with the Excession or the "higher beings" who use the Excession as a bridge between universes' (J. Clarke, 2018: 220). For the militantly atheist Banks, Subliming's suggestion of spiritual transcendence had to be rationalized (a goal of which he is mostly successful), as Clarke observes: 'the object of this SF sense of wonder is the manifestation of previously divine attributes into a non-theistic context' (J. Clarke, 2018: 216).

Topia: U/Dys/Ustopia, Anti-Utopia and the Cities of Handiness

The final part of Clute's framework – topia – discusses the social formations that potentially arise following a conceptual breakthrough, including utopia, dystopia, and variations thereof, as the final stage of sf's overarching narrative: 'the Jerusalem whose gates have been opened by Conceptual Breakthrough' (Clute, 2011: 27). Clarke and Banks offer a variety of different outcomes that are potentially utopian: (1) material, secular harmonious environments such as those of the Culture, or the Golden Age on Earth following the arrival of the Overlords; (2) the group consciousness of the Overmind which follows it; (3) Subliming, material transcendence into another dimension of existence, and often performed by a civilization *en masse*; (4) the unknown potential that would follow contact with the Excession; and (5) the results of the journey beyond the Star Gate and the alien message from beyond the Monolith.

In relation to the first potential topia, the realization of a material utopia for humans, the fiction of Clarke and Banks seems to reflect differing stances: Banks was a vocal utopian while Clarke's relationship with utopia seems complex at best, and anti-utopia at worst. Martin McGrath argues that, when such themes are mentioned in his fiction, 'Clarke's critique of utopianism is unwavering' (McGrath, 2011: 9). Clarke's novels, *Childhood's End* and *The City and the Stars* (1956), depict various utopian spaces – a harmonious Earth, overseen by benevolent extraterrestrials in the former, and the techno-utopia of Diaspar contrasting with the agrarian utopia of Lys in the latter. In all cases, human culture stultifies, reaching a state of *ennui*:

> It is this sterility that Clarke found repellent. Clarke, through his science fiction novels, sought to construct an idea of better societies and an improvement of the human condition – seeing us become better as a species, casting off old prejudices, coming closer to achieving our full potentials – while, at the same time, specifically rejecting utopia as a dead end. (McGrath, 2011: 9)

Banks conceived of utopia in the exact opposite manner, portraying it as the ultimate goal of a progressive civilization and techno-scientific development. He contested the problem of utopia as boring by arguing that only the rich have experienced anything approaching such a state: 'So we haven't tried it. We don't know that it's boring. We can always find things to struggle with. We make our own problems' (Nolan, 2014: 69).

Clarke was not simply an anti-utopian, however, as defined by Ruth Levitas as someone who 'actively opposes the imagination and pursuit of alternatives' (Levitas, 2013: 110). Instead, McGrath explores Clarke's thinking in terms of Michel Foucault's 'heterotopia' defined as 'something like counter-sites, a kind of effectively enacted utopia in which the real sites, all the other real sites that can be found within the culture, are simultaneously represented, contested, and inverted' (Foucault, 1986: 24). McGrath concludes that Clarke would have shared 'Foucault's belief that specific change can be achieved to improve society while still rejecting the idea of concrete utopias that might spring from wholesale, programmatic, revolutions' (McGrath,

2011: 13). Similarly, while Sherryl Vint (2006, 2008) and Patricia Kerslake (2007) read Banks's Culture as reproducing the dystopian logic of imperialism and empire-building, this reading can be rectified somewhat with the utopian content of Banks's series by considering the latter as an example of the 'critical utopia'. Initially developed by Tom Moylan in 1986, the critical utopia 'breaks with previous utopias by presenting in greater, almost balanced detail, both the utopian society and the original society against which the utopia is pitted as a revolutionary alternative' (Moylan, 2014: 43). Moylan subsequently acknowledged the work of Simon Guerrier and Michal Kulbicki, both of whom 'effectively argue that Iain M. Banks's series of "Culture" novels can be read as critical utopias' (Moylan, 2014: xxiii). So, too, would Clarke's work benefit from such sustained analysis in relation to Moylan's notion.

With the third potential topia, a kind of immaterial transcendence, the fiction of Banks and Clarke again offers conflicting views. The topia of *2001* is clear, with Bowman's transformation into the Starchild and subsequent uninhibited movement through space and time portrayed so vividly in both book and film. Becoming a being of pure energy, like the Monolith builders before him, Bowman becomes something much like the Sublimed in Banks's universe, returning to Earth at the novel's conclusion to intervene in the continuing Cold War and safely detonate a nuclear warhead in orbit – an action which suggests he pursues utopian goals of peace, and possibly continuing the cycle of conceptual breakthrough once more. Yet the Culture continually negates Subliming (entering a mysterious new dimension *en masse*), strongly criticizing the small minority of its citizens who choose to do so, seeing it as an insult, given that they have created a kind of material paradise on Earth already.

In this respect, Banks's fiction can be seen as an indirect response to Clarke's work, especially *2001*, which continually demonstrates a desire to seek *freedom from* matter by transcending it altogether, while Banks's series – for all of its wildness of style – advocates remaining grounded in the material plane based on the optimism that we may radically improve such a state from within. The Culture is enabled as a utopia by the existence of AIs, the Minds and drones, which are themselves the result of a conceptual breakthrough idealized within real-world scientific theory – the Singularity, or a spike in technological development that allows intelligent machines to radically advance their own intelligence beyond that of humans. Yet, as Gary Westfahl argues, Clarke 'intimates that advanced civilizations may reach a stage when they no longer need machines'. The Monolith builders eventually become, like the Starchild, free from corporeal reality and 'it appears, require machines only to interact with lesser species that are still bound to matter' (Westfahl, 2018: 42). All, it would seem, a stage too far for the Culture. The topia represented by the Excession remains mysterious, although its final message suggests that it has the potential to offer vastly increased – if not limitless – freedom of communication and movement through the universe; and perhaps the Culture would relish such an opportunity, given that it seeks to remain within the material realm. To Clarke, the BDO represents a potential for hope that knows no limitations, and overcoming the perceived flaws of human nature, whereas, to Banks, the BDO is perhaps a challenge to the potential utopian perfectibility of humanity.

Conclusion

Without Clarke, sf would clearly have been much different, the BDO remaining a relic in obscure space opera. Peter Nicholls places the BDO 'at the heart of what attracts many people to SF' (Nicholls, 1997), and such narratives continue today in the work of Stephen Baxter and Alastair Reynolds, among many others. Clarke's work displays the optimism for space exploration which characterized that era; yet by the time Banks published *Excession* in the mid-1990s, Clarke noted a 'current disenchantment with space travel' that 'may be due to disappointment with the real universe as compared with the glamorous one of fiction' following the fact that NASA space probes had revealed 'alas, no Martian cities or lush Venusian jungles' (Clarke, 1999: 399). At the time of writing however, fifty years after *2001* was released, the allure of Big Dumb Objects from outer space seems very much alive. On 19 October 2017, astronomers at the University of

Hawaii reported the discovery of the first interstellar object to enter our solar system, and aptly named it 'Oumoumou', meaning 'a messenger from afar arriving first' in Hawaiian (Kazmierczak, 2018). Such is the extent that Clarke's work has entered the popular consciousness that articles in several sources compared the object to *Rendezvous with Rama* and suggested that Rama was a popular proposed name for the object, while others drew comparison with Clarke's Monolith (Overbye, 2017). The SETI institute's Allen Telescope Array listened unsuccessfully for radio emissions in December 2017. In the early twenty first century, private enterprise has replaced government projects as the main instigator of space exploration and techno-scientific development, yet Banks, a socialist, remained hopeful about its prospects nonetheless. While Banks did not share Clarke's background as scientific researcher, practitioner and broadcaster, his sf has gone on to influence real-world science, just as Clarke's did in his own era, with Elon Musk's Culture-inspired projects, such as autonomous drones and mind-computer interfaces, continuing the real-world *technologiade* project.

BDO narratives are sf myths, stories full of anticipation at the prospect, not just of first contact, but of contact with something so radical that we cannot help but be automatically and radically changed ourselves. Often called a 'Macguffin', or derided as a cheap method of creating suspense, the prolonged or often incomplete revelation of detail relating to the real nature of the BDO in fact operates as a method for representing the unrepresentable. Intrinsic to BDO stories is a sense of promise and potential, of hope for the existence of something so much bigger than ourselves that it renders our problems and disagreements redundant, and reinforces the belief that radical, utopian change is possible. Yet the BDO also functions to reveal the significance of finding meaning in our day-to-day lives, even if the real universe cannot live up to the glamour of fiction. Banks's fiction serves to advocate a commitment to the material world over the spiritual or the transcendental: there is no Subliming, no extraterrestrial Overmind for the Culture, only its AIs. But the true purpose of BDOs like the Excession or Rama is ultimately less important than the way in which we small dumb humans react to that which we have not predicted and cannot comprehend. As Clarke said, 'I am an optimist; anyone interested in the future has to be' (Clarke, 2000b: 285), a trait that Banks shared – and sf needs their optimism now more than ever.

Works Cited

Agel, J. (2018) *The Making of Kubrick's 2001*. New York: Simon & Schuster.
Banks, I. M. (1991) *The State of the Art*. London: Orbit.
Banks, I. M. (1996) *Excession*. London: Orbit.
Botting, F. (2010) *Gothic*. London: Routledge.
Clarke, A. C. (1968/2000) *2001: A Space Odyssey*. London: Orbit.
Clarke, A. C. (1973/2006) *Rendezvous with Rama*. London: Orbit.
Clarke, A. C. (1999) *Greetings, Carbon-based Bipeds!* London: Voyager.
Clarke, A. C. (2000) *The Collected Stories of Arthur C. Clarke*. London: Gollancz.
Clarke, J. (2018) 'The Sublime in Iain M. Banks's Culture novels', in N. Hubble, E. MacCallum-Stewart and J. Norman (eds) *The Science Fiction of Iain M. Banks*, pp. 211–27. Canterbury: Gylphi.
Clute, J. (2011) *Pardon This Instrusion: Fantastika In The World Storm*. Harold Wood: Beccon Books.
Clute, J. and P. Nicholls (2018) 'Clarke, Arthur C.', in J. Clute and D. Langford (eds) *The Encyclopedia of Science Fiction*, URL (accessed 28 December 2018): http://www.sf-encyclopedia.com/entry/clarke_arthur_c
Csicsery-Ronay, I. (2008) *The Seven Beauties of Science Fiction*. Middletown, CT: Wesleyan University Press.
Duggan, R. (2018) 'Inside the Whale and Outside Context Problems', in N. Hubble, E. MacCallum-Stewart and J. Norman (eds) *The Science Fiction of Iain M. Banks*, pp. 227–49. Canterbury: Gylphi.
Foucault, M. (1986) 'Of Other Spaces.' Trans. Jay Miskowiec. *Diacritics* 16(1): 22–27.
Jameson, F. (2005) *Archaeologies of the Future: The Desire Called Utopia and Other Science Fictions*. London: Verso.
Kaveney, R. (1981) 'Science Fiction in the 1970s: Some Dominant Themes and Personalities.' *Foundation* 22: 5–34.
Kazmierczak, J. (2018) 'New Study Shows What Interstellar Visitor "Oumuamua" Can Teach Us.' *National Air & Space Agency* (27 March), URL (accessed 28 December 2018): https://www.nasa.gov/feature/goddard/2018/new-study-shows-what-interstellar-visitor-oumuamua-can-teach-us

Kerslake, P. (2007) *Science Fiction and Empire*. Liverpool: University of Liverpool Press.

Kincaid, P. (2017) *Iain M. Banks*. Illinois: University of Illinois Press.

Langford, D. (2012) 'Dyson Sphere', in J. Clute and D. Langford (eds) *The Encyclopedia of Science Fiction*, URL (accessed 28 December 2018): http://www.sf-encyclopedia.com/entry/dyson_sphere

Langford, D. and P. Nicholls (2018) 'Macrostructures', in J. Clute and D. Langford (eds) *The Encyclopedia of Science Fiction*, URL (accessed 28 December 2018): http://www.sf-encyclopedia.com/entry/macrostructures

Levitas, R. (2013) *Utopia as Method*. Basingstoke: Palgrave Macmillan.

McGrath, M. (2011) 'Against Utopia: Arthur C. Clarke and the Heterotopian Impulse', *Vector* 267: 8–14.

Mendlesohn, F. (2005) 'Iain M. Banks: *Excession*', in D. Seed (ed.) *A Companion to Science Fiction*, pp. 556–67. Oxford: Blackwell.

Moylan, T. (2014) *Demand the Impossible: Science Fiction and the Utopian Imagination*. Bern: Peter Lang.

Murray, I. (2002) 'Interview with Iain Banks, 29th November 1988', in I. Murray (ed.) *Scottish Writers Talking 2*. Edinburgh: Tuckwell Press.

Newman, K. (1986) 'Interview with Iain M. Banks', *Interzone* 16: 41–42.

Nicholls, P. (1997) 'Big Dumb Objects and Cosmic Enigmas: The Love Affair Between Science Fiction and the Transcendental', *Gregory Benford's Website*, URL (accessed 28 December 2018): http://www.gregorybenford.com/extra/big-dumb-objects-and-cosmic-enigmas/

Nicholls, P. (2016) 'Conceptual Breakthrough', in J. Clute and D. Langford (eds) *The Encyclopedia of Science Fiction*, (accessed 28 December 2018): http://www.sf-encyclopedia.com/entry/conceptual_breakthrough

Nolan, V. (2014) '"Utopia is a way of saying we could do better": Iain M. Banks and Kim Stanley Robinson in Conversation', *Foundation* 119: 65–76.

Overbye, D. (2017) 'An Interstellar Visitor Both Familiar and Alien', *New York Times* (22 November), URL (accessed 28 December 2018): https://www.nytimes.com/2017/11/22/science/oumuamua-space-asteroid.html

Palmer, C. (2006) 'Big Dumb Objects in Science Fiction: Sublimity, Banality, and Modernity', *Extrapolation* 47(1): 95–111.

Rawlison, L. (2009) 'Author Iain M. Banks: Humanity's future is blister-free calluses!', *CNN* (6 January), URL (accessed 7 January 2019): http://edition.cnn.com/2008/TECH/space/05/15/iain.banks/index.html

Sutherland, J. A. (1979) 'American Science Fiction since 1960', in P. Parrinder (ed.) *Science Fiction: A Critical Guide*, pp. 162–187. London: Longman.

Vint, S. (2006) *Bodies of Tomorrow: Technology, Subjectivity, Science Fiction*. Toronto: University of Toronto Press.

Vint, S. (2008) 'Cultural Imperialism and the Ends of Empire: Iain M. Banks's *Look to Windward*', *Journal of the Fantastic in the Arts* 18(1): 85–98.

Westfahl, G. (2018) *Arthur C. Clarke*. Champaign: University of Illinois Press.

Winter, J. (2016) *Science Fiction, New Space Opera, and Neoliberal Globalism: Nostalgia for Infinity*. Cardiff: University of Wales Press.

11

CLARKE DARE SPEAK NOT ITS NAME
DEFINING SEXUALITY IN *IMPERIAL EARTH*

Mike Stack

The year 2017 not only saw the centenary of Arthur C. Clarke's birth, but the year also marked fifty years since the partial decriminalization of homosexuality in the UK. This chapter will argue that any consideration of Clarke's life would not be complete without addressing the latter of these two anniversaries, or rather, the impact of the changes in both legislation and social attitudes towards homosexuality during Clarke's lifetime, and how this shaped his portrayal of sexuality in his writing.

For example, the 1990 edition of *Uranian Worlds* – Eric Garber and Lyn Paleo's ambitious attempt to list all instances of alternative sexualities in science fiction, horror and fantasy – includes five works by Clarke: *Imperial Earth* (1975), *The Songs of Distant Earth* (1986), *2061: Odyssey Three* (1987), *Cradle* (1988) and *Rama II* (1989), the latter two co-authored with Gentry Lee. Five of the four novels merit entry because they feature gay, lesbian or bisexual incidental characters. But it is the first, *Imperial Earth*, which stands out due to the prominence – and paradox – of sexuality on display. Garber and Paleo describe the book as having a 'strong homosexual foundation [which] underlies this fascinating extrapolation'. And yet, following a summary, they conclude: 'While Clarke shies away from expressing open approval of exclusive homosexuality, he portrays male bisexuality with great acceptance' (Garber and Paleo, 1990: 50). These two statements appear contradictory; 'a strong homosexual foundation' that 'shies away from open approval'. Surely to refuse approval denies the strength of such a foundation?

This ambiguous approach to sexuality, where same-sex relations are simultaneously explicitly referenced and hidden from view, reflects how Clarke presented his own sexuality. I will argue that contextualizing his life within a broader queer history will enable us begin to understand Clarke's ambivalence surrounding sexuality – not just the sexual orientation of characters within *Imperial Earth*, but also his own. Similarly, by examining the sexual politics within the novel, we begin to see how Clarke drew on, and anticipated, theoretical understandings of sexuality, enabling us to begin building a picture of how Clarke understood his own sexual sense of self.

Clarke's Sexuality: Neither In Nor Out

Hitherto, there has been some reluctance among critics to discuss Clarke's sexuality. Robin Anne Reid argues for discretion: 'Readers and fans of writers enjoy learning more about the life of a writer, but readers must also respect the right of a living writer to privacy' (Reid, 1997: 3). Similarly, Neil McAleer, writing in his revised edition of Clarke's biography, concludes:

> Decades of speculation over his sexual ambiguity spawned gossip, and the gossip was transformed into what became an 'open secret' that Clarke was indeed gay. But there was no fire – only smoke. [...] And, as Clarke aged and his admirers continue to read his works, the matter of his sexuality seemed to fade from view and, ultimately, became little more than a footnote (McAleer, 2017: 370).

Such evasion rather dictates what readers ought to think, and works against the details of Clarke's life and literary output. Indeed, Clarke seems to invite speculation because of the ambiguity and blurriness of the details surrounding the sexual area of his life. His marriage to Marilyn Mayfield is his only documented heterosexual relationship; they met on 28 May 1953, married on 15 June, and were separated by November (McAleer, 2017: 88-9, 97). Mayfield herself promised to reveal more details about Clarke after his death, but predeceased him. Conversely, Clarke apparently confided to the physicist Jeremy Bernstein that Mayfield was lesbian (Bernstein, 2008). Instead, it is Clarke's relationship with Leslie Ekanayake that appears to have held the strongest emotional significance. Clarke himself described the strength of the bond: 'He was the only man who ever said to me (several times) "I love you" without the slightest hint of embarrassment or mawkishness' (McAleer, 2017: 265). Such a statement raises many questions: was this love sexual or platonic? Was Clarke plaintively wishing more men had told him they loved him? Or indeed had others, but only Ekanayake's frankness and openness stood out? Yet McAleer's biography forecloses any speculation, casting the relationship in heteronormative terms (while also invoking an incest taboo): 'Ekanayake had become like a son to Clarke in many ways, the son he'd never had' (McAleer, 2017: 265). How the bond was forged is left unexplored.

Yet, in spite of McAleer's assertion there was no 'fire' regarding Clarke's sexuality, others have been more direct and forthcoming. For example, Michael Moorcock, writing a memorial after Clarke's death, unambiguously announced '[e]veryone knew he was gay' (Moorcock, 2008). Moorcock's assertion is striking for many reasons: not only a brazen disregard for the caution displayed by other authors, but also for its matter-of-fact assumption that 'everyone knew'. It is unsurprising, then, that McAleer describes Clarke's sexuality as an open secret, a fact known but not talked about, to remain unspoken in polite company. There are instances where McAleer directly confirms Clarke's sexuality in the same biography where it is dismissed; the author includes an anecdote from Kerry O'Quinn, editor of *Starlog* magazine, observing that Clarke proudly wore a lambda pin (a symbol adopted by the gay liberation movement) for the duration of a lecture tour on a cruise ship. O'Quinn is quoted as claiming: 'Arthur was gay – although in his era that wasn't the term' (McAleer, 2017: 238).

More gravely, any biography of Clarke's life must also include the allegations of Clarke's sexual abuse of underage boys made by *The Sunday Mirror* in 1998. Although these were subsequently discredited, he was nevertheless asked to release a statement announcing the postponement of his investiture of a C.B.E. (McAleer, 2017: 366). Yet it is possible to speculate that the slander made against Clarke was facilitated by the question marks surrounding his sexuality, suggesting that he had something to hide, in tandem with a tacit acceptance of homosexuality.

On closer examination, Clarke himself is the cause of such ambiguity. When interviewed by Luke Harding in *The Guardian*, Clarke dismissed sex altogether: 'I had an operation for prostate cancer 10 years ago [...] I haven't the slightest interest in sex'. Such disinterest is unsurprising: Clarke was then 82 years old. But Harding also reported that Clarke's standard reply to those asking him if he considered him gay was '[n]o, merely cheerful' (Harding, 2000). While this response playfully harks back to the earlier meanings of the word, it neither confirms nor denies whether he considered himself gay in the sexual sense. Such evasiveness from Clarke may account for McAleer's approach as official biographer, protective of his subject's privacy. Yet the paradox remains that Clarke did not deny he was gay, as if teasing his audience to delve deeper and ask the very questions he was avoiding. To understand why, I will briefly summarise a necessarily condensed history of homosexuality during Clarke's lifetime.

The Emergence of the Homosexual

So far, I have used the term 'gay' as a synonym for homosexuality; however the usage of the word is a relatively recent phenomena, predated by the more pejorative term 'queer' (see Cook, 2014: 7–8). Either way homosexuality itself is a contested and relatively recent concept. As the quote from O'Quinn suggests, the word 'gay' was not adopted as a popular term until relatively late in Clarke's lifetime. Michel Foucault famously pinpointed 1870 as the year in which 'the homosexual' first came into being:

We must not forget that the psychological, psychiatric, medical category of homosexuality was constituted from the moment it was characterized [...] less by a type of sexual relations than by a certain quality of sexual sensibility, a certain way of inverting the masculine and feminine [...]. The sodomite has been a temporary aberration; the homosexual was now a species. (Foucault, 1998: 43)

Foucault's multi-volume *History of Sexuality* (1976–2018) charts the evolution of power relations from familiar systems to those interiorized on the body after the Industrial Revolution; psychology and psychiatry were among such disciplines emerging in the 1800s that sought to categorise and control behaviour. Thus, whereas same sex relations had previously been an activity, they were now seen to reflect a distinct type of person.

The emerging psychological discourses concerning homosexuality coincided with the legislative changes regulating sexuality. Clarke was born in an era when the 1885 Labouchère Amendment was in force in Britain. The Act diverged from previous legislation that criminalized male homosexual behaviour in two key ways. First, rather than specifying a particular sex act, it criminalized 'gross indecency', a vague and subjective term covering a wide variety of behaviour; second, it forbade such acts 'in public and in private', imposing the law not just upon the street, but into the private, domestic sphere itself, creating an all pervasive sense of judgement. The law soon became to be known as the 'Blackmailer's Charter' (Weeks, 2016: 22). John Potvin summarizes the affective impact of the law: 'one could never truly be comfortable, even within one's home' (Potvin, 2014: 22).

The Labouchère Amendment was very prominently enforced in the Oscar Wilde trials of 1895, where the playwright's high profile added to the spectacle and hubris of his fall. The trials were still in living memory when Clarke was born. Alan Sinfield argues that it is through Wilde that the public perception of the figure of the 'homosexual' was formed. Wilde's own persona – that is his class, dandyism and femininity – shaped the stereotype of the homosexual man:

> Wilde appeared, suddenly but ineluctably, as one who consorted with male prostitutes. Yet he was still the effeminate dandy. So the two fig-

ures coalesced. [...] Indeed, as the sexologists were saying, he was a more specific figure than the sodomite – the homosexual. (Sinfield, 1994: 122)

Just as Foucault wrote of the homosexual as a figure inverting masculinity and femininity, Sinfield sees Wilde's personality as a violation of 'the cross-sex grid', patterns of behaviour acceptable to each gender, and thus by association, furthering the perception of homosexuality as a disruption of gender norms. Sinfield relays a story about the author Beverley Nichols being caught with a copy of Wilde's *The Picture of Dorian Gray* (1890), whereupon his father flew into a rage, 'Oscar Wilde! To think my son...' and who later sent him a note in Latin stating 'the horrible crime must not be named' (Sinfield, 1994: 130). The incident occurred during the First World War, around the time of Clarke's birth.

The paranoia of wartime further contributed to the repressive moral scrutiny of the era. In 1918, shortly after Clarke's birth, the MP Noel Pemberton Billing exploited a rumour that the German Secret Service had a list of 47,000 'sexual perverts' to vilify dancer Maud Allen, who, he claimed in an editorial entitled 'The Cult of the Clitoris', performed for such a corrupt audience. Allen attempted to sue Pemberton Billing for libel but lost (Weeks, 2016: 105–6). Thus, the Britain of Clarke's formative years portrayed and perceived homosexuality through the punitive and suspicious lenses of legislation, patriotism and psychology.

And yet, even in a climate of hostility, there were those who defended homosexuality. In 1908, socialist campaigner Edward Carpenter published *The Intermediate Sex* (an expanded edition of an earlier 1898 essay) arguing for the recognition of 'urnings' or 'uranians' who contribute to society through artistic and empathic sensibilities. Although positively described (and Carpenter swiftly glosses over sex), the book still draws upon notions of gender violation: Carpenter's urnings/uranians are 'men who might be described as of feminine soul enclosed in a male body [...] or in other cases women whose definition would be the reverse' (Carpenter, 2007: 11).

Similarly, queer cultures continued to exist in the era of the Labouchère Amendment. Clarke moved to London in 1936, aged 19 (McAleer, 2017: 34). A contemporary of Clarke's, raconteur Quentin Crisp (just nine years Clarke's senior) lived in London during the same era, and his 1968 memoir describes the sophisticated queer culture of the West End, albeit one structured along highly gendered lines between the 'roughs' and the 'bitches' (Crisp, 1985: 62), emulating the patterns of the cross-sex grid. Would Clarke have been aware of, and engaged in this culture? His biography is unclear. As a contrast between Clarke and Crisp, when the Second World War broke out, Crisp was declared exempt from National Service as he declared himself homosexual (Crisp, 1985: 118), whereas Clarke entered the RAF in 1941 (McAleer, 2017: 49). Clearly, if Clarke thought himself homosexual, he kept quiet. Stationed at Davidstow Hall in Cornwall, he would therefore have missed the influx of American GIs and the sexualised atmosphere (as Crisp saw it) in London during the latter part of the war.

Post-War is portrayed as an era returning to traditional roles, reinforcing the family and social puritanism. Historian Matt Houlbrook uses the Metropolitan Magistrates Courts and City of London Justice Rooms records to chart the increase in arrests of men for gross indecency in London post-war, rising three-fold from 211 proceedings in 1942 to 637 in 1947 (Houlbrook, 2006: 272). Yet Houlbrook cautions against interpreting such statistics as representative of a wider clampdown on homosexuality, arguing the distribution of arrests was restricted to a few Metropolitan Police districts, and hence motivated by individual officers. Indeed, there were further signs of change in attitudes to homosexuality in the post-War years. In 1948, American sexologist Alfred Kinsey published *Sexual Behaviour of the Human Male*, a survey based on the sexual histories of 5,300 American men. From his data, he argued that 37% of men had some homosexual experience, and developed the heterosexual-homosexual continuum, a six-point scale suggesting the fluidity of sexual orientation (Irvine, 2005: 32). In 1950s Britain, debates about homosexuality were becoming ever more prominent, with the Tory Home Secretary Sir David Maxwell-Fyfe announcing that homosexual men were 'a danger to others' (Weeks, 2016: 158). Public figures were increasingly implicated; in 1952, mathematician Alan Turing was arrested, before committing suicide in 1954 – Clarke later told Jeremy Bernstein that he had hoped Turing would emigrate to Sri Lanka alongside him (Bernstein, 2008). In 1953, Sir John Gielgud was arrested for cottaging, resulting in a call for his knighthood to be withdrawn (Weeks, 2016: 159). In 1954, the trials of Peter Wildeblood, Michael Pitt-Rivers and Lord Montagu put homosexuality onto the front page of many newspapers, just as the Wilde trials had done, sixty years earlier. Although the press was savage, Wildeblood himself was surprised to receive support from the public. The trials served as a catalyst for the formation of a Home Office Committee chaired by Sir John Wolfenden in 1954, which published its report in 1957 recommending the repealing of the Labouchère Amendment. While seeing the report as a positive step, Jeffrey Weeks sums up the limitations of the Wolfenden Report: 'It represented [...] a widespread acceptance, by a representative section of elite opinion, of homosexuality as an unfortunate condition' (Weeks, 2016: 165).

Following the Report, under pressure from the predominantly middle-class Homosexual Reform Society, the law was eventually changed in 1967. Although homosexual activities between men were decriminalised, there were conditions and limitations; the law only applied to those over 21 (the heterosexual age of consent was 16), the acts must be in private, and the law only applied in England and Wales (Weeks, 2016: 175). Clarke had left England by this point, leaving for Sri Lanka (then Ceylon) more or less permanently in 1956 (McAleer, 2017: 111). Although ostensibly to go skin diving, Bernstein has speculated this decision was influenced by the persecution of Turing (Bernstein, 2008). Nevertheless, Clarke was therefore outside UK when the impact following the change in the law began to shape and embolden gay culture in the UK, first with the formation of the Gay Liberation Front and the identity politics of the 1970s. And it was in this decade that *Imperial Earth* was published.

Imperial Earth

Clarke began writing *Imperial Earth* as far back as the 1950s (McAleer, 2017: 136), but it was finally published in 1975. It tells the story of Duncan Makenzie, part of a clone dynasty on one of Saturn's moons, Titan, in the year 2276. Duncan is the third generation of the Makenzie family; his father Colin was cloned from his father, Malcolm Makenzie. 'Grandfather' Malcolm, the family patriarch, originally made his money from hydrogen mining. Malcolm was married, but was unable to father children and hence obtained a clone to start a family. The genetic ideas of cloning, particularly repetition and variance, are embedded in the novel; the family name is the result of a misspelling – it was originally MacKenzie – that was ultimately repeated across countless documentation until it would be unable to correct it, as if echoing DNA replication.

The bulk of the novel follows Duncan, aged 31, on his first journey to Earth. As a representative of the Makenzie family, he has been asked to give a speech to Congress as part of the celebrations for the 500th anniversary of the United States. Duncan has also been asked to make new business contacts/strategies for the future of Titan, as well as to obtain a clone himself to continue the lineage of the dynasty. Mid-way through the novel, we discover a key aspect of Duncan hitherto unmentioned – Duncan is black:

> He had never given any more thought to his skin colour than to that of his hair [...] Certainly he had never though of himself as black; but now he realised, with understandable satisfaction, that he was several shades darker [...] (Clarke, 1975/1997: 125)

The revelation is surprising, as Clarke makes no prior indication to Duncan's race. This challenges what Richard Dyer has described as an *assumption of whiteness*: 'whiteness generally colonises the stereotypical definition of all social categories other than those of race. To be normal, even to be normally deviant [...] is to be white' (Dyer, 1997: 12). On the one hand then, Clarke's reference to race is radical. It defies the reader's preconceptions, reminding us that white heroes should not automatically be the default. And yet, simultaneously, the move erases any specificity of Duncan's race and culture. There is no attempt to draw out any particularities of Duncan's blackness, his reflection on his race is isolated to this one moment. In the same scene, Clarke optimistically attempts to erase racism from the future. Duncan is being introduced to his host, a landowner George Washington who has dressed up as his historical namesake, together with his black friend Professor Henry Murchison, who has dressed as Washington's slave. Washington accuses Murchison of 'overdoing it' with his impression of patois. The scene is particularly tasteless, a recreation of a master-slave scenario that appears to be played as a joke, rather than acknowledging the horrors of slavery. Clarke attempts to gloss over any racial tensions: as Murchison remarks: 'It's getting more and more difficult to find a *genuine* black skin' (Clarke, 1975/1997: 125). While this remark attempts to echo America's ideal of the melting pot, embracing and integrating all races and cultures, from a contemporary perspective in an era where racial tensions are increasing in the United States and Europe, the scene reads extremely naïve. However, the tension between a radical attempt at presenting a progressive culture, and the realities of identity politics, is present throughout *Imperial Earth*. Race is only one aspect; woven throughout the book are Clarke's own attitudes to sexuality, which, as we have seen, are ambiguous and ambivalent.

The second major character of the novel is Karl Helmer, Duncan's childhood friend. With the exception of a climatic scene, Karl is mostly referred to via flashbacks but his presence is felt throughout. Karl Helmer is the heir of another Titan dynasty, rivals to the Makenzies. Although Karl and Duncan were close in their formative years, we learn they are estranged as adults. Karl is five years older than Duncan, who idolised him as a boy. The character is frequently referred to in romantic terms: Karl has 'dazzling blue eyes' (Clarke, 1975/1997: 17), he possesses 'the slightly over-muscled build of the native born Terran' (Clarke, 1975/1997: 65), and is '[t]he boy with the hair like the sun' and 'one of those men upon whom, for their own amusement, the Gods had bestowed the fatal gift of beauty' (Clarke, 1975/1997: 66). Thus, Duncan's admiration for Karl is based very much on physical attraction. Yet this attraction manifests around a love triangle, as both men as teenagers were infatuated with Calindy, a visitor from Earth, their feelings continuing into adulthood. The first confirmation we have for Duncan and Karl being physical lovers is through a description of a teenage threesome with Calindy. As Duncan describes to his father, 'They *enjoyed* having me there, just to tease me! As least Karl did':

> He must have realised for a long time, without admitting to himself, that there was a very definite streak of cruelty in Karl. Certainly his love-making often lacked tenderness and consideration; there were even times when he had scared Duncan into something approaching impotence. And to do *that* to a virile sixteen-year-old was no mean feat. (Clarke, 1975/1997: 67)

This description provides at least two scenarios: Karl and Calindy with Duncan as a third; and Karl and Duncan alone, 'love-making'. There is no ambiguity to the sexual content; even Duncan's fear cannot render him impotent. On the night that Calindy returns to Earth, Karl and Duncan console each other 'this was the last night they would ever spend together' (Clarke, 1975/1997: 69).

How can we interpret these instances of explicit same-sex sexual interaction? Titan is a small colony, with relatively few inhabitants. It may be these are opportunistic sexual encounters in the absence of other human contact. Again, however, this scene is particularly radical. If Clarke had written the scene in the 1950s, then homosexuality in the UK was still illegal. Even post-1967 it presents a challenge: Duncan is stated as being aged 16, yet at the time of publication the age of consent was 21. On one level, this is extremely progressive; on another, it uncomfortably foreshadows the slander against Clarke regarding the sexual abuse of underage boys. The age of consent was only equalised to 16 in 2001 (Weeks, 2016: 260). In spite of the criminalization of homosexuality and unequal ages of consent post-1967, this situation was not uncommon in the Britain of Clarke's upbringing, due to the expansion of the single-sex public school system in the nineteenth century. As Dominic Janes demonstrates, homosexuality was tacitly accepted within public schools, and expulsion was avoided to prevent potential scandals, which in turn would undermine public schools (Janes, 2015: 134). To pretend that sex did not happen between teenagers because of the law is naïve.

What is particularly notable about the scene is, even though the relationship between Duncan and Karl is already established, the description of their sex only occurs *after* Calindy is introduced, and is involved in the first description of their intimacy. Does the heterosexual element nullify the homosexual side? Eve Kosofsky Sedgwick has described the dynamics within relationships between men that are mediated through the presence of a woman as a 'homosocial triangle':[1]

> The bond that links the two rivals is as intense and potent as the bond that links either of the rivals to the beloved, in that the bonds of the 'rivalry' and 'love', differently as they are experienced, are equally powerful and in many senses equivalent. (Sedgwick, 1985: 21)

While Sedgwick's work is a survey of English literature up to the nineteenth century, from eras when depictions of homosexuality were taboo, the same dynamics are on display in *Imperial Earth*. Although Karl and Duncan both idolise Calindy, her presence facilitates the sex between men (as a threesome and a reason for comfort). Establishing the infatuation for Calindy also helps to negate – or at least, complicate – a suggestion that Duncan and Karl are exclusively homosexual. Thus, Calindy's presence prevents *Imperial Earth* from being a 'gay' novel. On the surface, this is a shrewd marketing move – the novel is for a general audience. But equally, it helps Clarke portray sex between men without ever resorting to the characters defining themselves as 'homosexual'.

Sedgwick further explored the complexities of sexuality in her later work, *Epistemology of the Closet* (1990), summarizing two separate understandings that are circulation; a minoritizing approach, that is 'a distinct population of persons who "really are" gay', and a universalizing approach which sees 'sexual desire as a powerful solvent of stable identities' (Sedgwick, 2008: 85). The former sees homosexuality as a distinct, fixed identity, whereas the latter understanding considers sexuality to be a spectrum, that everyone may experience attraction for the same and opposite sex. Writing at the same time, Judith Butler challenged the notion of identities, arguing they are performative 'manufactured and sustained through corporeal signs and other discursive means' (Butler, 2006: 185). Performativity and universalizing provided the foundation for the discipline of queer theory, which, as well as celebrating diversity and dissent, sought to challenge notions of normativity and expectations of identity. In this sense, the novel depicts a queer world. Clarke portrays the future of *Imperial Earth* through a universalizing lens, where heterosexual exclusivity is no longer dominant. The word 'homosexuality' is absent.

Such universalizing of sexuality can be found in several of Duncan's encounters. On his voyage to Earth, Duncan arranges an illicit rendezvous with the ship's engineer Warren MacKenzie, 'a freckled red-head' (Clarke, 1975/1997: 98), to see its power source, the Asymptotic Drive. Such a liaison is forbidden, as Titan is a potential competitor in space engineering. However, at the mid-point of the journey, the gravity is turned off to allow passengers to fully experience space travel. Rather than a lofty appreciation of weightlessness, Clarke explains that passengers often exploit the period to experiment with zero gravity sex due to 'human nature having certain invariants' (Clarke, 1975/1997: 104). Duncan uses this period as a cover in which to take look at the Asymptotic Drive, remarking to Warren: 'It's just occurred to me [...] that if anyone does meet the pair of us at two o'clock in the morning of Turnaround, we'll have the perfect alibi' (Clarke, 1975/1997: 105). The line suggests, without stating outright, that Duncan at least sees it plausible that he and Warren could have sex. Later, during Duncan's tour of Earth, we learn that his host Bernie Patras has arranged escorts for Duncan. On one occasion with 'a cuddlesome and talented young lady', apparently Patras's own girlfriend, a possible threesome is suggested: 'when Bernie, as an interested party, wanted to join in the festivities, Duncan selfishly threw him out' (Clarke, 1975/1997: 204). Again, this scene is reminiscent of the homosocial triangle, with Patras's girlfriend facilitating the possibility for sex between Duncan and Patras himself. But Clarke again is careful to ensure that the (nameless) girlfriend is present before raising the possibility of two men together.

These throwaway references to threesomes, casual sex and open relationships contribute to the depiction of the future as sexually liberated. Such a portrayal is not unsurprising; the book was published after the sexual liberation of the 1960s, when the contraceptive pill freed sex from the consequences of reproduction. Yet, as Lynne Segal has observed of the permissive society: 'The issue of power was always present, somewhere, with women feeling that men were still in control, even when supportive of women's liberation' (Segal, 2015: 45). Again, we encounter another paradox of *Imperial Earth*, for in spite of its depiction of a liberated society, the role of women is restricted and overlooked. First, there is Duncan's wife, Mirissa, a character absent from the action of the novel; she is not granted a single line of dialogue. Our first encounter with her is when Duncan switches off a video chat with her, having said goodbye before departing for Earth and leaving her on Titan. Clarke's attempt to portray Duncan as heartbroken here is unconvincing: 'he was glad that the ordeal was over' (Clarke 1997: 86). When faced with the opportunities of zero gravity sex at the mid-point of the voyage, Clarke relates that 'Duncan had been tempted: Mirissa was beginning to fade and there was no lack of opportunity' (Clarke 1997: 104). Yet, we are told the voyage only takes twenty days (Clarke 1997: 79). Far from a heartfelt separation that leaves him yearning for his spouse, Duncan is forgetting her after little over a week. There are echoes here of Clarke's own marriage. As Marilyn Mayfield (then Clarke) told the *Wood Green Reporter*: 'Sometimes when he looks at me he doesn't even see me. He's way up on another planet!' Clarke even spent their honeymoon checking the proofs for *Childhood's End* (McAleer, 2017: 91–2).

There are only two other women of note in the book: Duncan's grandmother, who acted as a mentor to Duncan as a child but who remains on Titan throughout the novel, and Calindy herself. As the focus of Duncan and Karl's infatuation, Calindy is herself described in gendered terms: 'it was emotion that provided the driving force of Calindy's life; her will and beauty and intelligence were merely its servants' (Clarke, 1997: 65). Calindy's function in the novel is to be a glamorous object of desire, one that is emotional rather than rational. When Duncan meets with her once again on Earth, she has become an executive for Enigma Associates, a company that arranges high-profile tours. Her charm is now used for professional purposes as a hostess. When revealing that Karl has been physically abusive to her, Clarke's description undermines her: 'With another theatrical gesture, she slipped open her dress, displaying the upper left arm – not to mention her entire left breast' (Clarke, 1975/1997: 249). Rather than sincere, she is described as 'theatrical', and rather than emphasise the abuse, we are invited to imagine her breasts as if she is little more than a sex object.

Furthermore, there is something slightly artificial about Karl and Duncan's desire for her. This is highlighted when Duncan in reminiscing about her on Titan: 'When he thought of Calindy, and tried to conjure up her image, he did not see the real girl, but always his only replica of her, in one of the Bubble stereos that had become popular' (Clarke, 1975/1997: 64). Even when Duncan finally consummates his infatuation with her, Clarke hints at disappointment: 'Calindy no longer tasted of honey' (Clarke, 1975/1997: 252). Part of the Earthbound plot follows Duncan trying to track down Karl on Earth. Calindy reveals that Karl has obsessively followed her, behaving like an abusive ex-lover. She explains that on her final night on Titan, he had experimented with a 'joy machine' when making love – a form of electronic sex drug that had imprinted her on his consciousness. While this explains the need for Karl to console himself with Duncan earlier – and the subsequent diminishing of their relationship – it also suggests that Karl's heterosexual obsession with Calindy was only ever something artificial: 'It must have been flattering to have held in your hand the soul of someone as talented and beautiful as Karl – even if he had been enslaved accidentally, with the aid of a machine' (Clarke, 1975/1997: 247). So, although Calindy is an object of desire, this desire is artificially induced (for Karl) or disappointing when obtained (for Duncan).

While women are either absent, or reduced to tragic objects of desire, Clarke's most troubling portrayal of women occurs when Duncan visits the island of Dr Mohammed to arrange for a clone of himself. When touring the island at night, he encounters a party of the surrogate mothers who bear the clones in their wombs:

> Most of these women were extremely plain; some were ugly, a few were frankly hideous. And though Duncan noticed that two or three might even pass as beautiful, it only needed a glance to show that they were mentally subnormal. (Clarke, 1975/1997: 186)

Reid interprets the scene as highlighting the anxieties and moral complexities over reproductive technologies (Reid, 1997: 74), but arguably it expresses a deeply offensive attitude to women in general. It reduces women to be valued by their looks and assumes that such judgements are objective and universal. Even if Duncan's judgements were reasonable, it is ironic that in a technically advanced world, where space travel and cloning are possible, that any supposed cosmetic limitations cannot be altered surgically. The reduction of those mentally subnormal (again another value judgement made only with a 'glance') to surrogate wombs to be used is again ethically and morally suspect, raising issues of informed consent and exploitation. This is made all the more worrying by the statement that a 'purely mechanical womb could have served as well' (Clarke, 1975/1997: 182). Effectively, women are treated as cattle.

In the same scene, Duncan observes male nurses tending these women:

> [S]everal of the men looked *very effeminate*, and were treating their partners with what could only be called sisterly affection. They were obviously dear friends; and that was all they would ever be. [...] Duncan could never feel quite happy with someone whose affections were exclusively polarised towards one sex. What a contrast to the *aggressive normality* of Karl [...](Clarke, 1975/1997: 187, emphasis added)

Here Clarke undermines his universalizing approach to sexuality; instead resorting to a minoritizing description that draws upon the gendered psychological discourses that were drawn up in the nineteenth century. The nurses' heterosexual failure ('never more than friends') is directly aligned to effeminacy, thus a breach of the expectations of masculine behaviour. While the praise of bisexuality may seem progressive, it is undermined by the phrase 'aggressive normality'. The word 'normality' suggests prescribed expectations of behaviour.

'Aggressive' is a gendered word: aggression is seen as a masculine trait. In a novel where women are passive and overlooked, this simply reinforces the patriarchal power dynamics that Segal cautioned against in her appraisal of sexual liberation.

The novel does, however, conclude with a genuinely progressive twist. Towards the end, Karl is killed, and Clarke attempts to redeem the character by revealing that he was developing plans for a deep space telescope. Duncan returns to Titan inspired by the plans, and, rather than cloning himself, has cloned Karl instead. The scene is Clarke's only use of Duncan's blackness; the revelation is confirmed by a description of the baby's 'golden hair' (Clarke, 1975/1997: 284). At this moment, Clarke predicts ideas of the queer family, a disruption of heterosexual reproduction. The baby effectively has two fathers – Duncan and Karl. Kath Weston has argued that ideas of the queer family were consolidated in the late 1980s and early 1990s, as a response to the HIV/AIDS crisis. In particular, she argues the homophobic climate created by the crisis caused a necessity for gays and lesbians to rethink families, and celebrate the bonds created within the LGBT community (Weston, 1997). Similarly, also in the late 1990s, the advances in genetic research led to plausible scientific speculation about the possibility of cloning for same-sex reproduction (Baker, 1999: 312–14). Adoption and foster rights were only made equal for gay men and lesbians in the UK in 2002 (Weeks, 2016: 260). Clarke's novel anticipated these debates back in the 1970s.

The concept of cloning further disrupts the psychological dynamics with the family, in particular the Oedipal triangle between the son, mother and father. Leo Bersani has attempted to invert pathologizing psychological constructions of homosexuality by arguing that gay men bypass the Oedipal crisis; that is, the fear of castration by the father which causes the child to renounce the relationship with his mother, in turn causing him to see his mother as different from himself. Bersani suggests gay men's more empathic relationships with women as evidence of this: 'Freud's hypothetical homosexual has after all not abandoned his mother, but neither has he fantasmatically struggled with his father in order to have her' (Bersani, 2009: 54). Thus, Bersani speculates, a gay subjectivity is founded on the refusal of boundaries between the self and other built around confrontation, and Bersani suggests an 'impersonal narcissism' in homosexuality – an ability to see the self in another. Gay men are not repulsed by other men. The relationship between Duncan and Colin, his clone father, is similarly founded not upon any Oedipal crisis, as Duncan's subjectivity is built around his awareness as a clone:

> It was sometimes a great advantage, and sometimes downright embarrassing, to have a father who was also your forty-year-older twin. He knew all the mistakes you were going to make, because he has made them already. It was impossible to conceal any secrets from him, as his thought processes were virtually the same. (Clarke, 1975/1997: 66)

Such a moment challenges traditional psychological notions of family, just as Bersani is attempting to challenge the psychological conceptions of homosexuality. The notion of the father as threat to self, or even the presence of a mother as an original point of empathy, is disrupted in Duncan's perception of his father. (How his son as a clone of Karl will respond, of course, is open to speculation.) So it is the cloning backstory of *Imperial Earth*, which provides both a background and alternative future for Duncan, that is the novel's most radical theme. In portraying cloning, it is a pity that Clarke leaves the treatment of women unchallenged and that he does not explore the use of an artificial womb by Duncan. Likewise, it is disappointing that Duncan's blackness is erased by Karl's (cloned) whiteness in this otherwise queer family.

Conclusion

This chapter has explored *Imperial Earth* through the changes in understandings of homosexuality that occurred throughout Clarke's lifetime. David Halperin has suggested that gay male culture is a specific response to the discursive constructions of gendered behaviour, that is, the prescriptive notion that desiring men is a feminine attribute. Halperin highlights drag culture, cults surrounding the diva, and gay men's fascination with femininity, as attempts to challenge prescribed gender roles (Halperin, 2012). Yet, as we have seen, *Imperial Earth* takes a different approach; women are largely absent in the novel.

But then, *Imperial Earth* isn't a gay novel, or at least, Clarke would not want us to see it so. Clarke cautiously avoids any mention of the words homosexuality or bisexuality, and carefully frames the relationship between the two protagonists in a love triangle, deploying the homosocial triangle as a displacement of the relationship between the two men. But his own reluctance to expand or explore his female characters undermines this evasive technique. The homosocial triangle is nullified because Calindy is little more than a distraction. Instead, it is the clone subplot that simultaneously provides the novel's lowest point and most radical move: the scene of the clone mothers is, if not misogynistic, then, at best, written by an author oblivious to his male privilege. And yet, cloning also provides the opportunity for creating a queer family, consolidating the relationship between Duncan and Karl.

To ask if Duncan and Karl are gay is to be overly simplistic. Clarke himself scoffed at the idea: 'They'd just mucked around as boys' (McAleer, 2017: 316). I'd like to imagine he'd have more positively responded if asked whether they were 'cheerful', because that is how Clarke presented his own sexuality. In the end, *Imperial Earth* is a product of a man who is also a product of his time.

Note

1 Reid also refers to Sedgwick's homosocial triangle, although not in her chapter on *Imperial Earth*; instead when discussing 'Golden Age' science fiction in her chapter on *2061: Odyssey Three* (Reid, 1997: 140–1).

Works Cited

Baker, R. (1999) *Sex in the Future: Ancient Urges Meet Future Technology*. Basingstoke: Macmillan.

Bernstein, J. (2008) 'The Grasshopper and His Space Odyssey: A Scientist Remembers the Celebrated Science Fiction Writer Arthur C. Clarke.' *The American Scholar* (June 1), URL (accessed November 2019): https://theamericanscholar.org/the-grasshopper-and-his-space-odyssey/

Bersani, L. (2009) *Is the Rectum a Grave? and Other Essays*. Chicago, IL: University of Chicago Press.

Butler, J. (2006) *Gender Trouble: Feminism and the Subversion of Identity*, 3rd edn. New York and London: Routledge.
Carpenter, E. (2007) *The Intermediate Sex*. Middlesex: Echo Library.
Clarke, A. C. (1997) *Imperial Earth*. London: Vista.
Cook, M. (2014) *Queer Domesticities: Homosexuality and Home Life in Twentieth-Century London*. Basingstoke: Palgrave Macmillan.
Crisp, Q. (1985) *The Naked Civil Servant*. London: Flamingo.
Dyer, R. (1997) *White*. Abingdon: Routledge.
Foucault, M. (1998) *The History of Sexuality: The Will to Knowledge*, trans. Robert Hurley, 2nd edn. London: Penguin.
Garber, E. and Paleo, L. (1990) *Uranian Worlds: A Guide to Alternative Sexuality in Science Fiction, Fantasy, and Horror*, 2nd edn. Boston, MA: G. K. Hall.
Halperin, D. M. (2012) *How To Be Gay*. Cambridge, MA: Harvard University Press.
Harding, L. (2000) "The Space Odysseus", *Guardian* (28 September), URL (accessed November 2021): https://www.theguardian.com/books/2000/sep/28/sciencefictionfantasyandhorror.arthurcclarke
Houlbrook, M. (2006) *Queer London: Perils and Pleasures in the Sexual Metropolis, 1918–1957*. Chicago, IL: University of Chicago Press.
Irvine, J. M. (2005) *Disorders of Desire: Sexuality and Gender in Modern American Sexology*. 2nd edn. Philadelphia: Temple University Press.
Janes, D. (2015) *Picturing the Closet: Male Secrecy and Homosexual Visibility in Britain*. Oxford: Oxford University Press.
McAleer, N. (2017) *Arthur C. Clarke: Odyssey of a Visionary*, 2nd edn. London: Ashgrove.
Moorcock, M. (2008) 'Brave New Worlds', *Guardian* (22 March), URL (accessed November 2021): https://www.theguardian.com/books/2008/mar/22/arthurcclarke
Potvin, J. (2014) *Bachelors of a Different Sort: Queer Aesthetics, Material Culture and the Modern Interior in Britain*. Manchester: Manchester University Press.
Reid, R. A. (1997) *Arthur C. Clarke: A Critical Companion*. Westport, CT: Greenwood Press.
Sedgwick, E. K. (1985) *Between Men: English Literature and Male Homosocial Desire*. New York: Columbia University Press.
Sedgwick, E. K. (2008) *Epistemology of the Closet*. Berkeley: University of California Press.

Segal, L. (2015) *Straight Sex: Rethinking the Politics of Pleasure*. London: Verso.
Sinfield, A. (1994) *The Wilde Century: Effeminacy, Oscar Wilde and the Queer Moment*. London: Cassell.
Weeks, J. (2016) *Coming Out: The Emergence of LGBT Identities in Britain from the Nineteenth Century to the Present*, 3rd edn. London: Quartet Books.
Weston, K. (1997) *Families We Choose: Lesbians, Gays, Kinship*. New York: Columbia University Press.

12

Thirty Years is Ample Time
The Clarke Award and Literary Science Fiction

Nick Hubble

According to its website, the Arthur C. Clarke Award 'is given for the best science fiction novel first published in the United Kingdom during the previous year', but it has come to be identified in particular with the idea of literary sf, and the attendant arguments about whether sf is good literature and if this is a desirable thing or not. In the Clarke tribute anthology, *2001: An Odyssey in Words* (2018), non-fiction contributions by Neil Gaiman and China Miéville touch directly on such questions. Gaiman suggests that part of the fun of the Award is that it is contentious, and that this capacity to provoke argument is due to the element of unpredictability created by judges acting on radically different criteria from each other. However, while the perennial uncertainty as to which book will win, or even what will get shortlisted, probably contributes to the Award's enduring popularity, Gaiman proposes that the reason it is taken seriously is because of its capacity for 'bridge-building': 'The Arthur C. Clarke Award is the award that the world of sf offers, each year, to the world outside as an example of both what sf is and what it can be' (Gaiman, 2018: 186). On this view, arguments as to whether the Award has tended to favour mainstream authors who have written sf over genre authors who have written sf with mainstream appeal, or *vice versa*, are irrelevant. It is the Award, itself, which holds this unstable and historically disreputable field together, and offers it to the wider world as something of cultural value. Miéville neatly encapsulates the alchemy of the Award with a clever play on Clarke's Third Law by claiming that more than thirty years after its inception: 'More and more readers can now agree, as Clarke Award-watchers have long known, that any sufficiently advanced science fiction is indistinguishable from literature' (Miéville, 2018: 189). But far from being content with this victory, Miéville wants something more; for the Award to honour a book 'without a single explicit unreal, fantastic element' (Miéville, 2018: 191–2). The example he imagines is of a book that in its non-fantastical, radical estrangement of the everyday nevertheless reconfigures the world. For such a work to be recognized as sf would be an admission that sf is the name for any literature that seeks not merely to reflect, represent or understand the world, but to change it. For Miéville, therefore, the really exciting idea implicit to the history of the Clarke Award is 'that any sufficiently advanced literature must be indistinguishable from science fiction' (Miéville, 2018: 192). This chapter will investigate how such a radical inversion of cultural values has come to be associated with the name of Clarke and what it signifies for the future.

It is generally accepted (although there are different versions of what exactly was intended) that the enticement of Clarke in 1986 to give his name and money to the prize was part of an attempt to change the negative public image of sf. Therefore, the first point to consider is what it was about Clarke as a writer that made him suitable for this role. While Clarke was long established as one – alongside Isaac Asimov and Robert A. Heinlein – of sf's 'Big Three', this in itself did not betoken that he represented in anyway a bridge between sf and mainstream literary culture. He was, however, the one living British sf writer whom most British people would have heard of; possibly in connection with his collaboration with Stanley Kubrick on the screenplay of *2001: A Space Odyssey* (1968), and more probably for his two very popular television series, *Arthur C. Clarke's Mysterious World* (1980) and *Arthur C. Clarke's World of Strange Powers* (1985).

More particularly, his literary prestige within the sf field reached its zenith over the course of the 1970s. Following the success of *2001*, both book and film, Clarke signed an almost unprecedented triple book deal in the early 1970s. Of these novels, *Rendezvous with Rama* (1973) and *The Fountains of Paradise* (1979) both won the double of the Nebula and Hugo Awards. 'A Meeting with Medusa' (1971) also won the Nebula Award for Best Novella.

It is worth pausing to consider what these works are like. *Rendezvous with Rama* might be described as a classic tale of sf evoking a 'sense of wonder' at a 'big dumb object' (see Joseph S. Norman's chapter in this volume), in this case a colossal spacecraft hurtling through the Solar System. The novel combines these factors skilfully with narrative suspense surrounding how a team can get to the craft, explore it and get back out again within the constraints thrown up by the mathematics of fuel load and velocity. However, as a work of literature, it doesn't present much to think about beyond the contrast between the human activity and the enigmatic nature of the huge superstructure. Probably the passage most quoted today is the notorious throwaway line about the effects of weightlessness on female breasts. Of course, there is nothing wrong with it being a tale to be enjoyed rather than a text to be analysed; but it is a little odd perhaps when viewed in the context of the history of British sf because it reads superficially as though the New Wave of the 1960s never happened. While Clarke's 1950s fiction is marked, as Roger Luckhurst argues, by both an 'English imaginary' and 'a very British understanding of the rhythm of the rise and fall and rise of Empires over centuries' (Luckhurst, 2005: 134–5), *Rendezvous with Rama* also seems to depict 'a process of colonisation' (Butler, 2012: 58). Yet the novel is different in one respect; it possesses a grandeur of scale that exposes the limitations of human perspective, which is thereby decentred (even if this appears to have little emotional effect on Clarke's protagonists). This odd blend of old-fashioned liberal humanism with unknowable vastness was by no means restricted to Clarke and became indicative of a 1970s aesthetic as represented, for example, by the improbable length of time it takes for the imperial star cruiser to pass overhead in the opening scene of George Lucas's *Star Wars* (1977), but Clarke was indisputably one of its key practitioners. The (transposed) Sri Lankan setting of *The Fountains of Paradise* represents an advance in the way that it offsets the infinity of space with a sublime figuration of Earthly landscape, and thereby enables a more subtle vision of the relationship between humans and the universe, which is supported by the temporal shifts between antiquity and present day that occur within the novel. While the characters are not particularly any more three-dimensional than usual for Clarke's fiction, the framing generates an engaging level of complexity so that Peter Nicholls and John Clute are probably correct in their assessment that 'it is the most considerable work of the latter part of Clarke's career' (Clute and Nicholls, 2019). In short, Clarke's writing and sales in the 1970s were substantial enough to give him a level of respect outside the field. Once this respect (and, of course, the money his books earned) were taken into account alongside his historical status, public fame and British nationality, then he was the obvious choice to ask to be involved in a British Award. Whether any of the winners of that Award would resemble Clarke's own approach to fiction was a matter that was yet to be decided.

Edward James, who was involved with the establishment of the Award and its administrator for the first two years of its existence, explains that the initial impulse for what would become the Clarke Award came from the Science Fiction Foundation, which had been founded in 1971 with the mission of educating the public about sf. The idea was that the Award would help fulfil this mission by directing the public towards good sf but this gave rise to a quandary:

> Should the Award go to a work which the judges recognise to be solidly within the science fiction tradition, which should no doubt be applauded by sf fans, but be received blankly by an uninterested world? Or should the Award associate itself with a work which the outside world would actually recognise, to increase the standing of science fiction by hanging on the coattails of recognised literature? (James, 2002: 70)

A slightly different account is given by Paul Kincaid, also involved in the establishment of the Award and later to be its administrator from 1996 to 2007, who states that 'Clarke wanted to use the award to encourage British science fiction' but the organizers decided that there were too few British writers for this to work and so therefore, as is the case to this day, 'the award would be for the best science fiction novel receiving its first British publication in the year' (Kincaid, 2017). As Andrew M. Butler points out, the aims expressed by James and Kincaid 'are not incompatible' and in the end were arguably achieved by the winning books in 1990 and 1991 (the fourth and fifth Clarke Awards): 'Geoff Ryman's *The Child Garden* (1989) and Colin Greenwood's *Take Back Plenty* (1990) were popular winners by major talents who were integral to the British sf scene' (Butler, 2016: 78–80).

However, the first winner of the award, Margaret Atwood's *The Handmaid's Tale* (1986), was neither a British book, nor, according to some including the author herself, sf. In the long run, recognizing this work has been very much to the Award's credit (it failed, by comparison, to win the Booker Prize), but this was not obvious at the time. In fact, James was later adamant that 'it was not an auspicious start to the award' and that 'in retrospect, *The Handmaid's Tale* was clearly the wrong book' (James, 2002: 70). He argues it did nothing for sf because the book was not recognized as sf, and that it was just a perpetuation of a mistaken strategy of appropriating works such as Jonathan Swift's *Gulliver's Travels* (1726) and George Orwell's *Nineteen Eighty-Four* (1949) to the sf tradition in order to try and make sf more respectable. It is clear that such suspicions continued to dog the Award even after the successive victories of Ryman and Greenwood, as demonstrated by James's discussion of the controversy surrounding the award of the 1993 Clarke to Marge Piercy's *Body of Glass* (US title: *He, She and It*). The magnitude of the furore may be gauged by the fact that James devotes three entire pages of an eleven-page book chapter to it. John Clute complained about the Award being given to the work of a 'mainstream author [...] manipulating SF devices to illuminate her own concerns' (cited in James, 2002: 72). He went on to suggest that Clarke would not have liked the book and probably would have preferred Kim Stanley Robinson's *Red Mars* (1992) to win. Eventually as the debate raged on, Clarke himself was drawn in, writing to the letters column of *Interzone*:

In view of the present controversy, I dipped into the opening chapters of *Body of Glass* and will say at once that I was very much impressed. If Marge Piercy maintains the same standard throughout the whole book, there's no doubt it is an outstanding work of science fiction by any definition. (cited in James, 2002: 74)

This ended the controversy but, according to James, the problem would only get worse because with the disintegration of genre boundaries, more and more writers would be writing what was in effect sf, but which would be described by their publishers as anything but that; what was distinctive about sf was in danger of becoming indistinguishable from the mainstream. In other words, the possibility that Miéville finds so exciting in 2018 was viewed as a threat by James in the 1990s.

Making sense of this shift is key to thinking about the cultural value today of both sf in general and the Clarke Award in particular. Viewed from my own personal experience as an adult who had read sf since childhood but didn't then engage with sf fandom or criticism, it was Atwood's victory that eventually made me aware of the Clarke a few years after that award had been made. The first book I went out and bought because I heard about it winning the Clarke was *Body of Glass*. At no point did it occur to me that Piercy was not an authentic sf writer because she had written the *bona fide* sf classic *Woman at the Edge of Time* (1976). For that matter, I also enjoyed Paul Theroux's *O-Zone* (1986), which was the benchmark of awfulness that Clute rated *Body of Glass* against. It would, therefore, be easy for me to argue at this point that critics such as James and Clute were simply being over-precious in protecting sf heritage because I have never seen the problem the way that they saw it. However, it would be insincere of me – as a long-time academic in university English literature departments – to imply that I am unaware that the defensive attitudes of sf critics were rooted in bitter and protracted experience of the persistent distaste for sf manifested by the literary establishment in Britain.

Historically, this 'generic revulsion', as Fredric Jameson terms it, is a product of a 'literary "reality principle"' that is neither 'a matter of personal taste, nor is it to be addressed by way of purely aesthetic arguments, such as the attempt to assimilate selected SF works to the canon as such' (Jameson, 2005: xiv). When James asks the question of Clarke Award judges 'are they choosing a work for insiders or outsiders?' (James, 2002: 71), he is making the similar point that if mainstream-friendly books are picked to win the Award, then it cannot address the unseen ideological mechanisms that resist sf's potential to change the world. Yet, surely, few contemporary novels have shown more capacity to change the world than *The Handmaid's Tale*, with its radical estrangement of gender relations. In this context, the significance of Atwood's novel being the first Clarke winner lies not in its mainstream status and appeal to 'outsiders', which actually serves to enable the downplaying of its material effects by disguising them as 'literature', but in its continued sfnal capacity to disrupt the gender relations of the present. Retrospectively, the vindication of the first Clarke Award jury's decision lies not in the fact that *The Handmaid's Tale* is now regarded as a modern classic but that it is also now undisputedly regarded as sf. In effect, albeit with a built-in time delay, that first award has already achieved the identification between sufficiently advanced literature and sf that Miéville calls for.

The failure of James to realize this at the time of the Award or over the course of the next dozen or so years is not surprising when we consider Atwood's own insistence that *The Handmaid's Tale* was not sf but speculative fiction. This fine distinction was to reach its zenith in the introduction to her 2011 essay collection, *In Other Worlds: SF and the Human Imagination*, in which Atwood admits that she had (at that time) 'written three full-length fictions that nobody would ever class as sociological realism: *The Handmaid's Tale*, *Oryx and Crake* and *The Year of the Flood*', but that they were not sf in the same way that *Nineteen Eighty-Four* is not sf when compared to Ray Bradbury's *The Martian Chronicles* (1950) (Atwood, 2011: 2). To provide further clarification, Atwood proclaims sf to be those texts descended from H. G. Wells's *The War of the Worlds* (1898), 'which treats of an invasion by tentacled, blood-sucking Martians shot to Earth in metal canisters – things that could not possibly happen', whereas speculative fiction 'means plots that descend from Jules Verne's books about submarines and balloon travel and such – things that really could happen but just hadn't completely happened when the authors wrote the books' (Atwood, 2011: 6). Choosing to align herself with the adventure yarns of Jules Verne, rather than the writer of whom Orwell wrote 'the minds of all us, and therefore the physical world, would be perceptibly different if Wells had never existed' (Orwell, 1970: 171), is an eccentric choice given that Atwood's novels clearly follow the example of Wells in using sfnal devices to critique toxic aspects of society such as patriarchy and the instrumentalization of science in the same way that *The War of the Worlds* critiques colonialism. In many ways Atwood's insistence that she was writing speculative fiction rather than sf is best ignored as an idiosyncrasy. The point is that by the time she published this clearly labelled collection of essays on sf, she had published those 'three full-length fictions' which everyone read as sf. It would be excessive to suggest that Atwood has single-handedly changed the status of sf but she has probably done more than any other single author to make it respectable. In any case, her willingness to pose for photos, after winning the 2016 Kitschies Red Tentacle for *The Heart Goes Last*, with the award on her head suggests that she no longer feels the need to rigidly distance herself from the taint of genre.

The changing dynamic of Clarke Award winners and shortlists provides a different way of thinking about what happened to sf between the late 1990s and the early 2010s. As soon as one thinks about the Clarke Award in terms of male and female winners, it becomes impossible to think of it as a straightforward tale of progressive literary evolution from Atwood onwards. The fourteen awards made from 1987 to 2000 were split evenly between male and female writers despite books by women comprising only 31 per cent of the shortlisted novels. In contrast, during the ten years from 2001 to 2010, Gwyneth Jones was the sole female winner (in 2002 for *Bold as Love*) and only sixteen books by women (just over 25 per cent of the total) were shortlisted (including another two by Jones, the most short-listed author in the Award's history). In the ten years since 2011, however, books by women writers have comprised over 40 per cent of all shortlisted works and won six of the ten awards. Of these, neither Jane Rogers's *The Testament of Jessie Lamb*, the winner in 2012, or Emily St

John Mandel's *Station Eleven*, the winner in 2015, were initially marketed as sf and nor are their authors known as sf writers. Both these novels were elegant literary dystopias and so, in that respect at least, successors to *The Handmaid's Tale* but, significantly, neither provoked the kind of controversy that had arisen from the victories of Atwood and Piercy.

On the one hand, the first decade of the twenty-first century appears to be an interregnum between what can otherwise be presented as a story of a progressive closing of the gender gap in terms of recognition by the Clarke. On the other hand, this period also saw a transformation in the relationship between sf and mainstream literature so that, by the end, not only was Atwood publishing books on sf but other mainstream female writers were writing Clarke-winning sf. So what were the various Clarke juries of those years awarding when they selected China Miéville in 2001, 2005 and 2010, Christopher Priest in 2003, Neal Stephenson in 2004, Geoff Ryman in 2006, M. John Harrison in 2007, Richard Morgan in 2008, and Ian R MacLeod in 2009? An interesting suggestion was mooted by James Lovegrove in a 2007 review of four novels: the 2006 Clarke winner, Ryman's *Air*, Morgan's *Black Man* (published as *Thirteen* in the US and in later UK editions), which would win in 2008, Ken MacLeod's *The Execution Channel*, which would be shortlisted in 2008, and Ian McDonald's *Brasyl*, which (controversially) would not be shortlisted. Lovegrove argued that these novels showed that sf, which was 'written predominantly by white Western males', was starting to turn away from a preoccupation with using space settings to examine the world as it is and instead focusing on the 'others' around 'us' – those with 'a different language, skin colour, set of cultural signifiers, even gender' (Lovegrove, 2015: 143). While the encounter with otherness had always been a part of sf, Lovegrove is surely correct that there had been a paradigm shift at this time in the way major British male sf authors approached this encounter. This shift reflected a wider set of changes in Britain over the preceding decades, where eighteen years of Conservative Party rule from 1979 to 1997 had generated a politicised culture of resistance, based around multiculturalism and opposition to sexism and homophobia, which became firmly established and dominant – at least within the big cities. As a consequence, men read and wrote books in which the middle-class, white male viewpoint was not necessarily privileged or assumed as the universal default position of the reader. Indeed, many of the key novels mentioned above were not written predominantly from the viewpoint of white male protagonists at all. For example, Stephenson's *Quicksilver* includes probably his most complex and satisfying female protagonist; *Black Man* is unambiguously about a black man; *Air* and Ian MacLeod's *Song of Time*, the 2009 winner, are both long, complex novels woven around the perspective of non-white women. *Brasyl*, with its three intercut narratives and range of protagonists, including the 'bisexual and gender fluid' Edson (Morgan, 2017: 88), is inherently pluralistic. What these victories demonstrably celebrated was an association of sf with a cultural representation of difference that had hitherto been considered as the exclusive property of literary fiction. By the end of the decade, sf and literature were no longer considered antithetical terms but, indeed, equal components of a 'literary sf'. Indeed, the dominance of literary sf within the sf field in general was such that it led to an attempted counter-revolution in 2014 by the self-labelled Sad and Rabid Puppies attempting to put forward slates of nominees they found acceptable for the Hugos, the annual sf awards voted on by members of that year's Worldcon. The twentieth-century division between sf and literature had been transformed by the first decade of the twenty-first century into what Adam Roberts satirically classified as the division between:

> The Hard, politically conservative 'SF is about learning and respecting the inviolable laws of physics', masculinist, macho kill-and-rape video game, neo-Fascist Hugo ballot-stuffing crowd in one corner; and the Literary SF, 'science fiction is about the encounter with otherness', lovin-the-alien, polymorphous, feminist, queer, coloured, trans and politically liberal crowd in the other. (Roberts, 2015: 9)

This political division confirms that literary sf, as a category, is no longer defined by its proximity to mainstream realism but can now include the full panoply of aliens and generic tropes provided that their deployment is governed by a sensibility of openness to the other. It seems reasonable to think that Clarke himself would have welcomed this shift described by Lovegrove and Roberts as completing his own rather more mixed attempts to decentre universal human experience in relation to the vastness and unknowability of space.

However, the negative consequence of male writers dominating the Award for a decade by occupying the territory of difference was that women were unfairly represented. In an interview in 2010, Tricia Sullivan, who had won the 1999 Clarke with *Dreaming in Smoke* and been shortlisted in 2004 for *Maul*, pointed out that there had only been one win by a woman in the last decade, compared to five in the 1990s. This generated extensive discussion and a poll to decide the decade's top sf novels by women run by Niall Harrison on the *Vector* editorial blog (Harrison 2010). Six of the eleven books in the top ten (there was a tie for tenth) had in fact been shortlisted by the Clarke, and Gwyneth Jones's *Life* (2004) had not been published in the UK, but Justina Robson's *Natural History* (2003) looks a striking omission in retrospect. Robson, in particular, seemed to represent a worrying pattern in that her first two novels, *Silver Screen* and *Mappa Mundi*, had been shortlisted in 2000 and 2002 respectively but then she completely disappeared from the Clarke annals (even before writing the *Quantum Reality* series which might be considered science fantasy rather than sf). The poll winner was Sarah Hall's *The Carhullan Army*, whose inclusion on the 2008 Clarke shortlist had been overshadowed by the controversy surrounding *Brasyl's* omission. In retrospect, however, her victory in the poll despite being one of only two non-genre writers in the top ten (Audrey Niffenegger's *The Time Traveler's Wife* – shortlisted for the Clarke in 2005 – came fourth), pointed the way forward to the Clarke wins of Rogers and Mandel. In the wake of the poll, and extensive critical analysis and discussion commissioned and posted by Harrison, the 2011 Clarke jury shortlisted two women writers for only the second time since 2004: Sullivan's *Lightborn* and Lauren Beukes's *Zoo City*, an sf-fantasy blend as uncompromisingly urban as anything by Miéville, which won. Every subsequent shortlist, with the exception of the outlying all-male one of 2013, has contained at least two women writers.

James was being satirical when he suggested a future in which the 'Clarke Award ceremony is shown on prime-time TV [...] and [...] the cultural barriers between the science fiction and literary worlds have broken down and the world is thus a much better place' (James, 2002: 77). However, while Andrew M. Butler is not yet giving his chair-of-judges speech on live television, the irony is that most of this has come to pass. As Butler wrote during the run-up to the thirtieth anniversary of the Clarke, the Award is now well thought of and reported as prominently in the mainstream press as the Booker. Writers not inside the genre such as Rogers and Mandel have won and been happy to win, and victory now generates publicity and up to a 200% sales spike for winners (Butler, 2016: 81–2). He concluded his reflections with the hope that 'long may that silence at the announcement be unpredictable and the discussion that follows rich' (Butler, 2016: 83).

Well, there certainly was a momentary stunned silence – at least, on my behalf – a few months later when Butler announced the winner of the 2016 Award: Adrian Tchaikovsky's *Children of Time*. I had not thought that a novel about a generation starship and a planet populated by talking spiders would win the Clarke. It wasn't that I hadn't enjoyed it immensely but it had seemed self-evidently an example of the Clarke's relatively frequent propensity to include an enjoyable read on the shortlist as a nod to past genre conventions. For example in 2010, when the Clarke timetable still permitted an annual 'Not the Clarke Award' at Eastercon, the inclusion of Chris Wooding's *Retribution Falls* on the shortlist alongside what were obviously five more serious contenders – Miéville (who won), Jones, Roberts, Kim Stanley Robinson and Marcel Theroux (filling the non-genre writer slot) – was greeted by the panel, in those days of pre-puppy innocence, as a welcome return to old-fashioned adventure. Nevertheless, it was the first of the six to be discarded. Moreover, only four years before Tchaikovsky's unexpected win, online discussions around the Clarke had reverberated with Christopher Priest's broadside fired at the judges concerning the supposed deficiencies of the 2012 shortlist, which included his memorably pithy dismissal of Sheri Tepper's *The Waters Rising*: 'how can one describe it? For fuck's sake, it is a quest saga and it has a talking horse' (Priest, 2012). And now the Clarke had actually been awarded to a novel with multiple talking spiders. The 2021 Clarke was awarded – live on BBC Radio Four's *Front Row* – to Laura Jean McKay's *The Animals in that Country*, in which all animals talk to people infected by 'zooflu', with profound and disturbing effects.

There was concern in some quarters perhaps that, following the 2014 Clarke victory of Ann Leckie's *Ancillary Justice*, *Children of Time*'s win was indicative of a turn towards genre. Although the establishment of a Shadow Clarke Jury in 2017 (Allan, 2017) was not a direct response to the 2016 Award (having its roots in the 2016 Eastercon panel on 'Thirty Years of the Clarke Award', which took place before even the shortlist had been announced), some of the discussion reflected an anxiety about uncritical acceptance of commercial fiction. As a participant, I found involvement in the wider online conversation around the Shadow Clarke helped bring the contours of the new, twenty-first-century literary sf into focus. The victory of *Children of Time* had seemed unthinkable to me because it was outside the norms of the usual criteria for literary judgement; but once thought – and discussed and analyzed – it suggested a liberation from all the tired, old normative attributes traditionally associated with the 'literary'. This was not just because the spiders have names like Portia and Bianca, and suitably arachnoid matriarchal tendencies, but also because – to use Roberts's terminology – the 'lovin-the-alien, polymorphous, feminist' sensibility feels both modern and in line with an older sf idea that the future can be engineered into being. Here, the contrast between the humans constrained by their half-understood history and the spiders' belief in a Lamarckian progression underpinned by expanding scientific knowledge recalls the work of Clarke himself. Overall, Tchaikovsky's novel suggests the need for a move beyond the classical individualism that still retains authority in Western thought and is the implied viewpoint of canonical 'English Literature'. What has changed since the 1950s heyday of sfnal optimism in the future is that the rigidly constructed binaries of gender, sexuality and race, by which a conformist culture was maintained, have been significantly challenged; being open to otherness precludes the privileging of classical individualism. As a consequence, what we consider 'literary', which is just another way of saying what we value, has changed.

There is now a twenty-first-century readership, often but by no means exclusively university educated, which is perfectly comfortable in switching between experimental texts, genre material, fragmented complexity and talking animals. What there isn't at the moment is an established critical discourse that encompasses the full range of that readership and supports this new constellation. One way of facilitating the full emergence of such a discourse would be to rethink the history of English literature at least from the time of Wells, who, as suggested above, might be considered the key figure in facilitating the cultural break with Victorianism at the *fin-de-siècle* which gave rise to the birth of Modernism. For example, in the 1950s and early 1960s, literary commentators such as Angus Wilson had observed that postwar social realism was proving to be less realist than the modernist writing of Virginia Woolf it sought to replace, and that the solution was to turn to science fiction (Hubble, 2018: 38–9). Likewise, Kingsley Amis argued in *New Maps of Hell* (1960) – which, originating as a 1959 lecture series at Princeton University, was one of the first sustained attempts to discuss sf seriously as literature – that 'a new volume by [Frederik] Pohl or [Robert] Sheckley or Arthur Clarke ought, for instance, to be reviewed as general fiction, not tucked away, as one writer put it, in something called "Spaceman's realm" between the kiddy section and dog stories' (Amis, 1963: 129). Viewed from the conventional literary perspective of the late twentieth century, these might have appeared calls in vain but today we can argue that Wilson and Amis have been retrospectively vindicated by the emergence of the new configuration of literary sf in the twenty-first century. In fact, a key story of literature since the 1950s is the perpetual revolution of successive generations of sf writers making it new: the New Wave of the 1960s, the feminist sf of the 1970s, the cyberpunk of the 1980s, the New Space Opera of the 1990s and so on.

These successor generations were proleptically foretold in Clarke's *Childhood's End* (1953), which, in common with John Wyndham's *The Midwich Cuckoos* (1957), envisions the children of the time to be so different as to be alien. These texts did not just reflect the postwar emergence of the 'teenager' but a more profound understanding of how human nature is not a constant but radically contingent on technological development and socio-cultural change. To those, like sf writers, who were oriented towards the future it was clear that human behaviour and subjectivity would alter beyond recognition, and even if they couldn't anticipate what form those changes would make, they could at least represent the sense of how devastatingly total that disjunction would feel. While Wyndham conveys the magnitude of the situation by having his adults kill the children, Clarke's approach is more humanistic but also simultaneously bleaker because it demonstrates so clinically the meaninglessness of mid-twentieth-century humanism to the wider universe. As the alien Overlord, Rashaverak – whose own species are 'trapped in some evolutionary cul-de-sac' with the consequence that they will never transcend individualism – explains to the protagonist, George, the current generation of human children have reached 'Total Breakthrough' and are about to merge with the galactic Overmind:

> 'I've only one more question,' [George] said. 'What shall we do about our children?'
> 'Enjoy them while you may,' answered Rashaverak gently. 'They will not be yours for long.'
> It was advice that might have been given to any parent in any age: but now it contained a threat and a terror it had never held before. (Clarke, 1953/2010: 207)

When the children leave Earth, George and his wife join most of their peers in committing suicide; humanism comes to a tragic end. It would be trite, perhaps, to compare present-day media treatment of the 'millennial' generation as evidence of a similar incapacity on the part of those set in twentieth-century ways to adapt to the changed contexts of the twenty-first century, but such surface phenomena are indicative of fundamental shifts deeper in the culture. Where once New Wave writers turned from the outer space of the Golden Age to the inner space of altered consciousness, now writers – following a direction indicated by Clarke in the 1970s – have turned outwards to align that consciousness with the multiple and pluralistic possibilities of the universe. Today's literary sf is the product of aliens from the viewpoints of traditional literature and traditional sf alike. If academics, critics and cultural commentators want to engage fully with this contemporary sf – increasingly merged with what used to be thought of as the separate category of fantasy – then they need to abandon older concepts of individual interiority and character development, and engage with the way that genre forms have been retooled as vehicles for expressing futures free of twentieth-century social norms.

At one point in *Childhood's End*, Clarke provocatively states 'Fifty years is ample time in which to change a world and its people almost beyond recognition' (Clarke, 1953/2010: 75). In fact, thirty years has proved ample time enough for the Award bearing his name to change completely how we think about the relationship between sf and literature. By being the bridge, as Gaiman suggests, between the world of sf and the world outside, the Clarke has not just showcased the full range of possibilities of sf but also enticed mainstream literature within its portals. While some mainstream authors have been awarded for employing sf devices to illuminate their concerns, the net result has been, as Miéville implies, to make sufficiently advanced forms of sf and literature indistinguishable. One way of thinking about what this has achieved is to turn momentarily to the writer, born appropriately in the 1950s, who most obviously bridges the gap between Clarke's own work and twenty-first century literary sf: Iain M. Banks. At the end of *The Player of Games* (1988), playing the game of Azad on behalf of the Culture – Banks's particular vehicle for imagining a post-normative, post-scarcity future – against the Azadian emperor, the protagonist finally understands the ethos of his own society and beats his violent, patriarchal opponent with a strategic retreat that draws him into the heart of the Culture: 'The barbarians invade, and are taken over' (Banks, 1989: 276). And that is the story of the Clarke Award: the mainstream barbarians have been lured in and taken over. Today, sufficiently advanced literature from Atwood to Colson Whitehead, whose *The Underground Railroad* won the 2017 Clarke, is indistinguishable from science fiction. The success of the Award is therefore a fitting legacy for Clarke because it suggests that society – at least on the level of culture – now takes the prospect of future change seriously.

Works Cited

Allan, N. (2017) 'Announcing the Shadow Clarke 2017: An introduction and A Manifesto', URL (accessed 22 April 2020): http://csff-anglia.co.uk/clarke-shadow-jury/announcing-the-shadow-clarke-2017-an-introduction-and-a-manifesto/

Amis, K. (1963) *New Maps of Hell*. London: New English Library.

Arthur C. Clarke Award, The, URL (accessed 22 April 2020): https://clarkeaward.com/

Atwood, M. (2011) *In Other Worlds: SF and the Human Imagination*. London: Virago.

Banks, I. M. (1989) *The Player of Games*. London: Futura.

Butler, A. M. (2012) *Solar Flares: Science Fiction in the 1970s*. Liverpool: Liverpool University Press.

Butler, A. M. (2016) 'The Arthur C. Clarke Award: Thirty Years On'. *Foundation* 123: 78–83.

Clarke, A. C. (1953/2010) *Childhood's End*. London: Tor.

Clute, J. and Nicholls, P. (2019) 'Clarke, Arthur C.', in J. Clute and D. Langford (eds) *The Encyclopedia of Science Fiction*, URL (accessed 22 April 2020): http://www.sf-encyclopedia.com/entry/clarke_arthur_c

Gaiman, N. (2018) 'On Judging the Clarke Award', in I. Whates and T. Hunter (eds) *2001: An Odyssey in Words*, pp. 185–6. Alconbury Weston: NewCon Press.

Harrison, N. (2010) 'SF by Women, 2001–2010: Index', URL (accessed 12 September 2021): https://vector-bsfa.com/sf-by-women-2001-2010/

Hubble, N. (2018) '"The Choices of Master Samwise": Rethinking 1950s Fiction', in N. Bentley, A. Ferrebe and N. Hubble (eds) *The 1950s: A Decade of Modern British Fiction*, pp. 19–51. London: Bloomsbury.

James, E. (2002) 'The Arthur C. Clarke Award and Its Reception in Britain', in G. Westfahl and G. Slusser (eds) *Science Fiction, Canonization, Marginalization, and the Academy*, pp. 67–78. Westport, CT: Greenwood Press.

Jameson, F. (2005) *Archaeologies of the Future: The Desire Called Utopia and Other Science Fiction*. London: Verso.

Kincaid, P. (2017) 'Introduction (from *The Arthur C. Clarke Award: A Critical Anthology*)', URL (accessed 22 April 2020): http://csff-anglia.co.uk/

clarke-shadow-jury/introduction-from-the-arthur-c-clarke-award-a-critical-anthology/

Lovegrove, J. (2015) *Lifelines and Deadlines: Selected Nonfiction*. Alconbury Weston: NewCon Press.

Luckhurst, R. (2005) *Science Fiction*. Cambridge: Polity.

Miéville, C. (2018) 'Once More on the 3rd Law', in I. Whates and T. Hunter (eds) *2001: An Odyssey in Words*, pp. 187–92. Alconbury Weston: NewCon Press.

Morgan, C. (2017) 'Tipping the Fantastic: How the Transgender Tipping Point Has Influenced Speculative Fiction', in F. T. Barbini (ed.) *Gender Identity and Sexuality in Current Fantasy and Science Fiction*, pp. 83–103. Edinburgh: Luna Press.

Orwell, G. (1970) *Collected Essays, Journalism and Letters, Vol. 2*. Harmondsworth: Penguin.

Priest, C. (2012) 'Hull 0, Scunthorpe 3', 28 March, URL (accessed December 2015): https://christopher-priest.co.uk/hull-0-scunthorpe-3

Roberts, A. (2015) *Rave and Let Die: The SF and Fantasy of 2014*. Alconbury Weston: NewCon Press.

The Light of Other Minds
Collaborating with Sir Arthur C. Clarke

Stephen Baxter

APRIL 1998. *Oft, in the stilly night, / Ere Slumber's chain has bound me, / Fond Memory brings the light / Of other days around me ...*

I am sent a four-page outline by Arthur C. Clarke of a science fiction novel. The outline opens with the above quote from Thomas Moore. Am I interested in collaborating?

In one sense, I came to work with Arthur because of the last line of his 1973 novel *Rendezvous with Rama*. That last line read: 'The Ramans do everything in threes'. It was an obvious hook for sequels, a promise that was to be made good by Arthur and his first collaborator, Gentry Lee. In his later years Arthur, afflicted by post-polio syndrome, couldn't always fulfil his ideas alone, and collaborations became the norm for him.

And so, this new proposal about a 'remote viewer' – a Big Brother virtual camera you could tune to any event, anywhere. Arthur's outline follows the story of the entrepreneur who develops the viewer primarily as a news-gathering gadget, but step by step the device is used for other purposes: surveillance, blackmail, espionage, search and rescue, voyeurism.

But then it turns out that the viewer can be used to spy on events in the *past* as well as the *present*. Arthur lists plot possibilities laconically. '1. Destruction of religions based on charismatic founders. 2. Instant obsolescence of all history books, biographies. 3. Solution of all past crimes, mysteries. 4. Tremendous public demand for access to personal past ... ' But the outline has no plot closure, no real characters.

At first glance, I'm not sure if this is for me. The notion of a past viewer has been used in science fiction before, such as by Isaac Asimov in his story 'The Dead Past' (1956). (And Arthur had forgotten that Bob Shaw had already, very successfully, used 'The Light of Other Days' from the Moore quote as a story title in 1966! We ended up using the title, and dedicated the book to Bob.) But I recall that the Asimov story, for example, ends at precisely the point when it becomes most interesting – when *everybody* gets hold of an all-powerful time viewer – and Asimov steps back with a gasp of horror.

So where's the story? I ask myself the classic Hollywood question: Who has a problem with this? I begin to toy with the story of a fugitive, in a world where all the walls have turned to glass – where you have to imagine that everything you do is being witnessed by an army of scrutinisers *from the future*. How would you hide? How would you plan a crime – or, what if you were falsely accused of a crime? I start to realise, a bit belatedly, that the central notion has resonance for our own surveillance-saturated present.

I am becoming very interested in the idea. I reply with a tentative 'yes'.

*

I grew up with the books of Sir Arthur C. Clarke. Indeed I would say his work had the greatest influence on my writing of any author – and books like *Childhood's End* (1953) show enormous artistry in folding down transcendent concepts into heart-wrenching stories of individual humans.

I first met Arthur in person in 1992, when my first novel *Raft* was nominated for the Clarke Award. I didn't win but was the only nominee to turn up at the ceremony, which was held in Minehead, close to Arthur's birthplace in Somerset, to celebrate his 75th birthday. My wife and I met Arthur himself through the kindness of Arthur's brother, Fred, who remained a great supporter of his brother, and indeed a friend to us, until his death.

My publishers sent Arthur copies of my next few novels: Arthur was particularly taken by *The Time Ships* (1995), my sequel to H. G. Wells's *The Time Machine* (1895). In a way this was our first meeting of minds. He responded with a kind blurb, and with correspondence: he sent me a copy of the H. G. Wells Society's magazine, and even a little collectors' postcard of Wells himself. This was enormously generous; Arthur was almost exactly forty years older than me, had no need even to notice writers of my generation, yet he did. He followed the Clarke Award itself, endeavouring to read at least the annual winner – and thus, for example, encountered the works of China Miéville, as he once discussed with me.

And there is a sense of continuity here. Arthur never met Wells himself, but he did know Olaf Stapledon, who was a friend of Wells. And now I, and others of my generation, got to know Clarke.

A couple of years later I interviewed Arthur for *SFX Magazine*, by phone and email. Out of that, at my suggestion, grew our first collaboration, a short story that we eventually sold to *Playboy* – then a well-paying market for short fiction. That was how my name entered the frame after that when Arthur was looking for a new collaborator for the book that became *The Light of Other Days*.

*

JUNE 1998. The deal is somewhat complex, involving two major publishers, at least four lots of agents, and authors on different continents. Arthur is keen to get on with it. I'm working on other projects; I've learned from experience not to get too involved before a contract makes it real.

Meanwhile I'm jotting down developments, and sharing them with Arthur by e-mail and phone. Starting from that fairly open-ended outline by Arthur, we kick around ideas and outlines for some months.

I had been concerned that I would end up merely writing up somebody else's story. But all we started with was a few pages of notes, with one named character (which we don't use in the end); it is going to have to be a genuine collaboration.

And I respond to Arthur's enthusiasm. His motivation to collaborate is clearly that he has more ideas than he has time or energy to execute alone. As for me, after growing up on his books it will be a learning experience to get to see how Arthur C. Clarke's mind works from the inside.

In short, it will be fun.

We have taken to calling our novel LOOD.

*

SEPTEMBER 1998. Various contracts are being Fedexed around the world. It will not take as long to write the damn book.

Arthur is digging up provocative bits of history to revisit: 'Let's not be beastly *only* to the Germans ... '

I am working on a more complete outline. I'm keen to add in some transcendence for humanity – another key Clarke theme.

And I want to be sure the language and texture is up-to-date. Our past viewer is now called a WormCam.

*

NOVEMBER 1998. We have been emailing outlines and queries back and forth all autumn. We're coming close to figuring out a justification for the physics of the WormCam – enough to convince me, if not a physicist.

And we debate how to treat religion: we will have to visit Jesus. Arthur has in the past imagined religions melting away in the light of rationality and truth. But, I write, 'I wouldn't derive a vindictive glee over the debunking of Christianity but rather try to show a sense of loss as well as liberation, and go on to show us groping for new answers ... ' 'I quite agree,' Arthur replies. 'Probably a necessary evil for primitive organisms like us.'

*

JANUARY 1999. We are working steadily on Draft 1. Our story now shows the implications of the time viewer as worked out in the lives of a single family. But as usual, once the characters come alive, they start kicking our outline to pieces.

We agree reluctantly to cut some scandalous (fictional) speculations about the likes of Hillary Clinton and Bill Gates, revealed by the WormCam, partly because Arthur *knows* them – his contact network is astounding. But we do fix on the then fashionable theory that Abe Lincoln was gay. I suggest having Lincoln accepted in the near future as a gay icon, only to be 'outed' as straight by the WormCam. 'Splendid idea,' Arthur replies. 'Will annoy everyone.'

Arthur C. Clarke is surprisingly playful.

*

FEBRUARY 1999. We have a reasonably complete draft. I suggest running the novel past a few physicists, but Arthur demurs: 'I'm afraid they might say this is all nonsense'. We do send it to historians. One says this is 'the best Clarke novel [he's] read in a long while'.

*

SEPTEMBER 2000. First British publication. A British magazine calls me 'Clarke's ideal collaborator'.

LOOD wasn't an idea I would have come up with alone, and I suspect it didn't develop quite the way it would have if Arthur had worked on it solo. But it was indeed a lot of fun.

And I easily resist the mickey-taking of a friend who opens it at random: 'Your word or Clarke's? Your word or Clarke's?' The truth is, by now, after multiple drafts and revisions, I don't know.

*

After that first contact we worked together again. After LOOD we produced the three books of the *Time Odyssey* series (2002 onwards), and we collaborated on a new short story in the 'Tales of the White Hart' universe for PS Publishing. It was a joy and a privilege for me to work with a man who had such a profound influence on my life, and on the age we live in.

As I worked with him, I continued to be reminded of the Somerset farmer's boy who had got hooked on sf through a heady cocktail of Stapledon and the US pulps. He never forgot these roots. In 2001 Clarke sent me a portion of a letter to Stapledon from J. B. S. Haldane, dated 1945: 'Your utopia is a very exciting one. Why, though, must the intelligent animals forget the brutality of the past? ... *The final utopia must somehow redeem the past* [my emphasis], or else be something less than utopia.' Arthur wrote, 'Dear Stephen – This phrase [emphasised] haunts me – does it give you any ideas?' Well, it did, and though we never followed it up together, my own novel *Transcendent* (2005) was one result.

But the childhood on the farm left a legacy too. In our collaboration *Sunstorm* (2005), a disorderly sun threatens Earth. In fact the misbehaviour of the sun had featured in many of Clarke's works, beginning with 'Rescue Party' (1946), and including his novel *Songs of Distant Earth* (1986). I wondered if his attraction to this theme was a faint echo of that West Country farm boy, so dependent on the weather, on the sun.

When I interviewed him in 1997, I asked Arthur if he had any regrets about the way the twentieth century had unfolded: 'I would like to have seen a lot of things but I have seen infinitely more than I ever imagined in my lifetime. I've seen space travel. In *Prelude to Space* (1951) I predicted the first flight to the Moon in 1978 and I thought that was ridiculously optimistic. Of course by then we'd abandoned the Moon! I'd like to see men on Mars but I'm very happy with what we've done ... ' Arthur C. Clarke did vision, not disappointment.

I never actually met Arthur again in person after that Minehead event.

But I knew that to the end, Arthur remained fascinated by the future, and by the unfolding newness delivered to his study by the Internet. He was a terrific correspondent by email and phone. He would call, full of ideas or news, when it was convenient for him in Sri Lanka, sometimes at five in the morning UK time, often leaving a brusque answerphone message: 'This is Arthur, over and out!'

It was a joy and a privilege to work with a man who had such a profound influence on my life, and on the age we live in. His liveliness, curiosity and huge generosity of spirit make him a model of how I want to be when I grow up.

Goodbye, Arthur. This is Stephen, over and out.

Notes on Contributors

Stephen Baxter was born in Liverpool in 1957. Before becoming a professional author, he worked as a maths and physics teacher, and for several years in IT. His first short story 'The Xeelee Flower' (*Interzone*) appeared in 1987, and his first novel (*Raft*) in 1991. He is a former President of the British Science Fiction Association and a Vice-President of the H. G. Wells Society. His books include collaborations with Sir Arthur C. Clarke, Sir Terry Pratchett and Alastair Reynolds. He has won several prizes including the Philip K. Dick Award, the John W. Campbell Memorial Award, the BSFA Award, the Kurd Lasswitz Award and the Seiun Award. He is perversely proud to hold the record for the number of nominations for the Arthur C. Clarke Award without actually winning it.

Thore Bjørnvig has been enticed with all things outer space since pulling out his father's copy of *2001: A Space Odyssey* from his bookshelves at the age of 12. Subsequently this became an object of scholarly interest – his MA thesis was on the religious aspects of the Search for Extraterrestrial Intelligence. Since then, he has studied the relationship between spaceflight, SETI, science fiction and religion through various media. Currently he is researching the connections between environmental poetry and outer space in a project preliminarily entitled *Planetary Poetics and Astral Aesthetics*.

Andrew M. Butler is the author of *Solar Flares: Science Fiction in the 1970s* (2012), as well as books on Philip K. Dick, cyberpunk, Terry Pratchett, postmodernism, film studies, and Michel Gondry's *Eternal Sunshine of* the Spotless Mind. He has published chapters on cyberpunk cinema, Star Wars, Star Trek, and screen adaptations of William Gibson. He is managing editor of Extrapolation and the Chair of Judges for the Arthur C. Clarke Award. In his spare time, he collects shiny trousers.

Jim Clarke is Assistant Professor in English Literature and Cultural Studies at Cappadocia University. He is the author of *The Aesthetics of Anthony Burgess* (2017), *Science Fiction and Catholicism* (2019) and *Anthony Burgess's A Clockwork Orange* (forthcoming). He has also written extensively on J.G. Ballard, Iain M. Banks and *Doctor Who*. He is principal investigator on the *Ponying the Slovos* project, which investigates how invented languages function in translation. His work on Arthur C. Clarke forms part of a larger research project into Buddhist Futurisms.

Alexey Dodsworth-Magnavita is a Brazilian-Italian author and screenwriter of science fiction. He has two MAs in Philosophy and Astronomy, both obtained at the University of São Paulo. His doctoral thesis on transhumanism and space colonization was developed at both the University Ca' Foscari, Venice and the University of São Paulo, thanks to a dual title agreement and a grant awarded by the Erasmus Mundus Programme. He is a researcher at the Institute for Advanced and Convergent Studies at the Federal University of São Paulo, and in the Department of Philosophy and Cultural Heritage at Ca' Foscari.

Nick Hubble is Professor of Modern and Contemporary English at Brunel University London. They are the author of *Mass Observation and Everyday Life* (2006) and *The Proletarian Answer to the Modernist Question* (2017); and a co-editor of *The Science Fiction of Iain M. Banks* (2018). Nick reviews for journals such as *Strange Horizons* and *Foundation*, and is one of the judges for the 2021 and 2022 Arthur C. Clarke Award.

Lyu Guangzhao is a PhD candidate in Comparative Literature at University College London. His research project is a comparative study of the British SF Boom and the Chinese SF New Wave, focusing on the relation between the two movements and the broader socio-cultural transformations in post-Thatcherite Britain and post-socialist China. He is the co-founder of the London Chinese SF Group, a co-director of the London SF Research Community, and the 2021 recipient of the Support a New Scholar grant from the Science Fiction Research Association.

Notes on Contributors

Paul March-Russell is Senior Lecturer in English at Cardiff Metropolitan University. He is the editor of *Foundation*, series editor for SF Storyworlds (Gylphi Press), and co-founder of the feminist imprint Gold SF, published with Goldsmiths Press. His previous publications include *Modernism and Science Fiction* (2015) as well as chapters in *Popular Modernism and Its Legacies* (2018), *The Cambridge History of Science Fiction* (2019), *AI Narratives* (2020) and *The Edinburgh Companion to Science Fiction and the Medical Humanities* (forthcoming).

Joseph S. Norman teaches English and Creative Writing at Brunel University London. His research interests include science fiction, Weird fiction, utopianism and heavy metal. His monograph, *The Culture of The Culture: Utopian Processes in Iain M. Banks's Space Opera Series*, was published in January 2021 by University of Liverpool Press.

Patrick Parrinder is Emeritus Professor of English at the University of Reading and President of the H. G. Wells Society. His many contributions to sf and utopian studies include *Science Fiction: Its Criticism and Teaching* (1980), *Shadows of the Future* (1995) and *Utopian Literature and Science* (2015). He has taken a lifelong scholarly interest in H. G. Wells and his times, and was co-organizer of the 1986 international symposium, *Wells Under Revision*, at which Arthur C. Clarke was a guest speaker and took a prominent part in the proceedings.

Helen M. Rozwadowski is a professor of history and founder of the University of Connecticut's Maritime Studies programme. Her award-winning book, *Fathoming the Ocean: The Discovery and Exploration of the Deep Sea* (2005), chronicles the 19th century scientific and cultural discovery of the depths. Her recent book, *Vast Expanses: A History of the Oceans* (2018), won the University of Connecticut Sharon Harris Book Award in 2019, and has since appeared in a Korean edition (2019) and a Chinese edition (2020). She is co-editor of the new University of Chicago Oceans in Depth book series.

Andy Sawyer was, from 1993 to 2018, Librarian of the Science Fiction Foundation Collection at the University of Liverpool. From 2002 to 2012 he directed Liverpool's MA in Science Fiction Studies. He is now an Honorary Senior Research Fellow in English Literature at the University of Liverpool. He has recently compiled a four-volume collection

Notes on Contributors

of significant essays on science fiction for Routledge's Critical Concepts series (2020). He is currently researching science fiction of the 1950s, and the life and work of Jane Webb Loudon.

Mike Stack holds a PhD in Psychosocial Studies from Birkbeck, University of London. His chapter, 'Did the Doctor Change Sex or Change Gender?: Navigating the Sex and Gender Divide in *Doctor Who*', recently appeared in *Doctor Who and Science* (2020). His monograph on the *Doctor Who* story, 'The Happiness Patrol', is forthcoming in The Black Archive series (Obverse Books). He is currently an Associate Tutor in Psychosocial Studies at Birkbeck.

Index

Aderin-Pocock, Maggie 4
Agel, Jerome 91–92, 198, 209
Aldiss, Brian W. 2–3, 11, 49–50, 96–97, 105, 111–112
   'Blighted Profile' 111
   Canopy of Time, The 111
   Galaxies Like Grains of Sand 97, 111–112
   Greybeard 105
   Hothouse 96
   'Visiting Amoeba' 111
   'What Triumphs' 111
Allen, Maud 218
Amazing Stories 5, 45
American West 16, 118, 127–128, 133
Amis, Kingsley 248, 251
Amundsen, Roald 21
Antarctica 21, 33
anthropocentrism 158–159, 166, 169–170
apocalypse 9
Apollo 115, 134
Arrival (film) 4
Arthur C. Clarke Award 8–9, 235, 251
Arthur C. Clarke Foundation 8
Arthur C. Clarke's Mysterious World 7, 141, 236
Arthur C. Clarke's World of Strange Powers 236
Asimov, Isaac 2–3, 8, 11–13, 98, 101, 103, 111, 236, 254
   Caves of Steel, The 13, 101
   Foundation 8, 11–13, 33, 92, 101, 112, 173, 190, 209–210, 238, 251
   'Nightfall' 111
Asterank 159, 173
Astounding Science Fiction (magazine) 2, 7, 12, 16–18, 99, 112
atheism 78–79, 82
Atwood, Margaret
   Handmaid's Tale, The 9, 239, 241, 243
   Heart Goes Last, The 242
   Oryx and Crake 241
   Year of the Flood, The 241
Australia 122

Bamford, Peter 152, 154
Banks, Iain M. 10, 97, 106, 137, 193–211, 250–251
   'Descendent' 194

Excession 10, 193–195, 197–204, 207–210
Feersum Endjinn 197
Look to Windward 197, 211
Player of Games, The 250–251
'The State of the Art' 194
Use of Weapons 193
Baucom, Ian 101
Bauman, Zygmunt 184–189
Baxter, Stephen 4, 10, 36, 96, 154, 207, 253
  Raft 254
  Time Ships, The 255
  Transcendent 258
  with Arthur C. Clark
    Firstborn 154
    Light of Other Days, The 254–255
    Sunstorm 154, 258
    Time Odyssey 36, 154, 257
    Time's Eye 154
  Xeelee 96
BBC 15, 33, 247
BDO 193–194, 196–199, 202, 207–208. See also big dumb object
Beecham, Alice 29, 34
Benford, Gregory 47, 51, 210
Berlin 8, 76
Bernal, J. D. 63, 96
Berners-Lee, Tim 4
Bernstein, Jeremy 215, 220, 231
Bersani, Leo 229, 230, 231
Beukes, Lauren 245
  Zoo City 245
Bezos, Jeff 4
big dumb object 10, 193, 207, 210, 237. See also BDO
Billing, Noel Pemberton 218

bisexuality 8, 154, 213, 214, 228, 231, 244
Bjørnvig, Thore 9
Blackford, Russell 95, 111–112
Bletchley Park 6
Boards of Canada 4
  Tomorrow's Harvest (album) 4
Bonestell, Chesley 18, 34
Booker Prize 239
Bradbury, Ray 241
Brandreth, Gyles 75, 78, 92
British Interplanetary Society (BIS) 5, 13, 15, 33
Britton, Andrew 152, 155
Brookmyre, Chris
  Places in the Darkness 4
Buddhism 9, 75, 79–92, 93
Burma 86, 102
Butler, Judith 1, 10, 105, 139, 152, 155, 224, 225, 232, 237, 239, 246, 251
The Byrds
  'Space Odyssey' (single) 11

Campbell, John W. 2, 12, 16, 99, 141, 176
  'Twilight' 99
Caraccio, Marcio 139–140
Carnell, Ted (E. J.) 2, 6
Carpenter, Edward 218, 232
Carson, Rachel 8, 116
Carter, Howard 38
CBS News 7
Ceylon 8, 79, 86–87, 102, 121–123, 220. See also Sri Lanka
Chilton, Charles 9, 15, 26
  Journey into Space 15, 26, 28,

Index

33
Operation Luna 26, 33
World in Peril, The 26, 33
China 81, 176, 185, 190–191, 235, 243, 255
Christianity 55, 85, 92, 256
Christopher, John 2, 102
Christopherson, Peter 11
Cinefantastique 90, 93
Clarke, Arthur C.
  essays
    Challenge of the Sea, The 124, 129, 136, 138
    'The Challenge of the Spaceship' 17
    Exploration of Space, The 6, 22, 35
    Lost Worlds of 2001, The 42, 51
    Profiles of the Future 11, 35–36, 51, 124, 131, 136, 155
    Report on Planet Three 11, 155
  novels
    2001: A Space Odyssey 3–4, 7–8, 10–11, 35, 38–40, 42, 45–47, 81, 90–91, 95, 117, 139–143, 146–149, 152–153, 162, 168, 170, 178, 181, 187–188, 193–195, 197–201, 204, 206–207, 223, 235–237, 242, 258, 261
    2010: Odyssey Two 3, 10, 12, 139–141, 140–141, 146, 149, 151, 162–163, 168, 170
    2061: Odyssey Three 51, 154, 213, 231
    3001: The Final Odyssey 40, 51, 91–92, 154
    Against the Fall of Night 39, 41, 51, 98–99, 112
    Childhood's End 2–4, 7, 9–10, 23, 35–36, 38, 41–42, 44, 48, 50, 80, 83–85, 92, 95, 100, 140, 148, 155, 157, 167, 170, 177–178, 186, 188–190, 201, 203, 205, 226, 248, 250–251, 254
    City and the Stars, The 3, 7, 10, 13, 38–39, 41, 47, 50, 95, 97–102, 105, 112, 190, 205
    Deep Range, The 8, 10, 85–86, 88, 92, 117, 120, 122, 124, 127–128, 131, 136–137, 190
    Dolphin Island 8, 122–123, 127
    Earthlight 7
    Exploration of Space, The 6, 22, 35
    Fall of Moondust, A 26, 98, 124, 190
    Fountains of Paradise, The 8–9, 75, 77, 88, 90–92, 141, 237–238
    Imperial Earth 8, 10, 44, 51, 106, 141, 213, 214, 220, 221, 222, 224–226, 230–232
    Interplanetary Flight 22, 28
    Islands in the Sky 7
    Prelude to Space 22, 27, 32–33, 35, 102, 258
    Rendezvous with Rama 1,

8, 10, 38–39, 42, 44–45,
48, 50–51, 141, 161, 190,
193–194, 208–209, 237,
253
Sands of Mars, The 7, 23, 33
Songs of Distant Earth, The 8,
76, 92, 213
short fiction
'At the Mountains of
Murkiness, or Lovecraft
into Leacock' 7
'The Awakening' 46
'Call of the Stars' 25
'Dial F for Frankenstein' 4
'Encounter in the Dawn' 43,
47–48, 197
'Extra-Terrestrial Relays' 17
'Feathered Friend' 24–25
'Freedom of Space' 24
From the Ocean, From the Stars 124
'Greetings, Carbon-Based
Bipeds!' 44
*Greetings, Carbon-Based
Bipeds!* 41–42, 44, 51, 92
'History Lesson' 46
'Jupiter Five' 37–39, 42, 45,
50
'The Lion of Comarre' 100
'A Meeting with Medusa' 237
'The Nine Billion Names of
God' 9, 79, 81
'The Obsolescence of Man'
139, 144
'The Other Side of the Sky'
24, 31, 33
'Passer By' 24–25
Reach for Tomorrow 35
'Rescue Party' 7, 42, 258

'The Road to the Sea' 124
'Sentinel of Eternity' 140
'The Sentinel' 11, 25, 39, 62,
79–80, 140, 197
'Special Delivery' 24–25
'Summertime on Icarus' 194
'Take a Deep Breath' 24
Tales from the White Hart
100, 126
'Time's Arrow' 36
'Venture to the Moon' 23, 28
tv series
*Arthur C. Clarke's Mysterious
World* 7, 141, 236
Mysterious Universe 7
World of Strange Powers 7,
236
with Gentry Lee
Cradle 53, 213
Garden of Rama, The 154
Rama II 154, 213
Rama Revealed 154
with Mike Wilson
Boy Beneath the Sea 122
First Five Fathoms, The 122
Indian Ocean Adventure 123
Indian Ocean Treasure 123
with Peter Hyams
*2010: The Year We Made
Contact* 3, 140, 151
with Stanley Kubrick
2001: A Space Odyssey 3, 8,
40, 90, 92, 123, 139–142,
147–149, 151, 153–155,
195, 197–198, 201, 209,
236
with Stephen Baxter
Firstborn 154
Light of Other Days, The

Index

254–255
Sunstorm 154, 258
Time Odyssey 36, 154, 257
Time's Eye 154
Clarke Award 8, 10, 188, 235–236, 238, 240–242, 246–247, 250–251, 254–255. *See also* Arthur C. Clarke Award
Clarke, Jim 9, 75, 204
Cleaver, Val/A. V. 18, 20, 33
Clinton, Hillary 257
Clute, John 99, 112, 191, 194–195, 200–201, 204, 209–210, 238–240, 251
Cold War 15, 22, 27, 95, 127, 137, 142, 151–152, 201, 206
Colliers (magazine) 18
computers 81, 99, 103, 144, 146, 149, 208
Convention on the High Seas 19
Copernicus 144
cosmic horror 7
Cousteau, Jacques 118, 122, 124–125, 137
Cox, Brian 4
Crisp, Quentin 219, 232
Csicsery-Ronay, Istvan 194–195, 199–201, 209
Cuarón, Alfonso 4
Gravity 1, 4, 58, 64, 71
cyberpunk 248
cyborg 144

Dalai Lama 81–82
Dan Dare 7, 15, 22, 26, 28, 32
Darwin, Charles 85, 144, 190

da Vinci, Leonardo 46
Deism 77–78
Delany, Samuel R. 194
Nova 194, 196
Derrida, Jacques 140, 145, 155
Destination Moon (film) 16, 18–21, 26–27, 31, 33
Dhammapada 82–83
diving 8, 79, 102, 118–119, 121–124, 134, 136, 220
DNA 103, 221
Dodsworth-Magnavita, Alexey 10, 157
Doroga k zvezdam [*Road to the Stars*] (film) 16, 33
Dullea, Keir 151
Dunnett, Oliver 7, 11
Dunsany, Lord 10, 99–100, 112
Dyer, Richard 221, 232
Dyson, Freeman 196

Eagle, The (comic) 7, 15, 26, 30
Dan Dare 7, 15, 22, 26, 28, 32
'Dan Dare, Pilot of the Future' 7
Earth 1, 8, 10, 16–17, 19–20, 24–27, 30, 32, 34, 36, 38, 40, 42, 44, 46–48, 51, 57, 59–61, 64–65, 67–69, 76, 80, 82, 89, 92, 96, 100, 102–103, 105–106, 110, 112, 125, 132, 138, 141, 146–148, 153, 157–163, 165, 168–169, 171–172, 177–178, 180, 186, 201, 203–206, 213–214, 220–227, 230–232, 241, 249, 258

269

Eastercon 246–247
ecology 120
Edelman, Leo 98, 104–106, 111–112
 No Future 95, 104, 112
Egan, Greg 4
Ekanayake, Leslie 9, 88, 215
Erlich, Richard D. 188, 190
eschatology 9
ethics 10, 76, 158, 160–162, 166–168
Europa 142, 157, 162–163, 168, 170
Evening Standard (newspaper) 23

Faber, Michel
 adaptations. *See also* Glazer, Jonathan
fandom 5, 31, 240
Festival of Britain 12, 21, 33
First World War 5, 218
Flash Gordon 15
Fong, Kevin 4
Fort, Charles 7, 99
Foucault, Michel 97, 105, 112, 205, 209, 216–219, 232
Freud, Sigmund 85, 140, 142–144, 153, 155, 229
Fuller, Buckminster 8

Gaiman, Neil 235, 250–251
Galaxy 18, 63, 102, 178
Galileo 19, 30, 163
Garber, Eric 213, 214, 232
Gates, Bill 187, 257

Gay Liberation Front 220
Gemini 115
gender 10, 78, 218, 231, 241, 243–244, 247
Genesis 48
Geraci, Robert M. 63, 72
Gernsback, Hugo 5
 Amazing Stories 5, 45, 72
Gielgud, John 220
Gilgamesh 109
Gilroy, Paul 101
Goddard, Robert H. 16
Godwin, Tom 182, 189
 'The Cold Equations' 182, 189
Gollancz 12, 33–34, 51, 93, 112, 171, 193, 209
gravity 16, 21, 23, 53, 57, 59, 62, 64, 70, 143, 196, 225, 226
Gravity (film) 1, 4, 58, 64, 71
Greenland, Colin
 Take Back Plenty 239
Gregory of Nazianzus 78
Grisinger, George 122
Guerrier, Simon 206

Hadfield, Chris 4
Haldane, J. B. S. 11–12, 76, 96, 258
Hall, Sarah 245
 Carhullan Army, The 245
Halperin, David 230, 231, 232
Hampson, Frank 15
Hampton, Frank
 'Voyage to Venus' 15
Haraway, Donna 144, 155
hard sf 98
Harrison, M. John 101, 243
Harrison, Niall

245
Haskin, Byron 18
Hegel, G. W. F. 161, 172
Heidegger, Martin 140, 143, 148, 152, 154–155
Heinlein, Robert A. 2–3, 8–9, 12, 16, 19–21, 25–28, 30–33, 98, 236
'The Man Who Sold the Moon' 19
Stranger in a Strange Land 2
Herbert, Frank 79
Herrick, James 55, 60, 63, 72
H. G. Wells Society 255
Hinduism 79, 199
Hipgnosis 11
historical determinism 7
HIV 229
Hodgson, William Hope 96, 100, 112, 179, 190
Hollinger, Veronica 107, 112
Hollow, John 98, 112
homosexuality 6, 8, 10, 105, 107, 111, 151, 213–220, 223–225, 229–231, 257
Homosexual Reform Society 220
Houlbrook, Matt 219, 232
Hubble, Nick 10, 209, 235, 248, 251
Hull, Elizabeth 54
Hull, Seabrook 118
Hunter, I. Q. 149, 155, 251–252
Huntington, John 53–54, 72, 98, 184–185, 190
Huxley, Aldous 12, 100
Brave New World 100
Hyams, Peter 3, 140–142, 151
2010: The Year We Made Contact 3, 140, 151

Capricorn One 141

Illustrated London News 18
India 102, 171
Infinity Science Fiction (magazine) 24, 33
interplanetary travel 16
Interstellar (film) 4, 209–210
Interzone (magazine) 194, 210, 239
Islam 78

James, Edward 84, 92, 95, 238
Jameson, Fredric 39, 50–51, 202, 209, 240–241, 251
James, P. D. 105
Children of Men, The 105
Janes, Dominic 151, 155, 223, 224, 232
Jemisin, N. K. 96
Broken Earth 96
Jones, D. F. 147, 245
Colossus 147
Jones, Gwyneth 242, 245
Bold as Love 242
Life 245
Judaism 55, 78, 81
Jupiter 11, 37–40, 42, 45, 50, 140, 142, 146–147, 150–151, 160, 162–163, 198

Kaveney, Roz 193, 209
Kennedy, John F. 151
Kenya 102
Kerslake, Patricia 206, 210

Ketterer, David 55, 58, 72
Kincaid, Paul 194, 200, 203, 210, 238–239, 251
King's College London 6, 17
Kinsey, Alfred 219
Kipling, Rudyard 32–33
Klushantsev, Pavel 16–17, 33
  Doroga k zvezdam 16, 33
  Road to the Stars 16, 29, 31, 33
Kreuziger, Frederick 55, 56, 72
Kubrick, Stanley 3, 8, 40, 90, 92, 123, 139–142, 147–149, 151, 153–155, 195, 197–198, 201, 209, 236
  2001: A Space Odyssey 3, 8, 40, 90, 92, 123, 139–142, 147–149, 151, 153–155, 195, 197–198, 201, 209, 236
  Dr Strangelove, Or How I Learned to Stop Worrying and Love the Bomb 140, 148, 151
Kulbicki, Michal 206

Lacan, Jacques 104–105
Langford, David 95, 99, 112, 191, 195–196, 198, 209–210, 251
Lasser, David 5
  Conquest of Space, The 5, 28
Leckie, Ann 247
  Ancillary Justice 247
Led Zeppelin
  Houses of the Holy (album) 4
  Presence (album) 11
Leeds 5–6
Lee, Gentry 38, 154, 213, 253 with Arthur C. Clarke
  Cradle 53, 213
  Garden of Rama, The 154
  Rama II 154, 213
  Rama Revealed 154
Lem, Stanisław 44
Leonard, Garry 143
Leopold, Aldo 135
Lethem, Jonathan 1–3, 10, 12
Levinas, Emmanuel 185, 190
Lévi-Strauss, Claude 185
Levitas, Ruth 205, 210
Lewis, C. S. 23
Ley, Willy 17, 76
Life (magazine) 18, 42, 123, 126
Ligeti, György 141
Lilly, John C 127
  Man and Dolphin 127
  Mind of the Dolphin, The 127
Lincoln, Abraham 257
Lintott, Chris 4
literary adaptation. *See also herein* film, plays, radio drama and TV
Liu Cixin 10, 175, 189, 191
  Dark Forest, The 175–176, 179–185, 189–190
  Three Body Problem 10, 176, 179, 181–182, 184–185, 188, 190
Liverpool 5–6, 11, 51, 155, 210, 251
London 5–6, 11–13, 17–18, 21, 33–34, 50–51, 88, 92–93, 112, 121, 125, 138, 154–155, 171, 189–191, 209, 211, 219, 232, 233, 251
Lovecraft, H. P. 7, 10–11, 99–100,

Index

105, 110
'At the Mountains of Madness' 99
'Whisperer in Darkness, The' 99
Lovegrove, James 243, 245, 252
Lovejoy, Ray 141
Lucas, George 152, 237
   Star Wars 152, 237
Luckhurst, Roger 7, 12, 98, 101, 107, 112, 176–177, 191, 237, 252

MacLeod, Ian 244
   Song of Time 244
MacLeod, Ken 243
   Execution Channel, The 243
Mahayana Buddhism 80
Malaysia 102
Malmgren, Carl 181, 184, 191
Man and the Moon 18
Man in Space 18, 20, 34
Mandel, Emily St John 243, 245–246
   Station Eleven 243
March-Russell, Paul 1, 10, 95
Mars 7, 18, 23, 25, 33, 37, 160, 163, 167–168, 172, 239, 258
Mars and Beyond 18
Maxwell-Fyfe, David 219
Mayfield, Marilyn 6, 122, 215, 226
McAleer, Neil 3, 12, 22, 34, 79, 93, 121, 123, 137, 214–216, 219–221, 226, 231, 232
McAuley, Paul 4

McDonald, Ian 243
   Brasyl 243–245
McGrath, Martin 97, 112, 205, 210
McKay, Laura Jean 247
   Animals in that Country, The 247
McKechnie, Jack F. 86, 88
McKee, Gabriel 58–59, 59, 119, 127, 137
McLuhan, Marshall 10, 145
   Understanding Media: The Extensions of Man 145, 155
Mendlesohn, Farah 3, 12, 199, 203, 210
Mercury (planet) 37
Mercury (space probe) 115
Merril, Judith 25, 34
   'Daughters of Earth' 25
Midgley, Mary 64, 72
Miéville, China 155, 235–236, 240–241, 243, 245–246, 250, 252, 255
Minehead 4, 254, 258
Moon landing 7
Moon, the 7, 16, 18–24, 26–29, 31, 33, 40, 115, 118, 124, 140, 144–146, 148, 150–151, 158, 178, 187, 198–199, 258
Moorcock, Michael 6, 12, 215, 232
Moore, Osbert 86
Moore, Thomas 253
Morgan, Richard 243
   Black Man 243–244
   Thirteen 243
Moylan, Tom 97, 112, 206, 210

Musk, Elon 4, 208
Musson, Harold 86–88

Nebula Prize 1
Neumann, Kurt 21, 103
   Rocketship X-M 21
New Wave 1–3, 175, 194, 237, 248–249, 262
New Worlds (magazine) 2, 6, 12, 25, 34
New York 8, 11–12, 33, 44–45, 71, 72, 92, 92–93, 136–138, 140, 155, 172, 191, 209–210, 232, 233
Nicholls, Peter 176, 191, 196, 198, 200–202, 204, 207, 209–210, 238, 251
Nichols, Beverley 218
Nietzsche, Friedrich 91
Niffenegger, Audrey 245
   Time Traveler's Wife, The 245
Niven, Larry 194, 196
   Ringworld 194, 196
Nixon, Richard 151
Nolan, Christopher 4, 205, 210
   Interstellar 4, 209–210
Norman, Joseph S. 10, 111, 193, 209, 237
North Africa 8
North, Alex 141

oceans 10, 115–136, 158, 163, 187
O'Quinn, Kerry 215, 216
Orwell, George 202, 239, 242, 252

Nineteen Eighty-Four 239, 241
Outer Space Treaty 19
Outland 141

Pakistan 102
Paleo, Lyn 213–214, 232
Palmer, Christopher 199–200, 210
Paris 8
Parrinder, Patrick 9, 13, 35, 211, 263
St Paul 70
Peake, Tim 4
Pels, Peter 54, 72
Perry, W. J. 39
Pichel, Irving 18
   Destination Moon 16, 18–21, 26–27, 31, 33
Piercy, Marge 239–240, 243
   Body of Glass 239–240
   He, She and It 239
   Woman at the Edge of Time 240
Pintér, Károly 12
Pitt-Rivers, Michael 220
Playboy (magazine) 255
Pohl, Frederik 194, 248
   Gateway 194
polio 9, 123, 253
Poole, Robert 53, 55, 62, 72, 146–147, 158, 172
post-human 44, 49, 157, 168–169, 204
Potvin, John 217, 232
Pratchett, Terry 3, 261
Priest, Christopher 11, 101, 243, 246
Probe (newsletter) 76
propaganda 15, 18, 22, 32, 151

Purves, Philip 90–91, 93
Pynchon, Thomas 1
  Gravity's Rainbow 1

Rabid Puppies 244
Rabkin, Eric S. 98, 121, 137
race 2, 10, 27, 44, 48–49, 60, 65–67, 70, 84, 95, 106, 110, 118, 151, 154, 162, 170, 178, 181, 196, 221, 222, 247
radar 6, 17, 102
RAF 6, 17, 78, 102, 219
realism 20, 241, 244, 248
Reid, Robin 3, 13, 78, 93, 214, 228, 231, 232
religion 9, 54, 55, 56, 70, 71, 75, 78–79, 83, 85–86, 91, 110, 256
Revelation 48, 57, 59
Reynolds, Alastair 4, 207
Rieder, John 153, 155
Roberts, Adam 244
Roberts, Keith 101
Robinson, Kim Stanley 4, 40, 210, 239, 246
  Icehenge 40, 51
  Red Mars 239
Robson, Justina 245
  Mappa Mundi 245
  Natural History 50, 245
  Quantum Reality 245
  Silver Screen 245
Rogers, Jane 242
  Testament of Jessie Lamb, The 242
Rossiter, Leonard 151
Rozwadowski, Helen 10, 115, 117–118, 121, 137–138
Russell, Eric Frank 2, 99
  'Sinister Barrier' 99
Ryman, Geoff 239, 243
  Air 243–244

Sad Puppies 244
Samuelson, David 54, 75, 93
San Francisco 8
Satellite (fanzine) 99
Saturn 40, 140, 146–147, 163, 198, 221
Sawyer, Andy 9, 15
Scheider, Roy 142
Schweikart, Rusty 159
Science Fantasy (magazine) 6, 34
Science Fiction Foundation 238
Science Fiction Writers of America 8
Scott, Robert Falcon 16
Search for Extraterrestrial Intelligence 194. *See also* SETI
Second World War 13, 102, 116, 134, 219
Sedgwick, Eve Kosofsky 224, 231, 232
Segal, Lynne 226, 229, 233
SETI 194, 208. *See also* Search for Extraterrestrial Intelligence
sexuality 10, 23, 105–106, 213–218, 222, 224–225, 228, 231, 247
SFX Magazine 255
Shackleton, Ernest 21
Shadow Clarke 247, 251
Shaw, Bob 254

'The Light of Other Days' 254
Sheckley, Robert 248
Shelley, P. B. 45, 51
  'Ozymandias' 45
Shelton, Robert 142, 152, 154, 156
Shermer, Michael 148, 156
Sīlacāra 86
Sinfield, Alan 217, 218, 233
Singularity 63, 207
Sleigh, Charlotte 5, 13
Slusser, George 98, 251
Smith, Grafton Elliot 39
Social Darwinism 179, 188, 190
Society for Psychical Research 7
Somerset 4, 9, 254, 258
space 3–4, 7, 9–10, 15–32, 36–37, 39, 41–42, 47, 53–55, 57–60, 62–63, 65, 68–69, 71, 87, 89–90, 95, 97, 101–102, 115–121, 123–126, 129–135, 139–140, 143, 146–148, 150–151, 153, 157–160, 162–163, 167, 169, 171–172, 175, 182, 184, 187, 194–195, 197–198, 202, 206–208, 210, 225, 228–229, 231, 238, 243, 245, 249, 258
space opera 10, 194–195, 197, 198, 207, 211, 248, 263
Space Patrol (tv series) 20
space travel 15, 17, 22, 30, 32, 37, 39, 47, 115, 207, 225, 228, 258
Spinoza, Baruch 78
Sputnik 16, 18, 24, 118
Sri Lanka 8, 79, 83, 86–89, 91–93, 121, 123, 220, 238, 258. See also Ceylon
Stableford, Brian 95, 112
Stack, Mike 10, 102, 213
Stapledon, Olaf 5, 18, 35, 61, 96, 99–100, 196, 200, 255, 258
  'Interplanetary Man?' 18
  Last and First Men 5, 35, 61, 96, 99
  Star Maker 196
star gate 48
Stargate (tv series) 198
Starlog (magazine) 215
Stephenson, Neal 4, 243–244
  Quicksilver 244
Stockill, Peter 141, 153, 156
Stonewall 10
Strauss, Richard 141, 185
Strugatsky, Arkady
  and Strugatsky, Boris
  Roadside Picnic 1
Sturgeon, Theodore 107
  'The World Well Lost' 107
Sudan 102
Sullivan, Tricia 245
  Dreaming in Smoke 245
  Lightborn 245
  Maul 245
Sunday Mirror (newspaper) 9, 216
Sutherland, John 200, 211
Swift, Jonathan 239
  Gulliver's Travels 239
Sylvester, William 151

Tchaikovsky, Adrian 246–247
  Children of Time 246–247
telecommunications 6, 98, 126

Telstar (satellite) 6
Temple, William F. 5
 'Four-Sided Triangle' 5
Tepper, Sheri 246
 Waters Rising, The 246
Terrae Novae (fanzine) 6
Theravada Buddhism 79–81, 83, 92
Theroux, Marcel 246
Theroux, Paul 240
 O-Zone 240
Tibet 81
time 2, 5–6, 9, 13, 15, 18, 23, 25, 35–38, 40–41, 43–49, 57, 59, 61–62, 64–66, 69, 81, 86, 88, 90, 97, 99, 108, 110–111, 116, 122–123, 125, 127–129, 133, 135, 141, 143–144, 147, 150, 161–163, 175, 178, 185, 198, 200, 202, 205–207, 218, 223, 224, 231, 237, 239–243, 245–246, 248, 250, 254, 256–258
Titan 44, 221, 222, 223, 225–227, 229
Tom Corbett, Space Cadet (tv series) 20, 32
transcendence 9, 53, 54, 59, 60, 62–64, 67, 70–71, 71, 75, 78, 176–177, 179–180, 185, 187–188, 201, 203–204, 206, 256
transhumanism 10, 63, 157–158, 158–159, 167, 169
Transhumanist Declaration 158, 169–171
Tremaine, F. O. 99, 112
Trieste 115, 125, 132, 134

Trumbull, Douglas 140, 147
Tsiolkovsky, Konstantin 16–17, 59, 157–158
Tubb, E. C. 9, 16, 28, 28–32, 34
 'The Beatific Smile' 29
 'Bitter Sweet' 29
 'Blow the Man Down' 29
 'The Letter' 29
 'Like a Diamond' 29
 'The Troublemaker' 30
Tunguska 161
Turing, Alan 6, 103, 146, 220
Turner, Frederick Jackson 117, 125

Unknown (magazine) 7, 99
Unsworth, Geoffrey 141

Vance, Jack 96
 Dying Earth, The 96
van Vogt, A. E. 2, 107
 Slan 107
Vector (magazine) 112, 156, 210, 245
Venus 15, 46, 160
Verne, Jules 241–242
Vietnam 151
Vijrayana Buddhism 83
Village Voice, The 1
Villeneuve, Denis 4
 Arrival 4
Vint, Sherryl 144, 156, 206, 211
von Braun, Wernher 17, 124, 138
von Neumann, John 103

Wagner, Richard 141, 148
Watergate 151
Watson, James 103, 136, 138
Weeks, Jeffrey 217–218, 220, 223, 229, 233
Weird 10, 96, 100, 105, 107, 111–112
weird fiction 10, 96, 100, 105, 107, 111–112, 263
Wells, H. G. 1, 6, 8–9, 12, 26, 41–42, 50, 96, 100, 241–242, 248, 255, 263
  First Men in the Moon, The 26
  'The Star' 1
  Time Machine, The 96, 100, 255
  War of the Worlds, The 1, 18, 42, 50, 241–242
Westfahl, Gary 3, 13, 75, 84, 93, 98, 112, 207, 211, 251
  Cosmic Engineers 3, 13, 98, 112
Weston, Kath 229, 233, 251–252
whales 116–117, 124, 127–131, 128–129, 134, 136
Whitehead, Colson 250
  Underground Railroad, The 250
Wildeblood, Peter 220
Wilde, Oscar 217, 218, 220, 233
  Picture of Dorian Gray, The 218
Wilks, Anna 160, 173
Wilson, Angus 248
Wilson, Mike 121–122
  with Arthur C. Clarke
    Boy Beneath the Sea 122
    First Five Fathoms, The 122
    Indian Ocean Adventure 123
    Indian Ocean Treasure 123
Winter, Jerome 197
Wireless World (magazine) 6, 17
Withers, Jeremy 3, 13

Wolfe, Gene 96
  Book of the New Sun, The 96
Wolfenden, John 220
Wooding, Chris 246
  Retribution Falls 246
Woolf, Virginia 248
Worldcon 244
Wyndham, John 2–3, 12–13, 102, 248–249
  Midwich Cuckoos, The 248

zoocentrism 170

www.ingramcontent.com/pod-product-compliance
Lightning Source LLC
Chambersburg PA
CBHW071402300426
44114CB00016B/2158